MW01224396

THE ARMENIAN DIASPORA

Cohesion and Fracture

Denise Aghanian

University Press of America,® Inc.
Lanham · Boulder · New York · Toronto · Plymouth, UK

LIST OF CONTENTS

FOREWORD

This book provides an invaluable insight to the complexities of identity formation and cultural memory amongst the Armenian diaspora. This volume analyses the different ways that over time and place Armenians have found their way across national boundaries, while retaining their very distinct sense of identity. For those of us who are interested in diasporic studies and identity formation this book is an absolute must read.

Haleh Afshar
March 2006

PREFACE

This book is a case study of the Armenian diaspora in Manchester which examines the complex social and political processes at play that maintain, reinforce and shape their identity. My association with the Armenian community began over twenty years ago when I married an Iranian Armenian and we had four daughters. My interest in the Armenians, therefore, is not just of an intellectual nature but also personal. Why do Armenians feel a strong sense of belonging to an ethnic culture and are so fiercely proud of their heritage, replicating ancient cultural and religious customs in different settings. How can individuals feel 'Armenian' without the territorial or linguistic attachment that is usually associated with nationality and how do we explain their cultural longevity? Overall this book uses a comparative analysis in order to understand other Armenian communities throughout the world and indeed other self defined diaspora groups, locating similarities and differences. I begin by defining 'diaspora', setting the scene and creating a working definition for our subject. I then move on to examine contemporary and classical theories of ethnicity illustrating how we construct our sense of identity in different settings and by implication draw boundaries vis-à-vis others as well as how it changes in form and substance over time. This book narrates the long, rich and often traumatic history of the Armenian people: their adoption of Christianity in the fourth century, the rise of Armenian nationalism, the Armenian Genocide and the dispersion of the Armenians throughout the world and their eventual independence.

Essentially this book demonstrates how the Armenian people successfully balance lives rooted in a particular territory while also sharing very different cultural and social spaces. Empirical evidence in the form of focus groups and oral life histories is used to highlight the fact that the concept of diaspora can provide an analytical tool for the study of individuals in their country of settlement. Diaspora as a conceptual tool and empirical reality challenges the still widely held assumption that certain groups and their identities in some way automatically belong to a certain territory, of which the idea of national identity is the most prominent. One of the central ideas in this book emphasises the socially constructed nature of ethnicity and the ability of individuals to 'cut and mix' from a variety of ethnic cultures and forge their individual or group identities, thus forming an alternative to established writing about collective identity. Diaspora forces us to recognise the relevancy of patterns of identification whilst rejecting a discourse that is still based on the dichotomy of national and non-national. Their experience emphasises their ability to combine resources and networks from multiple locations (transnationally) in order to maximise their freedom and independence from the confines of any one nation state. Ethnic consciousness is experienced in a variety of ways, nevertheless, wherever and however they live—they feel Armenian.

Denise Aghanian
March 2006

ACKNOWLEDGEMENT

This book has benefited from a good deal of tender loving care and while I take full responsibility for the final text and its inevitable flaws, there are a number of people who have helped me along the way. I wish to thank Haleh Afshar and Rob Aitken for their insight, knowledge and constant encouragement throughout the research for this book. Their detailed attention to my drafts, constructive criticism and faith in me is always appreciated. My children, Danielle, Shariz, Talin and Tania for their patience and understanding and who often accompanied me on research trips to Manchester. I owe an enormous debt of gratitude to Scott Courts for his support and technical knowledge throughout this research: reading drafts and formatting the manuscript. Most of this entire book could not have been written without the help of the Armenian community in Manchester and elsewhere. My unreserved thanks go to those members of the community who participated in the focus groups and the oral life histories and who allowed me to gain intimate knowledge of their lives. I am also indebted to the Armenian Apostolic Church, the Armenian Institute, the Armenian Studies Group and CRAG (Centre for the Recognition of the Armenian Genocide) here in the UK for their assistance throughout this research. Finally this book is dedicated to the memory of those Armenian men, women and children massacred in the Armenian Genocide of 1915.

INTRODUCTION

The Diaspora[1] is a condition shared by approximately 4.5 million Armenians. Dispersion throughout Armenian history has been the result of de-stabilizing factors that have affected the historic Armenian homeland since early times. These factors range from political instability, conquest, religious persecution, massacre and deportation. Secondary catalysts of emigration from the Armenian homeland included the pursuit of foreign trade, educational opportunities and military careers. Between the fourth century AD and the Ottoman massacres and deportations of 1915, successive waves of Armenian immigrants and refugees have established hundreds of expatriate communities throughout the world.[2] By the turn of the nineteenth century some of these communities had disappeared and some had grown larger acquiring greater significance. There are approximately 18,000 Armenians in Greater London and Manchester. Most are first generation immigrants and their descendants, originating principally from Turkey, Lebanon, Syria, Iraq, Iran and Cyprus. They also include Armenians from Egypt and Palestine, as well as individuals from other countries who have had various experiences as Armenian émigrés before arriving in Britain.[3]

Every country has its immigrants, internal others, and each society, very much like the world we live in, is a hybrid.[4] As the import of goods became part of everyday activity, the cultural mixing of peoples became normal and necessary. A find of merchant's records from Asia show that laws and customs for the conduct of caravan trade were already well developed as early as the nineteenth century BC. Long distance trade therefore gave birth to permanent communities of aliens in major urban centres. Centuries later, beginning about 500BC, the rise of portable and universal religions a Buddhism, Judaism, Christianity and Islam provided an effective cultural protective shell for trading communities, insulating them from their surroundings in matters of faith and family as never before. Such faiths permitted followers of a religion that differed from the prevailing environment to maintain a corporate identity indefinitely, generation after generation. Jews and Armenians are particularly well known examples of polyglot communities who have settled in trading enclaves after leaving their homelands for economic or political reasons. Furthermore, the mixing of diverse peoples in urban centres through conquest, enslavement and long distance trade resulted in the creation of social spaces inhabited by various ethnic groups. Such groups entered into conventional and relatively well-defined relations with one another, and governments presided over ethnic diversity. The assumption that uniformity was desirable or that assimilation to a common style of life or culture was either normal or possible did not exist until nationalist ideals evolved in the nineteenth century.[5]

Migration has therefore been a continuous phenomenon throughout history, induced by trade, political or religious oppression, and more frequently, by the search for improved economic opportunities. Indeed immigration in Britain is anything but an unprecedented phenomenon. Throughout its history, Britain has been the recipient of immigrant inflows, thus all migration is in some sense, the latest episode in a long chain of events. It has nevertheless brought about a profound and indeed irreversible change in the whole character of the British social order. Clearly Britain is a visibly multi-racial society. Furthermore, it has become a much more poly-ethnic society. Thus, new and old ethnic communities, inspired as they are by cultural, religious and linguistic traditions, whose roots lie far beyond the boundaries of Europe, have significantly expanded the range of diversities covered by local British lifestyles.[6]

Armenians represent one of the older immigrant communities in Britain and the presence of Armenians in the British Isles can be traced to the Roman era, however, it was not until the nineteenth century that a sizeable community settled and struck roots in Manchester. The first Armenians who came to Manchester were not penniless refugees, their main purpose was to arrange trade connections and they or their families owned flourishing textile businesses in Constantinople, Smyrna or Trebizond. All were descended from the inhabitants of Ottoman Armenia, now eastern Turkey and they came to Manchester so that goods could be bought directly from the manufacturers and shipped by the merchants throughout the Ottoman Empire. Over the years more Armenians came from a wide range of places such as Isfahan, Tabriz, Tehran, Baghdad, and others came from the Caucasus, Tiflis, Athens and Alexandria. During the repressive rule of Sultan Abdul Hamid II over the Ottoman Christian minorities in the late nineteenth century and the massacres of the early twentieth century, more Armenians arrived from Sassun, Van, Moush, Karin and Zeytun. These Armenians created the nucleus of the present Armenian community and were the pioneers of the Diaspora in Britain.[7]

As a small-sized generally middle class and highly westernised migrant population, Armenian emigrants have generated relatively little interest in their countries of settlement. Despite their lengthy stays abroad and generally successful adaptation to their host countries, they seldom concede the permanence of their migration, refuse to identify with the country of origin and express a longing for their homeland, which they often visit and sometimes return to. Armenians often share many social features with other contemporary skilled migrant groups. These include settlement in cities of the developed West; possession of cultural skills, resources and networks that allow them to function in various settings; and close relations with the homeland and other Armenians in different host countries. In contrast, however, to many other ethnic communities settling in North

America and Europe, the existence of the Armenian Diaspora, very much like the Jews and Israelis, is much more likely to be examined from the vantage point of the country of origin rather than the host country. Furthermore, because Armenians are generally well educated, employed, and competent in the language of the host country and highly integrated into institutions, they have low visibility, receive little notice in the media and are neglected by the politicians, academics and social agencies that generally attend to migrant communities.[8]

Clearly the growth of ever more dynamic ethnic communities in Britain, demonstrates that most minorities are committed to cultural and religious reconstruction and the impact on British social and cultural institutions has largely remained peripheral. This is usually confined to specific areas such as popular music, art, fashion, sport and the food trade. What their presence has, however, in some cases precipitated is intense hostility amongst the British white indigenous population. From the outset, non-European immigrants were subjected to racial exclusionism, and to this day skin colour remains an inescapable marker. Nevertheless, despite widespread use as a trigger for exclusionary behaviour, and white hostility, physical characteristics or skin colour, are much less significant today. In contrast, the focus has shifted to the ethnic minorities' religious and ethnic distinctiveness. Thus, their very ethnicity is widely perceived as an unacceptable challenge to the established social and cultural order. It is rarely the case that ethnic groups coexist with equal power and without structural forms of discrimination. Rarely can diversity simply be celebrated as a source of pluralism that feeds the market of options. It is often the case that diversity in society is made up of injustice and because individuals in such groups do not experience the promised neutrality nor do they see the political debate address such inconsistencies, they rely on alternative moral codes and seek other avenues of self respect. In this context their ethno-cultural membership becomes the most relevant alternative.[9] There is, of course, much to be added to the logic of racial and ethnic polarization, but that is beyond the scope of this study. What is clear, however, is that Britain is a multi-ethnic society, even if it is one in which the English have long enjoyed a position of almost unquestioned hegemony. More importantly, whilst it is essential to keep these wider issues in view, the focus of this study is restricted to those people and ethnic communities who consider themselves Armenian.

In order to reflect upon the experience of Armenian emigrants, one must first identify those whom one intends to study. To answer this question we must ask what is an Armenian? Due to the Diaspora, differences have originated in defining and estimating the number of Armenians around the world. There are, however, basically four common definitions of whether a person is Armenian. Firstly, language—those who regard Armenian as their native tongue or who use the language at home. Secondly, religion—those who are members of the Armenian Apostolic Church or some other distinctly Armenian denomination (Armenian Catholic or Protestant). Thirdly, nation—those people who are biological descendants of Armenian ancestors. Fourthly, culture—those who define themselves 'Armenian' in some way, by inner self definition or outward behaviour, such as Armenian cooking, music, friendship patterns etc., Since individual nations differ in their use of these four definitions, huge differences in numbers result. The linguistic definition is the most conservative, because it excludes many Diaspora

Armenians who prefer to use a language other than Armenian. The national definition is the most liberal, since it virtually includes the other three entirely. By way of example, in the United States in 1980 there were 100,000 or 500,000 Armenians, depending on the use of the linguistic or nationalistic definition. Although electronic data management technology is making demography a more precise science, future statistics on Diaspora Armenians are likely to become less precise as acculturation[10] causes the gaps between the four definitions to widen.[11]

A further related obstacle that has apparently deterred research on Armenian demography is the scarcity of data. In each nation, Armenians tend to be demographic ghosts, they remain unseen except for sporadic appearances that are typically vague or misleading. There is little information about them in the official sources of the United States, Canada, the United Nations or private agencies.[12] For the purpose of this research I have assumed working definition of an Armenian, as a person who calls themselves Armenian, who has some knowledge of the Armenian language, their history culture and traditions, and who maintains some identity based association with other Armenians. Given this definition, we can examine what forces are at work to perpetuate the fundamental characteristics that constitute being an Armenian, 'Armenianness' (Haygaganoutyoun), across time and distance.

The examination of the growth and development of the Armenian Diaspora is one of great interest as these communities outside Armenia have thrived and prospered, within a developing world economy, which constantly undermines ethnicity. Factors relating to the Armenian Diaspora, however, are complex because the Armenian Diaspora itself is a very complex phenomenon. There is no single Diaspora. The Armenian Diaspora is a Diaspora of Diasporas, geographically dispersed, multi-generational, and with multiple waves of migrations within migrations. Indeed the ancestors of the majority of Diaspora Armenians were not themselves from within the borders of the present Republic of Armenia. By way of example, the Lebanese community is largely made up of descendants of the survivors of the genocide in Western Armenia. On the other hand, the larger immigrant community in the United States, particularly in Southern California, is made up of several layers: American-born third or fourth generation descendants or refugees from Ottoman Turkey who came from 1890 to 1922; later immigrants from Lebanon, Iran, Iraq or Syria; and more recently, Armenians from the Soviet and Independent Republic of Armenia. The large Diaspora communities in the countries of the former Soviet Union and its satellites, particularly Russia or Poland, are altogether different from those in the West and the Middle East. They are primarily Eastern Armenian in origin, dating from before 1920, 1920-91 and after independence.[13] Diaspora Armenians, therefore, vary in historical experience, economic conditions and cultural assimilation. Food, music, art, language, educational background and aspirations may vary between national sub-sections of Armenian communities. Nevertheless, the links between immigrant communities and homeland may persist over generations, providing the basis for long standing communicative networks, which unite people across borders and generations. Thus, the Diaspora is made up of a string of communities scattered throughout the world that are subject to the linguistic, cultural, social and political influences of their host countries, but embody a persistent sense of community.

These differences in experience and place of origin are reflected in cultural, economic and political manifestations, as well as linguistic patterns. There are those who are still predominantly Armenia speakers, (Eastern or Western), and those who speak predominantly the language of their host country, or indeed both. More interestingly, there are those who are trilingual as a result of transmigrations: Armenian-Farsi-English, Armenian-Russian-Polish, Armenian-Arabic-French to name just a few. Furthermore, it is important to remember, that host countries range across the full political spectrum, from traditional, autocratic or theocratic to modern, open, democratic secular states; from centralised to decentralised; from relatively homogenous to multi-ethnic polities. Host countries can be generally divided into three significant groupings: the Islamic and post-Ottoman world (Iran, Iraq, Syria, Lebanon and Egypt etc) where the idea of religious or ethnic communities with identity and self government has some continuity and tradition; the Western European and North American secular democracies (France, Britain, Germany, Greece, Canada and the United States etc); and the East European Slavic or Orthodox countries (Russia, Poland, Georgia etc), both of which maintain a secular framework of unitary citizenship, allowing for some cultural expressions of community life. The importance of these sweeping and rough generalizations is to emphasize that for Armenians in these three main configurations, the principles and practices of what is civic, political participation, and political rights and relations with the majority are drastically different. Thus, the social place Armenians occupy in each of these diverse societies, both as community and individuals varies enormously.[14] The survival of Diasporas, therefore, their genesis, and development, is determined by various factors and dynamic social forces operating in global, regional, and local environments.

Once Diasporas are established, they become intimately shaped by the host country's dominant ideology, political system, socio-economic structure, cultural traditions, and domestic foreign policies. In a dynamic, modern, global context, the question of identity for Armenians who are citizens of Britain, Canada, Iran, Russia, Syria or the United States is a paradoxically alienating abstraction. Based on these distinctions and variations in the politics, culture and society of host countries, one would envisage the structures of the various Armenian communities to differ from each other and exhibit unique adaptive traits. Nevertheless, despite these distinctions and variations in the politics, culture and society of the host countries, Armenian community structures seem to be similarly conceived, legitimised, and constructed, whether in Tehran, Beirut, Paris, New York or London. The reason why there is so much similarity between, say, Fresno, Paris and London, is because they are descendants of the first distinctive Diaspora post-genocide structures consolidated after 1918, essentially in the Middle East. There, the Armenian concept of community, identity and community organisations was derived from the ideal of the Ottoman 'millet'—a community within a larger polity, with self-administration, quasi-autonomous structures, and some form of legitimate representation, held together with a very pre-modern ideal of the 'political'. The stronghold of the Armenian millet was the church, and the criterion of distinction was religion.

At the wake of the Armenian genocide in 1915, the Dashnaktsutiun (ARF—Armenian Revolutionary Federation)[15], the Hunchaks (Social Democrats) and the

Ramgavars (Democratic Liberals) had emerged, influenced by the nineteenth century European revolutionary ideals, circulating in Paris and St Petersburg, and these parties attempted to foster a nationalist dimension to religious community identity. This process of transformation of the millet system within the overall progressive transformation of the Ottoman Empire, was a failure. Furthermore, the first Armenian Republic (1918-20) did not exist long enough to consolidate the secular, democratic transformation of the political parties. The Armenian political parties were exiled to Lebanon and Syria, where a large community of Armenians existed and where the ideal of the millet still functioned and composed the structure for political life. Once again, therefore, the church became both the symbol and definition of community identity. The separation of church and state never took place. Thus, denied the opportunity to participate politically, without a country and formal political structure, the Armenian political parties entrusted themselves the role of ensuring the physical protection and survival of the post-genocide Armenian communities. They became all encompassing guardians of ethnic Armenian identity and strongly resisted cultural assimilation. By way of example, the ARF, which had led the short lived Armenian Republic dominated the Armenian communities of Aleppo, Cairo and Beirut, however, its domination was sharply contested. It was enthusiastically celebrated by its adherents and fiercely resented by its opponents. This struggle served as the day to day generator of polemics in which notions of Diaspora were implicitly and explicitly elaborated. The Dashnaks maintained that Diaspora could not be an end in itself rather it was lived as temporary and transitory: the eventual return to the homeland was deemed essential and inevitable. This notion emerged when the aspirations of a generation of ARF affiliated leaders exiled from Soviet Armenia in the 1920's combined with the hopes of the deracinated survivors of genocide. The Diaspora was to think of itself as exilic, existing provisionally until its eventual return and while it waited, it had to engage in an organised struggle to sustain Armenian identity. [16]

The contemporary Armenian Diaspora communities have attempted to maintain their separate cultural and social identities. As a particular Diaspora develops, it creates indigenous institutions and structures, maintaining coherence through the church and political parties, charitable and social organisations, and a network of newspapers and journals published in Armenian and other languages, which shapes the individual and collective behaviour of Diaspora members, who also are influenced by ties to the homeland, interaction with other Diasporas, and the larger world environment. Thus the Armenian Diaspora varies from community to community in its form, unique characteristics and complexity due to each community's history and developmental circumstances. The organisational level of each community varies too and that also creates different and specific problems. Nevertheless most of the leaders and indeed many of the members of the Diaspora conceive of themselves as being in one Diaspora both vis-à-vis Armenia and in relation to one another. Migration to and travel between the Armenian communities is very common. The frequent movement of people, capital, ideas, cultural artefacts and electronic information have created positive conditions both for inter-Diaspora and Diaspora-homeland communication, thus decreasing isolation and increasing the possibility of nourishing Diaspora identity and commitment.

How relevant is the examination of the Armenian Diaspora to the study of politics in general? Essentially, this is a case study in micro politics, an analysis of ethnic groups, reflecting the aggregate result of choices made by individuals. Micro analysis is more concerned with understanding face to face interactions between people in everyday life, whereas macro analysis is concerned with the behaviour of collections of people and the analysis of social systems and social structures. Indeed, all ethnic communities can be seen as the result of interacting macro and micro structures. The macro structures include the political economy of the world market, interstate relationships and the laws, structures and practices established by the host countries. The micro structures are the informal social networks developed by the individuals themselves, in order to cope with settlement. Indeed our examination of emergent social structures across domains of human activity and experience leads to the assessment that historically, dominant functions and processes in the information age are increasingly organised around networks. While the networking form of social organisation has existed in other times, the new information technology paradigm provides the material basis for its pervasive expansion throughout the entire social structure. Today, many authors[17] emphasize the role of information, informal networks for finding work and adapting to a new environment in sustaining ethnic communities. Such networks include personal relationships, family and household patterns, friendship and community ties, and mutual help in economic and social matters. These links provide vital resources for individuals and groups, and may be referred to as 'social capital'—informal networks based on familial connections, or on a common place of origin, that bind Diaspora communities in a complex web of social roles and interpersonal relationships. 'It is not what you know, its who you know'.[18] The family and community are crucial in Diaspora networks and are dynamic cultural responses, which provide the basis for the processes of settlement, encourage ethnic community formation and are conducive to the maintenance of transnational family and group ties.

Indeed, from the very outset, the dispersed Armenian communities made extraordinary efforts to recover from the trauma of the 1915 genocide. These communities, in general, maintained with little change the old structures and models set up in the Ottoman Empire in the nineteenth century, developing their own political, social and economic infrastructures: places of worship, association, shops, professionals (such as doctors and lawyers) as well as other services. Moreover, there are many criteria that characterise the types of activity in which Diaspora members engage. They may involve cultural, linguistic, familial, religious, social, economic, political, educational, informational, or any combination of these and other interests. At the individual level, they may engage in a number of activities that interest them, some may engage only in activities that involve their extended families, whilst other specialise in the flow of information, become absorbed in religious, artistic or patriotic activities or focus on economic interests involving their homeland and other Diaspora communities of the same origin worldwide.

By way of example a major trend is notable in the organisational development of the London Armenian community: the tendency for the proliferation of
voluntary associations. The reasons for this are both historical and contemporary
as many of the associations being set up in London are branches of associations
with which the Armenians have been familiar in their respective countries of origin. London Armenians are reproducing over time the structure, if not the content, of the associational framework of the international Armenian Diaspora.
Indeed the most important factor in the growth of Armenian associations in
London is that being voluntary they are dependent on the commitment of individuals who do not gain their livelihood from their services to these institutions.
Furthermore, the multiplication of Armenian associations, despite the heterogeneity of the London community, implies that a large number of people have been
attracted towards a commitment to voluntary service, thus developing and sustaining their community.[19] Therefore, while Armenians travel across geographical
and national borders, many remain within familiar networks. These provide newcomers with resources and a sense of familiarity in otherwise unknown settings.
In other words, they may be in a different national environment, however, they
are able to maintain a way of life, socially, linguistically, and even in terms of
recreation and diet that is not so very different from the one they left behind. Accordingly, their experience of migration may be quite distinct from that assumed
in the established literature that suggests geographical movement necessarily
equates to loss of social ties and isolation.[20]

The advantages of embarking on such a realm of study are that it enables the
analysis of diverse factors, which condition and maintain Armenian ethnic identity. Because of the limited nature of the study, one is able to probe the social and
political processes in depth. Thus, the analysis and interpretative outcome of this
study consists mainly on judgements that are critical and qualitative rather than
quantitative. The purpose of this study is to extend the empirical base to enable
further debate and theoretical propositions, rather than produce readily testable
generalizations. As befits an ethnographic account, little attention is paid to the
quantitative aspects of the Armenian presence. Homogenous descriptions of
ethnic groups in the dominant public culture, assume that ethnic groups have no
differential identities. The possibility of a broad range of identities within ethnic
groups that are well integrated is the antithesis of what dominant populations pre-
sume about ethnic minorities. Fixed notions concerning the identities of people
are further complicated if we consider the complex influences convergent statuses
have on identity formation. Class, gender, age, region and language in historically
specific contexts all complicate what identity is and means for individuals.

Indeed it has become common for people to speak in the name of large
abstractions, for instance, the West, Slavic, Middle Eastern, Caribbean or Jewish
culture, Eurasian etc—labels that collapse religions and ethnicities into ideologies. These examples are not new, and they occur in times of deep insecurity
when peoples seem particularly close to and thrust upon one another, as the result
of expansion, war or migration. Furthermore, in both the colonial and post colonial context, rhetoric of general cultures went in two potential directions, one a
utopian line that insisted on an overall pattern of integration and harmony among
peoples, the other, a line which insisted that all cultures were so specific and

monotheistic as to reject all others. Among examples of the first are the language of the United Nations founded in the aftermath of World War II, where world governments declared the co-existence and harmonious integration of peoples and cultures. Among the second, the theory and practice of the Cold War and more recently, 'the clash of civilizations'. Samuel P Huntingdon's essay 'The Clash of Civilizations' appeared in 'Foreign Affairs' in the summer of 1993 announcing in its first sentence that 'The world of politics is entering a new phase': "the great divisions among humankind and the dominating source of conflict will be cultural . . . the clash of civilizations will dominate global politics."[21]

More recently scholars have begun to refute the essentialist notion that roots and origins are fixed and that there are marked and identifiable differences between people of different cultures. Barth (1969) argues that ethnic groups must be treated as units of ascription, where the social boundaries ensure the persistence of the group. It is not the cultural content enclosed by the boundary but the boundary itself and the symbolic border guards such as language, dress food etc that perpetuate the community and require anthropological enquiry. Difference is not so much a reflection of pre-given ethnic or cultural traits set in tablets of stone but is a complex ongoing negotiation.[22] Said (2000) argues that just as human beings make their own history, they also make their cultures and ethnic identities. This challenges the assumption that tradition is prescribed and static in a culture's history. To understand cultures, therefore, what it actually means for its members is always a democratic contest, even in undemocratic milieu. There are canonical authorities to be selected, revised, debated and dismissed. There are ideas of good and evil, belonging and not belonging. Moreover each culture defines its enemies, what stands beyond it and threatens it. It is also true that in addition to the official canonical, there are dissenting or unorthodox voices that compete with the official culture. Thus, no culture is understandable without some concept of the ever present sources of creativity, from the official to unofficial and to assume that there is complete homogeneity between culture and identity is to miss what is vital and intellectually productive.[23]

The realization that identities are constructed rather than naturally occurring has mainly been limited to the academic realm, however, people still think of and speak of identities as essential. Armenians, as many others, still tend to believe that they are a distinct cultural group with fixed origins and marked cultural characteristics. Armenian scholars highlight these essences which they claim enable Armenians to preserve their identity historically as well as in the present.[24] The aim, therefore, is to highlight the qualitative characteristics of Diaspora members, and to emphasize, that however similar all Armenians may appear they actually constitute a far more diverse community than is commonly understood. In other words, what culture today has not had a long and intimate relationship with other cultures? To assert a rigid separation among cultures is to dispute the overwhelming evidence that today's world is in fact a world of mixtures, of migrations, of crossing over. There are no insulated cultures or civilizations and any attempt to separate them does damage to their diversity. A single all-encompassing identity is nonsensical. The world we live in is made up of numerous identities interacting, sometimes harmoniously, sometimes antithetically. The question is therefore not about whether identities are hybrid but rather about the social processes that recreate and maintain these hybrid identities. Thus we can no longer assume that cultures are essential and that they exist outside of history. Therefore, this approach serves to demonstrate the difficulty of making generalizations that apply unequivocally to every section of Britain's ethnic population. What is required is the recognition that all contemporary ethnic communities are to some extent hybrid to understand the micro politics of local and global interactions.

As a constantly shifting entity, hybridity is not easily understood. Inhabiting an intersecting space between local traditions and global modernity, hybridity requires a flexible methodology grounded in a flexible epistemology. As a tried and tested method of cultural inquiry focusing on everyday life, ethnography has for a long time been the method par excellence. The internationalization of cultural studies requires new ethnographic methods if we are to understand the expression of local conditions with global processes. This re-direction of the ethnographic lens was advocated by Appadurai who invited ethnographers to investigate the micro politics of locality: 'the task of ethnography now becomes the unravelling of a conundrum: what is the nature of locality as a lived experience in a globalized, deterritorialized world?[25] In order to understand the mutual expression of local and global processes, ethnographers must be able to negotiate their intersection. Thus people whose national or cultural identity is mixed by virtue of migration, overseas education or parentage belong simultaneously to both local and global realms.

Furthermore, the concept of citizenship, its rights and responsibilities is undergoing rapid change in Europe. As the European Union creates another level of civic belonging, Diaspora ethnic and religious ties also increase in importance. The networks, experiences and influences of Diasporas have an important impact on the host societies, as well as the global economy, politics and indeed security. Questions are raised as to the loyalty of Diaspora communities and their level of commitment to the host society. For most individuals in Diaspora communities, the layers of identity and multiple connections are not a source of conflict, but rather a source of enrichment of the individual, the ethnic group and society at large. Although Diaspora communities may, and usually are, studied as ethnic minorities, they also justify analysis as actors in international politics and world affairs. Globalisation has accelerated the flow of people so that practically every country has Diasporas. The political and economic activities of Diaspora organisations blur the distinction between domestic and international affairs, supporting links that condense the sovereignty of states and also extend the scope of their foreign policies. With this in mind, it is necessary to pay attention to Diasporas as increasingly important factors in world affairs. It is hoped, therefore, that this research will stimulate further exploration of ethnic communal political integration[26] and nation building, which is both important to our understanding of modern society and politics, and which can only lead to a more profound understanding of humanity.

Chapter One begins with an examination of the various definitions of Diaspora. The concept Diaspora has been used to describe a wide variety of groups and as such is imprecise. What do we mean by Diaspora? How is Diaspora historicised and politicised and how does it connect with ideas of transnationalism?

In the current discourse on Diasporas confusion arises because of the multiplicity of meanings assigned to this word.[27] Indeed, the word Diaspora was fairly limited until the 1990's, when there was a rapid surge of interest with the appearance of a new journal 'Diaspora', edited by Robin Cohen. One interpretation of the word 'Diaspora' has been dominant, which highlights the catastrophic origin, the forcible dispersion and the estrangement of Diaspora peoples in their countries of settlement. In academic discussions, however, there is contention between two approaches. First, according to the classical approach, the pre-requisite of being a Diaspora is to have been expelled by force from a homeland, the Jewish and Armenian cases serve as archetypes for this definition. Second, a Diaspora is considered to be a mass of people who live outside their country of origin, without necessarily having been expelled from it. The individual maintains ties with that mass and homeland, and engages in collective efforts to maintain an identity. Diaspora is being used today to describe a wide range of dispersions, and there exists an overlap with words such as migrant, exile, expatriate and refugees. The meaning of the term Diaspora has therefore been extended to encompass the dispersed communities outside the Jewish and Armenian Diaspora.

Indeed, in any typology of Diasporas, the origin of emigration is always a first point of contention. A second general characteristic is the persistence of the dispersed peoples as a distinct ethnic group, either because, as with Jews and Armenians, there is a desire not to be assimilated or, as with African Americans in the United States, there is a reluctance to offer assimilation to the community of the dispersed. Thirdly, Diasporas are characterised by continued practices of representation. These practices often, but by no means always religious in origin, distinguish the social group's identity from that of the host country's majority and establish real or illusory links with a homeland's identity. In this context, there is a further characteristic of Diasporas, an orientation towards the homeland, a developed rhetoric and actual behaviour of returning to the actual homeland. This rhetoric can foster expectations both in the Diaspora and indeed the homeland which are frequently misinformed, as the work of Razmik Panossian on recent Armenian homeland Diaspora relations and Yossi Shain on American Jews and Israel demonstrates.[28]

Diaspora as a conceptual tool and empirical reality challenges the still widely held assumption that certain groups and their identities in some way automatically belong to a certain territory of which the idea of national identity is the most prominent example. Diaspora has made a dynamic comeback in the debates around ethnicity, nationality, boundaries and identity and can be utilised as an important analytical concept. This is because the concept can relate simultaneously to both the country of origin and the country of exile. In this way it can describe the transnationalism of migrant communities in general. The concept can take into account this transnational reality and it can bridge the analytical dichotomy between country of origin and exile, as well as bridge the gap between the periods before and after migration. The concept of Diaspora is thus an important tool since it is able to provide ethnic studies with an undivided perspective of its area of research. A concept that has transformed in time, Diaspora has returned to address the understanding of migration and people's multiple sense of belonging and loyalties beyond national boundaries.

Armenians have not commonly been included in the discourse of transnationalism nor have they seen themselves as part of it. Nevertheless, given the Armenian legacy of dispersion, oppression, marginality and cosmopolitanism, their experience clearly corresponds to this position. A growing body of scholarship has addressed the ways by which groups have used transnational strategies to cope with problems associated with migration. The literature on this topic suggests that such links and resources can provide useful benefits. Transnationalism draws upon the language of Diaspora and unlike established studies of Diaspora does not privilege fixed relations with co-ethnics and a single homeland. It emphasizes new identities generated as individuals and is grounded in environments called transnational social spaces or communities, which includes people and networks in points of origin and settlement who exchange outlooks, expectations, and resources that are a product of their unique interaction and experience. This chapter therefore also examines the developing theme of the transnational community, which generally refers to migrant communities who maintain economic, political, social, cultural and emotional ties with their homeland and with other Diaspora communities of the same origin in different parts of the world.[29]

How do transnational immigrants differ from ethnic communities? The transnational community is defined in terms of transnational social space whereas the ethnic community is nation specific. According to theorists of transnational immigration, the distinction is made possible because of technological advances in communication over the past century. Personal computers, telephones, reduced cost air travel and other forms of modern telecommunications have made it relatively easy for immigrants to maintain personal contact with people in the homeland and other Diaspora communities. Essentially contemporary immigrants are different from their predecessors insofar as modern technology has strengthened the rate and extent of circulation between homeland and host country. Furthermore, not only does cheap, high speed travel allow frequent physical contact but it also accelerates the movement of goods, services and ideas.[30] As a result of this change, a paradigm shift has occurred in the field of Diaspora, replacing the earlier frameworks to what social scientists call the transnational community. Though often conceived in terms of a catastrophic dispersion, widening the definition of Diaspora to include trade and cultural Diasporas can provide a more nuanced understanding of the often positive, relationships between migrants' homelands and their places of work and settlement.

Chapter Two examines contemporary and classical theories of ethnicity. Ethnicity is a term being applied to the most diverse empirical situations of self-other ascription and is now seen as a major feature of social structure, personal identity, transnational networks and political conflict across the world. Given its increasing prominence in contemporary social and political debates, it is perhaps understandable that ethnicity in conjunction with related debates on nationalism, has come to have a major place in a number of social science disciplines. Ethnicity is a concept widely used in contemporary social science and yet, perhaps because of it, it is one of the most ambiguous of concepts. Every society in the modern world contains sub-sections, groups of people, more or less distinct from the rest of the population and the most suitable generic term to describe these sub-sections is an ethnic group. Indeed words like ethnic group, ethnicity and ethnic conflict have become common terms in the English language. Furthermore, the dichotomy between a non-ethnic 'us' and ethnic 'others' is implicit in concepts used within the fields of ethnicity and nationalism.[31] The major source of confusion, however, is the tendency to conflate ethnicity and nationality, and my aim here is to situate ethnicity conceptually, by distinguishing our subject from other central concepts widely in use in political discourse. The parallel between nationalism and ethnicity is obvious in that most nationalisms are based on ethnic ideologies. A fundamental difference between ethnic ideology and nationalism is that the latter predicates the existence of an abstract community, one that is loyal to a legislative system and a state. The nation, therefore, only exists if one is capable of imagining its existence.[32] Like ethnic ideologies, however, nationalism stresses the cultural similarity of its adherents and, by implication, draws boundaries vis-à-vis others, who thereby become marginalized or excluded. The distinguishing mark of nationalism is its relationship with the state: a nationalist holds that political boundaries should be coterminous with cultural boundaries, whereas many ethnic groups do not demand control over a state. Thus the difference between nationalism and ethnicity is clear if we adhere to this distinction, however, in practice the distinction can be much more complex.[33]

Why do people identify themselves as members of a particular ethnic group? Definitions of ethnicity vary according to the underlying theory embraced by researchers and scholars intent on resolving its conceptual meanings. The fact that there is no widely agreed upon definition is indicative of the confusion surrounding the topic. Here, attention is given to the various theories of ethnicity. The existing approaches tend to fall into two broad categories, the primordialists and the constructivists, those theorists who emphasize the socially constructed nature of ethnicity. The aim of this chapter is to provide an overview and systematic assessment of the main theoretical issues involved, thus enabling a framework of patterns and ideas to develop. I have tried to include many of the different concepts and interpretations that divide scholars of ethnicity, highlighting common ground as well as divergence between contrasting patterns of ideas. The focus will be on the literature and debates, which have been particularly influential in this area. During the late eighties, early nineties, we have witnessed an explosion in the growth of scholarly publications on ethnicity and nationalism, particularly in the fields of political science, history, sociology and social anthropology. In the case of social anthropology, ethnicity has been a main preoccupation since the late sixties, with the work of Frederik Barth and Abner Cohen, and it remains a central focus today. Anthropology has the distinct advantage of generating direct knowledge of social life at the level of everyday interaction. This is largely where ethnic consciousness is created and recreated. Ethnicity emerges and is maintained through social institutions, thus anthropology from its vantage point directly at the centre of local life, is in a unique position to investigate these interactive processes. This enables us to explore the way in which ethnicity is defined and perceived by people; how they talk and think about their own ethnic group as well as other ethnic groups, and how different perspectives are being maintained or contested. Therefore the significance of ethnic membership of a Diaspora group can most effectively be investigated through detailed grass roots research, which is the hallmark of anthropology.

This chapter also examines related debates in cultural studies and factors relating to diasporic identities. According to Jonathan Friedman 'ethnic and cultural fragmentation and modernist homogenization are not two arguments, two opposing views of what is happening in the world today, but two constitutive trends of global reality'.[34] Thus research on globalisation stresses the need to account for the relationship between the global on one hand and the local on the other. This perspective is the starting point for many post modernist theorists who argue that traditional sociological and political categories have become too ossified to embrace the fluidity of the contemporary world. As such the nation state is no longer an appropriate synonym for the ideal society.[35] Networks of communication, migration, trade, capital and politics cross virtually every boundary. For post modernists the collective identity of homeland and nation is a vibrant and constantly shifting set of cultural interactions. Post modern scholars discuss fluid bases of identity in which points of origin and settlement become blurred and are associated with multiple connections to various groups and practices. One of the central ideas is the socially constructed nature of ethnicity and the ability of individuals to 'cut and mix' from a variety of ethnic heritages and cultures to forge their individual or group identities. Such analyses examine diasporic identification and belonging thus forming an alternative to established writing about collective identity.[36] This debate openly acknowledges that the world is a less orderly place than we assumed. Essentially it is a response to the contradictions of relativism but most importantly post modernism is finally a recognition that ethnicity is subjective, inconsistent and definitively socially constructed.[37]

A study of this type would not be complete without an historical examination outlining the origins of the Armenian people thus providing an historical framework for Armenian dispersion and Armenian nationalism. Methodologically speaking the study of the modern Armenian Diaspora should, in my opinion, contain a study of the Armenian ancestral homeland. This is central to any informed analysis and understanding of the dispersal of the Armenian people. The Armenians who left the ancestral homeland, coerced or otherwise, brought their cultures, ideas and world views in all of its cultural richness and diversity and this has remained very much alive in the receiving countries as circumstances allowed.

Central to the perception of historical legacy among Armenians is the concept of the ancient Armenian homeland.[38] In the wake of the collapse of the Soviet Union, the new government of the independent Republic of Armenia assumed the legitimacy of independence and full statehood on the basis of a confident claim to antiquity as a nation and the historic responsibility for the Armenian people. Furthermore, citizenship was granted not only to those living within its territorial boundaries, but to those Armenians in the Diaspora who wished to exercise that right, thus as well as a new state, a new concept of nationhood was being invented for the world's Armenians.[39] Chapters Three and Four examine the historical legacy of the Armenians and also highlight the processes, which have had the greatest impact on the values and behaviour of Armenians; the adoption of Christianity in the fourth century; the rise of Armenian nationalism; the 1915 Genocide; the Soviet Republic of Armenia and its eventual independence in 1991.

When analysing the transnational setting of the Armenia Diaspora, one should first note the pre-eminent position of the Armenian Apostolic Church. One of the most commonly mentioned essences of Armenian identity, both in the past and in the present has been the church. No other institution has had a greater impact on shaping the national identity of Armenians than the Armenian Apostolic Church. At the present time, however, the church is divided into two rival branches: the Mother See in Etchmiadzin, Yerevan, and the Cilician (Sis) See in Antelias, Lebanon. Both are headed by a Catholicos or Pope and each presides over a transnational, ecclesiastical hierarchy termed respectively, the Diocese and the Prelacy. The Mother See in Etchmiadzin administers the church in the former Soviet Republics, and in most of Europe, South America, Australia and parts of North America. The jurisdiction of the Cilician See covers Lebanon, Syria, Iraq, Iran and many areas in North America and Venezuela. In addition, there are Armenian Patriarchates in Istanbul and Jerusalem, each of which has been in existence for hundreds of years, and owes nominal allegiance to the Mother See in Etchmiadzin, but in effect is self-administering.[40]

Despite the internal division of the Armenian Church, the Armenian Apostolic Church has served for centuries as the institutional focal point for Armenian nationhood. The Armenian Church has been independent of the Greco-Roman Church since the sixth century when, following the example of the Coptic and Syrian Orthodox Churches, it refused to accept the definition by the Council of Chalcedon in 451, of the relationship between the divine and human natures of Christ—often termed monophysite, rejecting what it regarded as unacceptable doctrinal innovation. Armenian theological scholars, however, reject the monophysite label, in contrast to the Copts, pointing out that Gregorians admit Christ's real human nature, although not the true mortality of his body. Gregorian rejection of the Council of Chalcedon, Armenian scholars contend, came about because the Council confused the two natures.[41] Nevertheless, the Armenian Church with its sister churches resented the growing ecclesiastical power of Byzantium and Rome and the fading prestige of Alexandria and Antioch, as leading Christian centres. Furthermore, a schism had arisen between the Gregorians and the orthodox Byzantine church decades before this doctrinal divergence when the former insisted on consecrating its own ecclesiastical head. The Gregorians argued that "there is a parallel to French rejection of 'the Donation of Constantine', because Armenia had never belonged to the Roman Empire, thus it need not recognise Constantinople's ecclesiastical jurisdiction."[42] Consequently, it held to the earlier Christological definition of St Cyril of Alexandria at the Council of Ephesus (431), "the one nature united in the Incarnate Word of God". To speak of the two natures after union, the Armenians insist, is to revert to heresy and endanger the doctrine of redemption.[43]

Although there are Diaspora Armenians of almost all world religions, the overwhelming majority of Armenians, including non-believers, still regard the Armenian Apostolic Church as a symbol of national integrity and identity. The adoption of Christianity as the state religion at the beginning of the fourth century, and the origination of a thirty six character, phonetic alphabet a century later, under church sponsorship, played a fundamental role in maintaining a distinct ethnic identity, for "in a real sense Armenians did not even fully become

'Armenian' until they acquired their own distinctively Armenian religion."[44] Armenians view themselves as the 'flock of new Israel' uz-hod nor Israeli, unreservedly committed to the Christian faith, which eventually became the ideological foundation of a peculiar religio-cultural nationhood centred in the Armenian Apostolic Church. Their faith and the invention by St Mesrop Mashtots of a unique alphabet for their Indo-European language has contributed significantly to the survival of Armenian identity.[45]

Armenians could certainly be considered an ethnie by about the early fourth century. By that time, the Armenians had adopted a unique religion, which distinguished them from their pre-Christian and later Muslim neighbours. According to Anthony Smith, 'religion has provided the most intense energy for many pre-modern ethnies, especially those that have evolved a myth of ethnic election'.[46] Those communities that managed to formulate and cultivate such beliefs have succeeded in prolonging the specific collective life of their members over many generations. The creation and dissemination of the belief that 'we are a chosen people' has been crucial for ensuring long term ethnic survival. Armenians perceive their church as the focal representation of their cultural traditions, and the one core institution that survived whilst their country suffered persecution from foreign empires. To this day, the church has more than an ecclesiastical significance and it remains a fundamental point of reference for individual identity. Thus, Armenian pride in being the first Christian nation cemented their belief in ethnic election and divine mission, a belief that the Armenian clergy vigorously nurtured throughout the communities. More importantly for most Armenians, Christianity has become essentialized as if all Armenians are somehow born Christian.

The Armenian Church still guards Armenian identity, with its own distinct practices and calendar, though these are not everywhere observed, and its hold, like that of other churches, has been loosened by the secularization of the modern era. The patterns of migration and settlement, however, over the last fifteen centuries of dispersion clearly point to the epicentric role of the Armenian Apostolic Church as preserver of ethnocultural identity. The church followed the immigrants wherever they went, and church buildings functioned as the centres of Armenian cultural life. Complete adherence to boundary mechanisms, in matters like endogamy were strongly enforced. Thus, the Armenian Church transcended its spiritual role to become the cultural overlord of the Diaspora. Fundamentally, the Armenian Church, with an unbroken institutional life of seventeen centuries, remains potentially a powerful, organisational force both in the homeland and the Diaspora communities.[47]

In the early nineteenth century, the unique millet system of self-government for the non-Muslim minorities of the Ottoman Empire apparently satisfied the Armenians, to the degree that the Ottomans knew them as the 'loyal community'. Pre-modern Armenians conceived of themselves as a religious community and much of what we understand to be nationality today was embodied in religious identification in earlier times. In the long years of Ottoman rule, religious identification was institutionalized in the Armenian millet, the political arrangement through which the Armenians were governed indirectly by the Ottoman authorities through the Armenian patriarch at Istanbul. It was religion that defined a people rather than language or ethnicity in the Ottoman world. In the Russian Empire also, the Armenians were united into a single religious community under the religious and educational authority of the Catholicos at Echmiadizin. It was the emergence of a new national consciousness in both Turkish and Russian Armenia that emphasized the ethnic culture of all Armenians, the vernacular languages of ordinary speech, and the desire to engage the modern world politically. The very concept of the Armenians as a religious community was challenged by Western ideas of secular nationality.[48]

The rise of nationalism, however, and the decline of the multi-national Ottoman Empire, began to change this situation throughout the nineteenth century, as one by one the various Christian nations on the Ottoman frontiers in the west broke away. During the late nineteenth century when the Armenian political parties began their activities, marking a new phase in Armenian realities, Western Armenians continued to consolidate their cultural structures and reinforce their identity. An extensive network of schools was set up, and numerous printing presses and libraries attended to the needs of a growing and cultivated readership. Armenian literature flourished acquiring its distinct features and very own canon. Numerous Armenian periodicals were published and widely distributed raising topical issues relating to social realities in Constantinople and throughout the provinces. Thus the Armenians were able to consolidate their unity and maintain adequate channels of communication, but most importantly this unity and Armenian distinctness was apparent in the pursuit of reform in the provinces. The reconstruction of Western Armenia was the overall goal of the Armenian Question. During the latter half of the nineteenth century and the first quarter of the twentieth, the relationship between the Armenians and the Ottoman Turks was to change significantly.

In 1878 the Balkans were granted liberty from Ottoman rule in the Treaty of Berlin. The Armenians sent a delegation to the Conference petitioning for some form of self government but found their hopes ruined with the promise of reforms but no provisions made for their enforcement. The self government, which began to work for the Christian nations of the Balkans, however, did not prove appropriate for the Armenians because unlike these other nations, the Armenians were concentrated in Anatolia, the heartland of the Ottoman Empire, and in addition constituted a minority in the very land they sought as their own autonomous or even independent state. Armenian independence, therefore, for the Ottomans was a logical absurdity and a threat to their very existence. These events had two important effects on Ottoman perceptions of the Armenians and the development of Armenian movements for autonomy respectively. Firstly it increased the Ottoman authority's suspicion and distrust of the Armenians who had turned to the European Christian powers, in particular Russia, with their demands for self government. A position that was no doubt exacerbated by the Ottoman Empire's loss of administrative control over the Balkan territories. Secondly, it encouraged the growth of nationalist movements among the Armenians who increasingly adopted policies of direct action to achieve reforms. These factors increased the tension between the Ottoman authorities and the Armenians which reached its peak under Sultan Abdul Hamid in 1895-6.[49] The First World War brought the Armenian Question to its frightful conclusion, resulting in the extinction of Turkish or Western Armenia in a series of deaths through deportations, massacres, disease, famine and war which the Armenians and many others refer to as the first genocide of the twentieth century. This chapter clearly illustrates the primacy of coercion—the massacres and expulsions that occurred in Ottoman Armenia in the late nineteenth and early twentieth centuries as causal factors of large-scale Armenian emigration from the historic homeland.

There is now a consensus among scholars that the Armenian genocide (1915), which was the first large-scale genocide of the twentieth century, is the prototype of much of the genocide that has occurred since 1945. Some of the patterns found in the Armenian case, have repeatedly appeared: there is a divided or plural society in which one ethnic group strives to dominate other distinct groups. This can lead to a quest for separation, even independence, and the challenge, real or imaged, to the control of government by the ruling ethnic group. Such demands are most likely to be employed at a time of political crisis, whether due to internal or external causes and in the process there is often a heightened emphasis on nationalism. Furthermore, if civil or international war breaks out, the likelihood of genocide is greatly enhanced as genocide can now proceed under the cover of war, and the victims can effectively be blamed for their own destruction.[50]

According to Suny, historians have generally excused the Ottoman deportations and massacres of the Armenians during the First World War as the result of incompatible ideologies, religious or nationalist, or as the unique political reaction of the Young Turks to a perceived danger to the Ottoman state. Such ideological or political explanations necessarily focus on the leadership of the two peoples as if by understanding the attitudes and behaviour of the two peoples the causes of the genocide may be understood. Certainly whilst it is necessary to focus on the political elites to understand the events of early 1915 that precipitated the Armenian tragedy, the scope of the killing, the degree of popular violence and the wide participation of various social classes requires an analysis which examines the social environment in which the Turks, Kurd and Armenians existed. For the Armenians an investigation is required to understand the passivity of the majority of Armenian victims as they met their death and the resistance of a small minority. For the Turks the principal examination should address how the benign symbiosis of several centuries broke down into genocidal violence.[51]

Both Armenian and Turkish scholars tend to examine their respective peoples from rather ethnocentric perspectives, largely ignoring the multi-national context in which they lived in Anatolia. Armenian scholars write as if Armenians continued for centuries to maintain their traditional national consciousness and aspirations of independence. Turkish scholars examine the Ottoman Empire almost exclusively from the point of view of the dominant people. Arguably, through a less ethnocentric history which broadens the contextual debate it may be possible to move forward the debates between Armenian and Turkish historians beyond the provocation thesis which asserts that Armenians caused their own destruction by engaging in revolutionary activities. Are we to assume that the national interest of one people validates the physical extermination of another? Are dual declarations to a single territory to be settled by deportation or massacre? If Armenians and Turks are to erase the pathological penalties of the mass murders that bind them together in historical memory, then these crimes must be recognised and their causes examined unemotionally. As Suny suggests, 'the courage must be found to rethink the unthinkable'.[52]

In December 1920 Armenia became a Soviet republic. The Sovietization of Eastern Armenia formalised the duality in the life of the Armenian people between those living under semi-indigenous authority and those in dispersion. Indeed, the sheer existence of a geographical unit in the name of the Soviet Socialist Republic of Armenia, no matter what its political system or degree of independence and sovereignty, had a unique significance for the Armenians, primarily because it was a novel phenomenon in the life of a people which had been deprived of its own state for several centuries. The establishment of Soviet power over a legally designated territory introduced important elements of stability: the promise of physical security and cultural autonomy for the Armenians living in the republic and those living throughout other parts of the Soviet Union. Many Armenians have played leading roles in Soviet society. The former president of the Soviet Union, the late Anastas Mikoyan, was an Armenian. Abel Aganbegyan, the chief economic adviser to Mikhail Gorbachev, is another prominent example. More importantly, however, the role of the Diaspora changed from being the source of aspirations for a future homeland, to one of assisting or indeed opposing a homeland that existed in reality. For the Dashnaks, who espoused a nationalist and irredentist cause, the destiny of Armenians lay in a free and independent Armenia. By contrast, the conservative Ramgavars accepted Soviet rule in 1920 as an inevitable and beneficial step towards ensuring eventual independence by providing a great power mandate over the beleaguered Armenians. In their view, Soviet rule was infinitely preferable to an independence threatened with annihilation by numerically and militarily superior Turkish forces.[53]

During the period 1915-1985 the Armenian Diaspora underwent a number of crucial stages in the construction of its identity and its relationship with the homeland. The genocide of 1915 created a new Diaspora, while at the same time a new homeland emerged in Eastern Armenia which was to become the foundation of a future Soviet homeland. Between the collapse of the independent republic and the recognition of the Soviet republic, the Armenians of the Diaspora slowly adjusted to the increasing reality that returning to their ancestral homeland was not an immediate option. Thus the recognition of Diaspora permanency was a gradual process which the Diaspora struggled with, to a greater or lesser extent, throughout the Soviet period. Increasing contact with Soviet Armenia simultaneously strengthened the Diaspora's homeland orientation and reinforced the political and cultural differences between the Diaspora and the homeland. At the same time, events in the homeland had a profound impact on the Diaspora in many ways. By way of example, Soviet Armenian policy towards the Diaspora exacerbated the cleavages within the Diaspora, providing a rallying point for unity in moments of national crisis. Moreover the renewal of national consciousness in the homeland during the 1960's fostered a similar revival in the Diaspora, and contributed to the emergence of new movements and organisations which challenged the hegemony of the traditional Diaspora organisations.[54]

The momentous events, and subsequent developments in the Soviet Union since 1985, have had a powerful impact on the Armenian Diaspora, in terms of its institutional structure, ideological orientation, morale and sense of priorities. Notwithstanding their earlier differences, between 1985 and 1991, the period of glasnost and perestroika, all Diaspora parties more closely identified with the social, political, and economic aspirations of the Soviet Armenian citizenry. These changes were primarily triggered by the devastating earthquake in Northern Armenia in December 1988, the demise of Soviet power, the proclamation of Armenia's independence, the Karabagh crisis and the resultant Azeri-Armenian confrontation. The impact of these crises galvanised the Armenian communities outside the Soviet Union. As the full realities of the troubles affecting Armenia began to unfold, it became clear that the external Diaspora would be called upon to play a crucial role in sustaining the new Armenian republic. The survival of Karabagh and the newly independent republic required a mobilised Diaspora that could provide not only economic assistance, but also political support and even military aid. These were alarming burdens for the geographically disparate Armenian communities.[55]

Chapter Five outlines the Methodology used for this research. This research is an ethnographic study of members of the Armenian Diaspora community in Manchester. Ethnography is a wide-ranging term with different traditions within different academic disciplines; however, common features often identified are that it involves empirical work in order to study people's lives. Essentially, all ethnographic studies examine people and aspects of their lives, and social worlds, which result in the production of a research text. Moreover, this text aims to be qualitative and non-reductive, incorporating change and process without resorting to simplistic aetiological or causation frameworks. Data for this research was collected in the form of focus groups and in-depth life history interviews. All interviews were tape-recorded and transcribed, and all respondents in this research are anonymous. Respondents were obtained from a variety of sources, including the Armenian Apostolic Church and associated organisations in Manchester, published lists of Armenian individuals and Armenian businesses as well as snowball referrals. Great care was taken in the selection of respondents to ensure that the selection represented the various sub-groups and categories within the Armenian community. Because visible activists, professionals, the clergy and self-employed business people are among the established elite of the Armenian community, the more recent immigrants, and young people were interviewed to gain a more rounded picture. In addition the sample includes Armenians from Iran, Iraq, Greece, Lebanon, and Egypt and their accounts inform us of Diaspora communities in their countries of origin. Thus, the respondents for this research include Armenians from a variety of backgrounds.

Chapter Six deals with my case study on the Armenian Diaspora community in Manchester. While the primary focus is on the group in question, this research is informed by theories from the broader fields of migration, ethnicity and Diaspora studies. This chapter examines the social and political processes that maintain and shape Diaspora identity. In particular, this case study analyses the ways in which Diaspora peoples balance lives rooted in a particular territory while also sharing very different social spaces. This is a case study in micro politics reflecting the aggregate result of choices made by individuals. The micro structures are the informal social networks and cultural links developed by the individuals themselves which bind ethnic communities in a complex web of inter-personal relationships. Diaspora as a conceptual tool and empirical reality, understood as a transnational social network relating to both the country of origin and the country of settlement can give a more profound understanding of the social reality in which migrants live. The concept of Diaspora, therefore, challenges the still widely held assumption that certain groups and their identities in some way automatically belong to a certain territory of which the idea of national identity is the most prominent. Empirical evidence from the Armenian Diaspora in Manchester is used to highlight the fact that the concept of Diaspora can provide an analytical tool for the study of individuals in their country of settlement.

Scholars of ethnicity[56] discuss fluid bases of identity in which points of origin and settlement become blurred and are associated with the recent literature on hybridity—the ability of individuals to 'cut and mix' from a variety of ethnic cultures to forge their individual or group identities. Such theories form an alternative to established writings about collective identity. These two discourses theorise the relevancy of patterns of identification while rejecting a discourse that is still based on the dichotomy of national and non-national. Diasporas can be thought of as positioned between host society, homeland and images of the Diaspora themselves. They are forced into a discourse about themselves since their presence is contrary to that of home and host. As Robin Cohen states 'the Diaspora provided an opportunity to construct and define their own historical experience—to invent their tradition'.[57]

This research illustrates that the cohesion and maintenance of the Armenian community does not derive from homogeneity or a collective ideal, it is maintained and reinforced from an acceptance of a symbolic framework which is multi-layered and expressed in a variety of ways. These feelings can be directed at a generalised tradition or the orthodoxy of immigrant religion. More often, however, they displace this desire on churches and cultural organisations, necessitating the recreation of tradition or rather a symbolic tradition, whilst at the same time living their lives as pragmatic responses to the society in which they reside. Among some people there exists a degree of ethnic awareness which is not a daily lifestyle but instead is only or mainly activated in times of interaction with other members of the same ethnic group or in times of crisis or on national holidays. Symbols of the genocide, the exilic Armenian, the Armenian homeland, language, and the Armenian Apostolic Church, gain strength from their ambiguity. It is because of the inherent ambiguity of symbols and their partial subjectivity that they are 'ideal media' through which people can speak a common language, behave in apparently similar ways and participate in similar rituals without subordinating themselves to a 'tyranny of orthodoxy'.[58] Individuality and commonality are thus reconcilable. Symbolic ethnicity provides the rallying point despite the communities' fluid boundaries and there is a strong continuity despite the shift in how the symbol is perceived. Therefore, the change in ethnic expression between generations in the Armenian Diaspora represents a change in form but not in substance. The ethnic identity of the later generations still maintains certain core values and symbols which are interpreted in such a way that it makes sense to that generation. As Herbert Gans[59] suggests all the cultural patterns which are transformed into symbols are themselves guided by a common pragmatic imperative: they must be visible and clear in meaning to large numbers of third generation ethnics, and they must be easily expressed and felt, without necessitating undue interference in other aspects of life. In this sense ethnic identity in a modern pluralistic society is highly relativistic and individualistic.

As with other immigrant groups in the United Kingdom, the Armenian community is unstable and changeable. Its cohesion is complicated by intergenerational divisions, by various degrees of identification with the homeland and by different extents of assimilation to and distinction from the main stream culture. The diversity of background is reflected in differences occurring between Manchester Armenians. They speak two major forms of the Armenian language; Western and Eastern Armenian. In Manchester, it is commonly Armenians of Iranian origins that use the Eastern inflection and reference to Eastern Armenian speakers is often synonymous with Armenians originating from Iran. Western Armenian speakers, however, originate from a number of different countries so that when reference is made to Western Armenian speakers it may incorporate a wide range of nationalities. Furthermore, the historical contexts of particular waves of immigrants within single groups contrast one another. The composition of different waves of immigrants may vary in class and region. Furthermore, once arriving in Britain very few immigrant cultures remain discrete, impenetrable communities. The more recent groups mix in varying degrees—they may intermarry with other ethnic groups. Thus the boundaries and definitions of Armenian culture are continually shifting and being contested from pressures both inside and outside the community. The reason to emphasise the dynamic fluctuation and heterogeneity of the Armenians is twofold. If minority immigrant cultures are perpetually changing in their composition and sometimes signifying practices as well as in their relationship to one another, it follows that the majority or dominant culture with which minority cultures are continually interacting with is also unstable and unclosed.

CHAPTER ONE

CONCEPTUAL CONSIDERATIONS OF DIASPORA

Large-scale international immigration has given rise to interdisciplinary discussions on the production and maintenance of ethnic identity within host countries. Concepts like Diaspora[1] in current discourse have acquired considerable significance as an analytical tool in the analysis of the emerging processes in societies where immigrants have settled. Confusion arises, however, because of the multiplicity of meanings assigned to this word. For over 2,500 years, one notion of the word Diaspora has been dominant, which highlights the catastrophic origin, the forcible dispersion and the estrangement of Diaspora peoples in their places of settlement. First used in the 'Septuagint', the Greek translation of the Hebrew scriptures explicitly intended for the Hellenic Jewish communities in Alexandria (circa 3rd century BC) to describe the Jews living in exile, Diaspora suggests a dislocation from the geographical location of origin and a relocation in one or more territories.[2] It has, however, assumed different meanings and interpretations since its early usages, and is currently employed in a wide variety of contexts. Indeed, it is often used as an all embracing phrase to categorise all migrations.

Therefore, broadly speaking we may think of a Diaspora as any community of individuals living permanently outside their real or imagined homeland, who identify themselves in some way with the state or peoples of that homeland, and maintain relationships with their homeland. The concept of Diaspora highlights the migrants' continuous relation to their countries of origin. Any such community consists of members who maintain some degree of consciousness of being different from its host society and act individually to express their identity and, more significantly, may organise themselves collectively in various ways to achieve their goals. Rarely, if ever, do individuals organise as a single collectivity. Consequently Diaspora organisations often conflict with each other, or simply seek different goals. Thus, the term Diaspora, which was once employed to imply meanings of exile, loss, dislocation, powerlessness and pain, is being used today to describe a wide range of dispersions.

In this sense, it has been argued that the labels Diaspora, migrant, refugee, expatriate and exile disclose differences in evaluation and orientation, differences in critical dealings with the phenomenon of migration, rather than differences in the migratory process as such. Thus, exile conveys a sense of loss, expatriate a sense of wealth and voluntary detachment and migrant a desire for upward mobility and so on. Beyond these labels, however, lies the migratory process whereby people operate as transnationals, interacting with people or institutions across the borders of nation states, rather than operating within circumscribed fields.[3] According to Khachig Toloyan[4] Diaspora communities now serve as 'exemplary communities of the transnational moment' where the Diaspora culture goes beyond and challenges several national boundaries. Among the variety of transnational communities that exist today such as transnational corporations (TNC's) and non-governmental organisations (NGO's), Diasporas emerge as symbols of transnationalism because they personify the question of borders. Thus, the concept of Diaspora is a useful analytical tool for an understanding of the transnational social reality in which immigrants live.[5]

The word 'Diaspora' is etymologically derived from the Greek dia 'through' and speirin 'to scatter seeds'. When applied to peoples, the ancient Greeks viewed Diaspora as 'migration and colonization'. According to Webster's Dictionary, Diaspora refers to 'dispersion from', thus the word embodies the idea of a home from where the dispersion occurred and it invokes images of a journey. Not every journey, however, can be understood as a Diaspora. Diasporas are clearly not the same as casual travel or temporary residence paradoxically diasporic journeys are essentially about settling down, and establishing permanent roots.

By contrast, Diaspora has been primarily associated by social scientists and historians with the dispersion of the Jews and Armenians,[6] thus the expression acquires a more sinister and brutal meaning, highlighting a collective trauma, a banishment where one dreamed of home but lived in exile. A further historical reference is the Black African Diaspora beginning in the sixteenth century with the slave trade, forcibly exporting Africans out of their native lands and dispersing them to the 'New World'—parts of North America, South American, the Caribbean and elsewhere that slave labour was exploited.[7] Therefore, when we talk of a trauma affecting a group collectively, it is perhaps possible to isolate those particular events in which the rapidity, scale and intensity of factors unambiguously compel migration or flight. Clearly, being dragged away in manacles, as were the Jews and Africans, and the forced expulsion of the Armenians from the Ottoman Empire appear qualitatively different phenomenon from the prevailing pressures of over population, poverty, hunger or unsympathetic political regimes. The Jews and Armenians were dispersed to such an extent that their Diaspora population greatly outnumbered the original homeland population, while the number of Diaspora Africans amounts to about forty million people, approximately one tenth of the black African population.[8]

The Palestinians also have an unambiguous case of almost complete dispersal. In 1947-48 they were violently displaced by the Israeli Zionists who asserted the right to a Jewish state. Some 780,000 Arabs were expelled from the territory controlled by the Israeli army, while a further 120,000 Palestinians were later classified as refugees because they had lost their land and livelihoods, but not their homes. In 1991, in the aftermath of the Gulf War, the Kurds captured world attention as an ethnic group struggling for self-determination. For a brief period, during March 1991, the Kurds controlled the territory that they considered to be their natal homeland—Kurdistan in Iraq. Within a month, however, government troops had pacified large areas of Kurdish resistance, and thousands of Kurds were dispersed. By some accounts as many as half a million Kurds fled to Turkey and 1.5 million to Iran. The cases of the Irish and Lebanese are also dramatic in terms of the number of people affected. The Irish lost twenty five per cent of their homeland population between 1845 and 1851, the years of the potato famine. Lebanon also experienced heavy population losses, around twenty five per cent of the population before 1914 and a similar amount during the civil war of the 1970's.[9]

All these traumatic historical events clearly bind these particular Diasporas. Fundamentally, they are 'victim Diasporas' in their historical experience. This does not mean, however, that they do not share characteristics with other self-proclaimed Diaspora communities it merely proves that their victim status is self affirmed and widely accepted by outside observers as their determining characteristics. There may also be compelling factors in the history of other Diasporas, but these may have involved fewer atrocities and may have had less effect on the natal society. It is clearly possible, therefore, to isolate those events in which the scale and intensity unequivocally compel migration. Indeed, until a few years ago most characterizations of Diasporas emphasized their catastrophic origins, their mass nature and their disturbing effects. Not every Diaspora, however, conforms to such a definition. There are Diasporas that emerged for reasons other than genocide or any other catastrophic event in the past. By way of example, Cohen distinguishes between victim, imperial, labour, trade and cultural Diasporas, among which only victim Diasporas by definition have a history of tragic origin.[10] Thus the concept has been generalized to refer to any people living outside their traditional 'homeland', who have maintained strong collective identities, and who have in recent years defined themselves as Diasporas, though they were neither active agents of colonization or passive victims of expulsion.

Certainly, the voluntarist component in the history of Jewish migration should not be overlooked, nor that all Jewish communities outside the natal homeland resulted from forcible dispersion. Jews do not have a single migration history. Indeed there is a rigid distinction by Jewish thinkers between 'galut', implying forced dispersion, and Diaspora, implying free and voluntary migration. Although 'galut' always implies a negative origin and condition, the word Diaspora is used similarly in the Jewish tradition.[11] Similarly, there is a distinction by Armenian scholars between the term 'spiurk',[12] the Armenian term for Diaspora and 'kaghuts' meaning colonies and 'kaghutahayutin', Armenians of the colonies. Communities of recent immigrants from Armenia are referred to as 'kaghuts' and Diaspora is a different term, one that assumes political integration, as dispersion has been part of Armenian reality for centuries. The distinction is significant because the new 'kaghuts' consist of people who left the Independent Republic of Armenia for economic reasons.

A further point emphasised by Marienstras is that time has to pass before we can know that an ethnic community has become a Diaspora. In other words, one does not announce the formation of the Diaspora the moment they arrive in the host country. As noted earlier, Diasporas are not synonymous with casual or temporary travel they are places of long-term settlement. Many members of a particular ethnic community may voluntarily wish to lose their prior identity and achieve individualised forms of social mobility. The changing of ethnically identifiable names by new immigrants illustrates this point, or they may inter-marry with the locals and gradually disappear as an identifiable ethnic group. Some assimilate in their host country and maintain only a marginal or selective interest in their homeland, whereas, by contrast, others remain rooted in their homelands and view their host country as only a temporary abode.

By way of example, the response from Armenians to life in dispersion, as with many other ethnic groups, was to make intense and lengthy efforts to maintain identity through communal insularity, until ties to the homeland were broken due to the passage of time or distance that made communication difficult or impossible. Inevitably, what ensued was assimilation. There was, however, an inverse relationship between the rate of assimilation and the incompatibility of the religious and cultural environment, and hostile Diaspora surroundings, thus the rate of assimilation was much lower in Muslim countries than in Christian countries.[13] A similar situation exists with the African Diaspora in the Americas where strong discrimination makes assimilation impossible, therefore, the more inhospitable the host country, the greater the survival of ethnic identity. Essentially, a strong attachment to the past, or a block to assimilation in the present and future, must exist in order to enable a diasporic consciousness to emerge or be retained.[14] Thus, Diasporas are not static, their membership expands or contracts, not just for demographic reasons but also because individuals may identify more or less with their homeland or host country, for changing reasons. Who is identified as a member of a community changes across time: similar peoples may be absorbed or peripheral elements may disappear.

According to Sanguin[15], Diaspora is used in both general and specific terms. In its general use, Diaspora refers to the movements of any distinct ethnic group to other parts of the world, whilst its specific use restricts the definition only to movements that have been massive and where the numbers who have left their homeland greatly outweigh those whom remain. In its general usage, this could apply to virtually any migration but the latter clearly could only refer to the movements of such peoples as the Jews, Armenians, Palestinians, Kurds and Lebanese. Sanguin further suggests that Diaspora could have a middle-range usage, referring to those ethnic groups from countries where there is still misery, over population, insecurity, dictatorship, or religious or racial persecution. Migratory movements that fall into this Diaspora category would be many and there does appear to be a common theme in creating Diaspora peoples, as more and more people are being expelled or pushed out of their homeland. Perhaps one of the reasons why the term Diaspora is becoming a central theme in migration studies is the increasing number of refugees or asylum seekers in the world. The redefinition of some refugees as 'economic migrants', the awareness of economic and environmental factors in the homeland, as well as political persecution, could render those places intolerable, thus blurring the distinction between refugees and other types of migrants. Consequently, this emphasizes the need to examine forced movements of people alongside other forms of migration within a unified framework.[16]

Kotkin (1993) views Diaspora cultures as expansionary groups being manipulated to exploit new opportunities in what he refers to as 'the making of global tribes'. Kotkin argues that strong Diasporas are the key to determine success in the global economy, and are likely to possess three characteristics, namely: a strong identity; an advantageous occupational profile; and a passion for knowledge. A strong ethnic identity fosters distance from the larger society that can be used for creative purposes. Furthermore, their unwavering loyalty to the Diaspora community inspires confidence born from their strong sense of identity. Certainly the persecutions suffered in the homeland, the denial of the opportunity to develop their own country, and their minority status in dispersion has combined to drive the Armenians to succeed whenever conditions were favourable. Therefore, the persistent quest for economic well being and educational achievement in Diaspora settings was a form of compensation for the Armenians' inability to develop their homeland as well as a device to achieve a sense of security in foreign environments.[17] Thus, Diasporas are outsiders as well as participants, comparing and learning from their experiences in the host country and other societies. Those members of society who belong to a Diaspora characteristically have an advantageous occupational profile, are more strongly represented in the professions and are less vulnerable to a volatile labour market. Finally, a passion for knowledge is characterised by a desire for education, specifically degrees, vocational or professional qualifications, which are the passports of the successful members of a Diaspora.[18]

Scholars of Diaspora acknowledge that the Jewish tradition is at the heart of any definition, and provides the basis for an ideal type. The most precise definition of Diaspora is Saffran who proposes that the concept of Diaspora be applied to minority communities whose members share several of the following characteristics:

1. They or their ancestors have been dispersed from a specific original 'centre' to two or more 'peripheral' or foreign regions;
2. They retain a collective memory, vision or myth about their original homeland—its physical location, history and achievements;
3. They believe they are not—and perhaps cannot be—fully accepted by their host society and therefore feel partly alienated and insulated from it;
4. They regard their ancestral homeland as their true, ideal home and as the place to which they or their descendants would (or should) eventually return—when conditions are appropriate;
5. They believe that they should, collectively, be committed to the maintenance or restoration of their original homeland and its safety and prosperity and they continue to relate, personally or vicariously to that homeland in one way or another, and their ethnocommunal consciousness and solidarity are importantly defined by the existence of such a relationship.[19]

Thus it is possible to distinguish five components of Diaspora: Dispersion; Myth, Alienation; Idealization and Commitment. Most importantly the term

Diaspora is used with regard to the ethnic community of people dispersed from their homeland to two or more foreign territories. This dispersal is the initial attribute without which the phenomenon simply would not exist.

Myth

The Diaspora-homeland relationship is to varying degrees defined by a myth of election. The original homeland for Diaspora communities may be an ideological construct or myth, but no less significant to them than specific homelands to which other migrant communities relate, thus the idea of a shared origin and birthplace is a common feature of Diasporas. By way of example, the Armenians claim to be descendants of Noah, whose ark came to ground on the top of Mount Ararat, where the earth was reborn. The Jews say they are the 'chosen people', all descendants of the prophet Abraham, and the Lebanese claim they are Phoenicians. The Indians, or at least the Hindu element, look back to the complex of gods and goddesses, notably Vishnu, Shiva, and Shakti, who gave birth to the sacred land of India and the River Ganges. Indeed the more ancient the myth, the more Diaspora groups utilise it as a form of social distancing from other ethnic groups, essentially giving rise to an air of superiority, even when faced with hostility and discrimination. Thus, a member's adherence to a Diaspora community is perpetuated by a collective memory and myth about the original or idealized homeland, which cements the diasporic consciousness and gives it legitimacy.[20]

Furthermore, the creation and dissemination of the belief that we are a 'chosen people' has been crucial for ensuring long-term ethnic survival. A myth of ethnic election should, however, not be equated with plain ethnocentrism—where ethnic communities have quite commonly ignored or derided other ethnic communities. A myth of ethnic election is more demanding. To be chosen is to be placed under certain moral, ritual and legal obligations. The classical expression of such beliefs among the ancient Israelites is to be found in the Book of Exodus, Chapter 19: 'Now therefore if ye will obey my voice indeed and keep my covenant, then shall ye be a peculiar treasure unto me from all peoples; for all the earth is mine; and ye shall be unto me a kingdom of priests and a holy nation'.[21] The covenant refers to a code of morality, law and ritual, set out in detail in the book of Deuteronomy. It is only by keeping these laws and ceremonies that the community and its members can be saved.[22]

A powerful myth of election also emerged in the kingdom of Armenia after its conversion to Christianity in 301AD. As founders of the first Christian state, Armenians have always felt a great sense of pride as the bearers of the divine grace and view themselves as the 'flock of new Israel' uz hod nor Israeli, unreservedly committed to the Christian faith which eventually became the ideological foundation of a religio-cultural nationhood centred on the Armenian Apostolic Church. Such ethnocultural identity served as the ideological underpinning of Armenian nationhood for 1500 years both in the homeland and Diaspora. It is significant because Armenians throughout the ages have regarded themselves not simply as a people but as a nation even after the loss of independence which persists in diverse Diaspora settings.[23] This conception imposes a heavy burden on the chosen people who are continually required to maintain strict moral standards. Indeed this close relationship with God and its inevitable moral demands on a community became the social and psychological motive of Jewish and Armenian survival. The intensity of identity produced by older sacral myths, based on but not always co-extensive with distinctive religions, has never been exceeded by modern secular myths.[24]

Since the birth of the anthropological tradition myth has been, together with magic and religion, among the most examined of its subjects, which is significant of the troublesome nature of this concept than of its disciplinary success. Myth as a term has been employed anthropologically to refer to the stories told by indigenous peoples about their origins. Mythical stories are said to present a nonsensical world where identity is fragile, causality perverse and time erased and distorted. It is through myth that people relate a particular metaphysical understanding of why things are or who they are. What anthropologists have viewed as myth has been understood as a problem of rationality that must be explained. In other words, while the scientist tells us of reality, the content of myths belongs to the domain of illusions.[25]

Nevertheless current scholarly analysis more or less accepts two basic premises. First, myths express, call to mind and deal with, if not directly at least consciously, people's reality claims about the world and second, mythic truths relate more to a moral, evaluative or important universe of meanings than to a natural one. Myth is one of the ways in which ethnic groups establish and determine the foundations of their own being. It is the content of the myth that is important not its accuracy or historical content. Increasingly, anthropologist are also accepting a third premise, namely that knowledge is not tied solely to reason and the material world of natural law and that there are many types of knowledge, empirical, rhetorical and metaphorical, social, moral and aesthetic knowledge among others.[26]

The role of myth emphasises the need to pay more attention to the subjective elements involved in ethnic survival. The reason being that long term ethnic survival depends in the first place on the active advancement by specialists and others of a heightened sense of collective distinctiveness and mission, by nurturing myths of distant origins and symbols of a golden age of former glory which have allowed for our particular humanity and those of our enemies of whom we must beware. Thus we find that myths of identity are equally myths of alterity, or significant otherness, for to state identity is also to speak of difference. Such a community is thus made to feel that their historic community is unique and myths of ethnic election have helped to mobilize communities and ensure their survival over long periods of time. It may also strengthen a community's attachment to its historic territory. Only the sacred land where their forefathers lived, their heroes fought and their saints prayed are fit for the elect. The ethnic myth is a dramaturgical story that links the present with a communal past, and one that is widely believed. This helps to draw members into a distinct ethnic community, conferring on them that of the elect, the chosen. In this view, the stress is placed upon the value of myths to society, in that it serves to reinforce social cohesion and unity. Furthermore, through its symbolism it strives to unify different classes and regions, spreading ethnic culture outwards from the urban centres and the specialists who guard such traditions, thereby creating a more shareholder society.[27]

According to Schopflin such myths are placed beyond question by making them sacred or taboo.[28] If they were questioned the society would either shift its sacralised sphere somewhere else or it would fragment. The essential foundations of a society cannot be left open to investigation by Enlightenment rationality. Sacralisation can take a variety of forms. It can be accomplished by creating and maintaining a state over a very long period of time, so that its origins are unclear and the populace accepts it as the only feasible form of living. There is, however, generally more to sacralisation than an uncomplicated cognitive closure. The most effective way of constructing consent is to base it on culture and it is here that this examination arrives at its most contentious point—that of linking consent to ethnicity. The core of the argument is that one of the characters of a shared culture is that it encompasses the links of solidarity that inform the members of a collectivity what their implicit obligations are to one another, what they share and what they do not. Solidarity, however, does not assume consensus, indeed solidarity makes a variety of disagreements possible by establishing the boundaries of disagreement. Thus the name given to this cultural solidarity is ethnicity. What this means is that an ethnic community will do virtually anything to ensure that it survives and it makes use of instruments to ensure its cultural reproduction. The ultimate aim of an ethnic group is to gain universal recognition for itself as a community of moral worth, as a bearer of collective values on the same terms as all other ethnic groups. Ethnicity is a central means of creating unity and order. Through this unity individuals identify mutual bonds and responsibilities. Essentially they acquire moral worth in their own eyes by being members of a community of shared solidarity.[29]

As discussed, myths of origin are powerful strategies that have the potential to make sense of the present, legitimise the existing political order and offer group identity. In contemporary ethnic groups and nations, history is used in the same way. In a very influential volume entitled 'The Invention of Tradition',[30] historian and anthropologists investigate how the past can be manipulated in order to validate a particular view of the present. Examples discussed include the Scottish Highland tradition and rituals invented by colonial authority in order to justify that the colonial empire was ancient and innate. According to Eriksen, however, there is no need to limit oneself to traditions that are recent and conceal political agendas, the past can be viewed in a whole host of ways as any comparison of history will reveal.[31] Obviously the history of the Ottoman Empire is not described in identical ways to Turkish and Armenian school children. As the present changes, so does the past and all interpretations of history are selective.

Alienation

Diasporas do not quickly assimilate into the host country. Through a combination of preference and social exclusion, they maintain their ethnic identity and unity over extended periods of time. This historical dimension of Diaspora formation is emphasized by Marienstras who argues that time has to pass before we can know that any community that has migrated becomes a Diaspora.[32] According to Gold, Jewish communities have provided their own members as well as co-ethnics abroad with education and assistance and have played important roles in helping their members resist assimilation into the Christian societies in which they lived.[33] After three generations the Armenian community in France, although French speaking and well established economically, maintains its Armenian solidarity and applauds, when it does not directly support, terrorist actions against Turkish targets.[34]

It is important to remember, however, that the maintenance of an ethnic or Diaspora identity is about cultural differentiation. Identity is always a dialectic between similarity and difference.[35] Ethnicity emphasises cultural distinctiveness. Ethnic ideologies stress the cultural similarities of its adherents and by implication draw boundaries vis-à-vis others. For difference to be socially marked, it follows that there has to be something to utilise as its marker, no matter how minor or arbitrary. Ethnicity occurs when cultural differences are made relevant through interaction. Thus the very nature of Diaspora emphasises the inability or unwillingness to be fully accepted by the host country, thereby fostering feelings of alienation, exclusion, superiority, or other kinds of difference.

Diaspora consciousness may also be heightened by the Diaspora's relationship with the host country. In some host countries alienation and discrimination are recurrent themes, rather than political integration or assimilation, resulting in a defective relationship with the host society. Unfortunately, a defective relationship with the host country is a common feature of a Diaspora community and most groups have at some stage experienced discrimination in their host countries. The Irish in England, Caribbean peoples in Europe, Sikhs in Britain, Poles in Germany, Italians in Switzerland, Turks in Germany, Kurds in Turkey, and more recently Albanians in Greece.[36] All these peoples, and many others, have experienced overt hostility and legal or illegal discrimination. Indeed some ethnic groups have become the recipients of extreme violence and racial hatred in their countries of migration. When a Diaspora community faces persecution by the host government, its interests in the homeland will typically intensify. What makes this form of inter-ethnic tension different is that Diaspora groups can reach outside their immediate communities to other Diaspora communities, for comfort, comparison and identification, and nurture the possibility of returning to their homeland, real or imagined, thus reinforcing solidarity with Diaspora members in other countries.[37]

The higher the socio-economic status of immigrants, the easier it is for them to maintain connections with their homeland. Communication with relatives and financial remittances are the most common form of exchange. Indeed Armenian emigrants send approximately $250 million per year to their relatives in Armenia, an amount equivalent to nearly half the annual state budget.[38] These valued characteristics, however, may also facilitate their integration in their host country and reduce their incentives for maintaining homeland relationships. For instance, the number of Israeli academics and professionals who have settled abroad poses an important concern for Israeli policy makers. They include scientists, doctors, engineers and computer specialists who have sought professional advancement and increased earnings, not to mention Israeli students who, after studying overseas and graduating found greater rewards elsewhere.[39]

Migrant communities may look to the homeland and perhaps to its government for cultural reinforcement in the form of teachers and religious leaders.

More importantly, the links between Diasporas and their homelands can be politicised, and this is their major significance in the study of international relations. They may, therefore, take a vital interest in political developments in the homeland and even be mobilised and focused to influence political outcomes in the homeland, to provide economic, diplomatic and even military assistance to the homeland. Individual migrants may be significant actors or collective associations may be powerful pressure groups in the domestic politics of their host countries as well as in the international political arena, usually prompted by the political plight of a country of origin—the Jewish, Armenian and Irish lobbies in the United States are the obvious examples. Sheffer emphasises how the growing role of new non-governmental transnational organisations in the political arena e.g., groups such as Armenian organisations linked together in the United States, France and the Middle East, demonstrates how transnational communities are amongst the world's most sophisticated political lobbyists.[40] According to Milton 'the scope and intensity of Diaspora activities, including those that affect international relations, are determined by three factors: the material, cultural and organisational resources available to them; the opportunity structures in their host country; and their inclination or motivation to maintain their solidarity and exert group influence'.[41] Thus alienation is a factor, though not a necessary condition, for Diasporas to retain or cultivate homeland connections.

Idealisation

The contrast between the current condition of the Diaspora and its imagined past is resolved by the actual return or assistance given to return movements within the Diaspora. Indeed the return of the community to its ancestral home, from which it had been exiled, became the precondition of collective redemption. Zionism is the classic example with its secular fulfilment of ancient Jewish aspirations as well as Philhellenism, Pan-Africanism, Garveyism, and the attempts to recreate Greater Armenia. All these are represented by the political vanguards of the Diasporas as the only stable means to overcome their uncertain and isolated existence in exile.[42] Since historical times, Armenians have perceived the Diaspora as a temporary phenomenon, a transient existence that would culminate in the inevitable return to the homeland. The return to the homeland is seen almost as an eschatological concept being viewed as the precondition of collective redemption. Many Armenian clerics use the Christological illustration of death and resurrection when describing the Armenian experience of the genocide and the spiritual imagery of re-birth is often used to describe the re-establishment of the Armenian homeland. This psycho-spiritual predisposition has been a pervasive and persistent feature of the Armenian dispersion, although with the passage of time many Armenians have had to establish roots and a sense of permanence.[43]

As it is for other peoples, the homeland for Armenians is and has been a contested and evolving notion. It is shaped by the personal memories, experiences, ambitions and hopes of people at particular times and by the desires and plans of intellectuals, priests and political leaders. For centuries there has been no single, clearly defined homeland for all Armenians. The confusion increases as political parties emphasize ideological notions of homeland, detached perhaps from personal experience but rooted in the past and in contemporary political events. The land that is now the Republic of Armenia or Hayastan as Armenians call it was previously a small corner of ancient historic Armenia. It declared a brief independence between 1918-20 and then became part of the Soviet Union. It is one construction of the Armenian homeland for those who live there and for many Diaspora Armenians. The importance of its survival is one of the few things that almost all Armenians there and in the Diaspora agree upon. A second homeland is also called Hayastan—the ancient homeland rooted in the 2,500 year history, the ancestral home of most of those now in the Diaspora. This is the homeland for intellectuals and activists. A return to at least some of this land, in particular Mount Ararat, forms a major platform for the Dashnak Party.

Indeed the dominant discourse portrayed the Diaspora as a temporary deviation for Armenians. Moreover, at least in rhetoric, the Diaspora was presented as a means to an end, the end being the homeland, its restoration and security. The myth of return functions as a source of purpose and destiny for the Diaspora in that it is providing an ideological justification for the perpetuation of the Diaspora and its structures. Whilst the homeland may have moved on, the Diaspora communities cling desperately to pre-Diaspora customs and structures because they view themselves as the custodians of national heritage. Thus, while the myth of return looks forward to the restoration of the homeland, it is also backward looking in that it often seeks a return to an historical era which, in most cases, is no longer plausible. This gives the Diaspora communities a rather nostalgic and romantic character—the institutions of the old world are idealised and the geography of the homeland sentimentalised. Essentially, the Diaspora community's image of the homeland is far removed from the current reality.

At the same time, however, there is an increasing willingness to acknowledge that, given the opportunity, most Diasporans would not return to the homeland, at least not to live. Indeed following the collapse of the Soviet Union only a small number of American-Armenians returned to the homeland on a permanent basis. Nowhere is this more evident than in the Western Diaspora communities since modern pluralist democracies such as the United States, Canada, France and the United Kingdom offer a fair degree of tolerance and security for ethnic minorities. Furthermore, there are obvious economic advantages in remaining in these countries, and very little to lure the Diaspora back to the homeland on a permanent basis. Diasporas living in the United States or the United Kingdom are less likely to forfeit the comfort of their life style to return to a poor or unstable homeland. Interestingly Robin Cohen recognises this as a further characteristic of Diasporas—'the possibility of a distinctive creative, enriching life in tolerant host countries'.[44] Even victim Diasporas can find their experiences in modern nation states fulfilling and creative. The Jews considerable intellectual and spiritual achievements simply could not have happened in a tribal society such as Ancient Judaea. The Armenians and Irish have thrived materially and politically in the United States. The Palestinians are characteristically more prosperous and better educated than the locals in their countries of exile. Africans in the Diaspora have produced influential music forms such as jazz, samba and reggae and generated major innovations in literature and poetry.[45]

By way of example, in 1991, the Los Angeles Times featured an interesting article which examined homeland orientation in the light of Armenia's new found independence. The article explained that for many American-Armenians the 'myth of return' was for decades at the core of their lives, however, as one interviewee was quoted as saying 'now the dream is a reality, what do you do? "We are and most of us will remain Diasporans" exclaimed one respondent. Of the many Diasporans who have visited Armenia since 1988 only a few were likely to settle there permanently. There are marked differences in culture, mentality, political culture and socio-economic conditions between the homeland and the Diaspora and over time, these differences have become practically irreconcilable. A recent immigrant was bewildered by all this talk of return and viewed the exiles as idealists who have no concept of what life was like in Armenia.[46]

Despite the effectiveness of the Diaspora to the homeland, however, Diaspora members are not always welcomed home. For example, they are often perceived as too Westernised or even politically dangerous. Furthermore, cultural disparities run both ways and the Diaspora and the homeland have often drifted apart to the point where it becomes useful to ask whether they should be considered two separate nations. Differences also exist between the nationalist ideologies of the two parts of the nation, particularly with regard to the question of identity and what constitutes membership of that nation. The Diaspora response to the uncertainty of the Diaspora-homeland relationship is typically to engage in re-imagination. As Marienstras writes both the Jews and Armenians produce numerous definitions of themselves to understand what they are.[47]

Commitment

Members of a Diaspora believe they should be collectively committed to the maintenance or restoration of their original homeland and its safety and prosperity. They continue to relate, personally or vicariously to that homeland in one way or another, and their ethnocommunal consciousness and solidarity are importantly defined by the existence of such a relationship.[48] There are, however, many criteria that characterise the types of activity in which individuals may engage. At one extreme, migrants act only as individuals and display no sense of solidarity with fellow migrants. A bond of loyalty to the country of settlement can compete with ethnic solidarity. There is frequently a considerable reluctance by those who have travelled quite far down the path of assimilation to accept too close an association with a discriminated or low-status ethnic group. At the other extreme, they eagerly join associations, political parties and other movements designed to promote various causes. This may involve cultural, linguistic, familial, religious, social, economic, political, educational, or any combination of these or other interests. Some may engage in activities that only involve extended families or native villages.[49] Others specialise in the flow of information or focus on economic interests involving their homelands. Some engage in all these forms of interaction, whereas others may focus on just one.[50]

For instance, soon after the earthquake in Armenia in 1988, Armenians throughout the world initiated successive campaigns to despatch funds, medicine, equipment and basic essentials to provide short-term aid to the thousands left destitute. The Azerbaijani-Turkish blockade and the Soviet government's failure to implement reconstruction programmes further highlighted the imperative of systematic planning in the various Diaspora communities in order to provide comprehensive assistance to Armenia's economy on a long term basis. One such case was the establishment of the United Armenian Fund, composed of seven major Diaspora Church and relief organisations, backed by Kirk Kerkorian's[51] Foundation, which despatched plane loads of supplies to the homeland on a regular basis. At the same time, Armenian political groups lobbied their host governments to extend economic assistance to the Armenian homeland.[52]

Nonetheless, these protracted efforts brought about a gradual realization that the resources of the Diaspora were insufficient to sustain Armenia's economy, and a conflict of priorities soon beset the Diaspora communities. This conflict in priorities became exacerbated by the needs of a growing number of economic migrants from Armenia and other parts of the former Soviet Union. Furthermore, it is unusual for individuals to support a single organisation, thus conflict between different Diaspora groups is commonplace. Indeed the chronology of Diaspora communities often creates overlapping communities with different perspective and goals. Historically, Armenian intra-communal politics has involved struggles amongst leaders, ideologies and political groups seeking to dominate the Church and the community. These political conflicts are often exacerbated by generational and gender distinctions as well as class conflicts and cultural cleavages between newcomers and older immigrants and amongst groups of immigrants from different countries of origin.[53]

By way of example, Robert Mirak[54] comments on the alienation of the more recent Armenian immigrants from the Republic of Armenian (Hayastantsis) in California who are charged with living off the welfare system, an anathema to the self-reliant older generation, and therefore excluded in many instances from communal assistance. By contrast the recent Armenian immigrants have accused the older Armenians of failing to retain their ethnic identity, since these older Armenians, or at least their children, do not speak fluent Armenian. The newcomers clearly identify themselves as more loyal to the Armenian historic culture. Similarly, how American Jews relate to Israeli immigrants is complex. While American Jews have a notorious record for supporting the Israeli state, they have often viewed Israelis settling in the United States with ambivalence. American Jews see themselves playing a vital role by contributing money and ensuring political support for the Israeli state. The role of Israelis, however, in their view, is to inhabit, develop and defend Israel, thus leaving the Jewish state, has been perceived negatively to American Jews.[55]

In summary, the early literature on Diasporas no doubt started from the observation that the Jewish Diaspora experience had apparent counterparts elsewhere. This launched an exploration to determine the extent to which similar characteristics could be found for use in theoretical analyses and explanations. Diaspora communities generally speaking possess a number of characteristics. Regardless of their location, members of a Diaspora share an emotional attachment to their ancestral homeland, are aware of their dispersal and if conditions warrant, of their oppression in the countries in which they reside. Members of a Diaspora also tend to possess a sense of racial, ethnic or religious affiliation which transcends geographic boundaries, share some broad cultural similarities and sometimes articulate a desire to return to the homeland. No Diaspora community manifest all of these characteristics or shares with the same intensity an identity with its scattered peoples. Indeed in many respects Diasporas are not actual but imaginary and symbolic communities.

In order to simplify the definitional process one overriding factor can be ascertained from Saffran's criteria. All five criteria emphasize the awareness or consciousness of being a Diaspora. Essentially if Diaspora as an analytical concept is to be a useful tool for scholarly analysis, it must include some notion of consciousness. The reason is that much of what is interesting about Diasporas is their relationship with their homeland and indeed their host country. If a Diaspora is not aware of being a Diaspora then these relationships cease to be important, the community is no longer a politically significant presence and the Diaspora community becomes another minority sub-culture within a pluralistic society. In such cases the community may be a Diaspora in the literal sense of the word—a dispersion of people but it has no meaning as an analytical concept.[56]

Once conceptualised as an exilic dislocation from homeland, Diaspora has therefore acquired new epistemological and political identities. Thus Diaspora is now employed to describe the dispersed communities outside the Jewish and Armenian experience. The Diaspora communities of the twenty first century are in a position to extend their connections to their home countries with growing intensity and establish networks globally. Globalisation has improved the practical, economic and effective roles of Diasporas proving them to be particularly adaptive forms of social organisation. Their relative solidarity and integration are particularly evident in relation to the local populations amongst whom they live Certainly many powerful and wealthy actors profit from globalisation, however, there is often a striking discrepancy between Diaspora communities and the local working class, where unemployment, temporary contracts, and the unstable job market have virtually destroyed any sense of solidarity. The profile of Diasporas with many being educated and professionally qualified has allowed them to avoid the worst impact of global restructuring.[57]

Globalisation and Transnationalism

Notions of globalisation have grabbed many an intellectual imagination over the past two decades and the concept of globalisation is employed across disciplines, across theoretical approaches and across the political spectrum. We are surrounded by globalizing developments: global communications; global markets; global commons. Yet ideas of globalisation tend to remain as elusive as they are pervasive. Persistent ambiguity over the term has fed considerable scepticism about 'globaloney' and 'global babble'.[58] Globalisation is often equated with the notion of liberalization. With this understanding globalisation indicates a process of removing legitimately imposed limits on movement of assets between countries in order to form an open and borderless world economy. Thus globalisation is about contemporary neo-liberal macro-economic policies. Although various theoretical approaches are represented in the literature, most authors suggest that nation states are becoming progressively less sovereign in terms of control over their own affairs. The most influential argument for considering the world a single economic system comes from Wallerstein (1990). His primary unit of analysis is the world system, which has the capacity to develop independently of the social processes and relationships which are internal to its components societies or states. Wallerstein states:

> The capitalist world economy has seen the need to expand the geographic boundaries of the system as a whole, creating thereby new loci of production to participate in its axial division of labour. Over 400 years, these successive expansions have transformed the capitalist world economy from a system located primarily in Europe to one that covers the entire globe.[59]

Many academics, corporate executives and policy makers support neo-liberal recommendations with the undertaking that world scale liberalization, privatization, de-regulation and financial restraint will bring wealth, freedom and democracy for all. Critics oppose neo-liberal policies arguing that a laissez-faire world economy creates greater poverty, inequality, social divergence, ecological damage and cultural damage. According to Giddens (2002) a fundamental failing of this type of approach concerns the interpretation of the growing unification of the nation state system. The sovereign power of modern states was not formed prior to their involvement in the nation state system, even in the European state system, but developed in conjunction with it. Thus, the sovereignty of the modern state was from the first dependent upon the relations between states. No state, however powerful, held as much sovereign control in practice as was enshrined in legal principle. A further shortcoming is that World systems theory concentrates solely on the economic influences as being responsible for global change.[60] Certainly large scale globalisation and widespread economic liberalization have emerged simultaneously in the past quarter of a century. It is something else, however, to conflate the two concepts. Such an equation can transmit the unconvincing and potentially harmful implication that neo-liberalism is the only available policy framework for a global world.

Globalisation is also interpreted as internationalization. From this global standpoint ideas, merchandise, money and people cross borders between nation states. Authors like Hirst and Thompson[61] suggest that the global is a particular component of the international. Indeed most accounts of globalisation as internationalization stress that contemporary trends are replaying earlier historical scenarios. 'As we coin new terms such as globalisation to capture the newness of developing conditions, we exacerbate the confusion by pouring old wine into new bottles'.[62] In other words, how far do contemporary trends compare with earlier historical belle époques of globalisation, namely the period 1890-1914.[63] If globalisation is nothing other than internationalization, except possibly for larger amounts of it, then why bother with new terminology.

A further conception of globalisation is often defined in terms of Westernization. Appadurai[64] traces this interconnedness back to the late fifteenth and early sixteenth centuries, when the West's encounter with the rest of the world created an overlapping set of ecumenes in which conquest, money, migration and commerce began to form durable cross cultural bonds. The problems of distance and the confines of technology, however, have generally restricted the interactions of the past, so that it was very difficult, and costly, to sustain dealings between culturally and spatially separate groups. Therefore, it is really only over the last century, with the advent of modern technology, particularly in transportation and communication that we have entered into a more profound global condition, which encompasses in varying degrees, those traditionally most remote from each other.[65] Globalisation in this way is often interpreted as colonization or imperialism. Indeed globalisation has often introduced patterns of Western social relations more extensively across the world, often concerning violent imposition that could merit descriptions as imperialism. Nevertheless it is one thing to assert that globalisation and Westernization have had interconnections and quite another to equate the two developments. Globalisation could in principle take non-Western directions e.g., Buddist or Islamic. Also it is by no means clear that globalisation is intrinsically imperialist given that there are emancipatory global social movements as well as exploitative processes.[66]

A more recent definition, not least in anthropological circles, defines globalisation as the spread of transplanetary and more particularly supraterritorial connections between people. This perspective refers to the intensification of global interconnectedness, suggesting a world full of movement and mixture, contact and linkages, and persistent cultural interaction. It is a world where borders and boundaries have become increasingly more porous, in which a myriad of processes, operating on a global scale, cut across national boundaries, integrating cultures and communities. People become more able physically, legally, culturally and psychologically to engage with each other in one world.[67] It is a world where the rapid flows of capital, people, goods, images and ideologies draw more of the globe into webs of interconnections, compressing our sense of time and space, and making the world feel smaller and distances shorter. In this usage globalisation refers to a shift in the nature of social space.

The term globality resonates of spatiality.[68] It says something about the arena of human action and experience, in particular globality recognizes the world as a whole as a site of social relations in its own right. Talk of the global illustrates that people may live together not only in the local, national and regional realms but also in transplanetary spaces where the world is a single space. There is no doubt that the world as a whole is experientially shrinking. No statistical measures of global consciousness are available, however, it seems safe to assume that people today are generally more aware than ever before of the world as a single place and are more inclined to regard the earth as humanity's home. Knowledge in the classroom, world weather and news reports, and global products in the cupboard all point to a global mindset. Globality is thus part of everyday awareness for hundreds of millions of people across the world.[69]

Globality has two qualities: the more general feature, transplanetary connectivity has figured in human history for centuries. The more specific characteristic, supraterritoriality is relatively new to contemporary history but is evident in countless features of contemporary life. By way of example, jet airplanes transfer people and goods across any distance within twenty four hours. Telephone and computer networks effect instant interpersonal communication between points all over the earth, so that a call centre for customers in the United Kingdom may be located in India. The global mass media spreads messages concurrently to transworld audiences. Currencies are examples of direct transplanetary circulation particularly when in digital form. In the field of organisations, voluntary organisations and regulatory agencies coordinate their respective activities across transworld domains. Ecologically, developments such as climate change, stratospheric ozone depletion, and losses of biological diversity unfold simultaneously on a world scale. The worldwide dissemination of AIDS and other epidemics is an instructive, if grotesque example that globalisation is not limited to contact mediated by abstract structures such as the mass media, contact across regional and national borders can be physical and direct.[70] Global human rights campaigns do not measure their support for a cause as a function of the territorial space and territorial borders that lie between advocates and victims. Indeed such manifestations of supraterritoral connectivity have reached unparalleled levels during the past half century. Earlier periods did not know jet travel, intercontinental missiles, satellite communications, the Internet, instant transplanetary television broadcasts, transworld retailers, global credit cards and a continuous diet of global sports tournaments. Contemporary world history is supraterritorial to degrees well beyond anything previously known.[71] Thus globaility means that we have been living for a long time in a world society in the sense that the notion of closed spaces has become illusory. No country or group can shut itself off from others.

It is not necessarily the case, however, that the world is shrinking for everyone and in all places. The experience of globalisation is an uneven process. By way of example, many people may possess the political and economic means to travel around the world but many more have little or no access to transport and means of communication. Furthermore, there are places only superficially tied into such global webs of interconnection. According to Allen and Hamnett[72], whole areas of Africa are quite literally off all kinds of maps, maps of telecommunications, maps of world trade and finance, and maps of global tourism etc., Thus, while the world may be full of complex interconnections, there are also many people and places whose experience is marginal or indeed excluded. Therefore, not everyone and every place participates in this complex web of movement.[73]

Nevertheless, Eriksen argues that the fact that a cultural phenomenon is global does not imply that it is known to everybody or concerns every individual on the face of the earth. Even Coca-Cola or McDonalds possibly the single most famous drink and meal respectively in the world is not known to everyone. The point is that such phenomena are disembedded from specific places. An event like the Winter Olympics or the PGA Masters Golf Tournament has a truly global dimension, even if the majority of the world's population is ignorant of it. One can follow such a sports event simultaneously in Milan, Leeds or Istanbul, thanks to newspapers and television. This does not imply that everyone who relates to these cultural forms perceives them in identical ways. Global symbols and globalized information are interpreted from a local vantage point. Many cultural phenomenons may be global in the sense that they are not located in a particular place, at the same time, however, they are local in that they are always perceived and interpreted locally.[74]

Anthropology is concerned with the articulation of the global and the local. In other words, how these globalising processes exist in the context of the realities of particular communities and are to some extent concerned with related concepts such as the transnational community and transnationalism. Transnationalism refers to a series of economic, socio-cultural and political practices which transcend the territorially bounded jurisdiction of the nation state, which enables migrants to sustain simultaneous connections with two or more nation states. New technologies, especially involving telecommunications serve to connect such networks with increasing speed and efficiency.[75]

Thus the transnational community generally refers to migrant communities, living in their host countries but maintaining economic, political, social and emotional ties with their homeland and other Diaspora communities of the same origin. To designate a community as transnational, it should possess certain qualities and characteristics including the community's recognisable presence in different parts of the world. By way of example, at one extreme Diasporas may be concentrated in one or two countries such as Mexicans in the United States or the Cubans in the United States and Venezuela. At the other extreme Diasporas are widely distributed in many countries. A normal pattern of concentration might involve many countries, with the largest community concentrated in one specific country, like the Armenians and Jews in the United States, and the rest scattered in smaller clusters. The American Armenian community is estimated at 1.5 million of which nearly half live in California. The growth of the community has led to an unprecedented church building effort along with the establishment of many full time community schools, cultural and athletic organisations, and the multiplication of newspapers and journals. Because of its growing size and wealth, the American Armenian community has assumed a dominant role in the development of the homeland and the Diaspora.[76] Influence and leadership in Diasporas is probably linked with density of settlement, thus the more immigrants settle in one place, the more influence the concentrated Diaspora will have by comparison with those who live in more scattered locations. Increasingly, however, we find transnationals who are often involved in several countries and may feel equal degrees of attachment to two or more countries. These feelings may range from very intense to mildly sentimental, and, of course, they may increase or diminish over time.

A further characteristic of a transnational community is transnational relations with relatives in other Diaspora communities and also with their home country. Transnational relations have important implications for both the sending and receiving society. There are two types of transnational relations i.e., vertical and horizontal. The vertical relations refer to the participation of immigrants in the host country. In this form of relationship, the Diaspora actively participates in the social, economic and political domain of the country thus becoming an important social and economic force in the host state. The horizontal relations, on the other hand, are manifested in the form of maintaining, reinforcing and extending the relations between the migrant communities and their places of origin.[77] By way of example, sending remittances by the immigrants, to their families and friends in their homeland, arranging and participating in marriage, and other ceremonies, as well as sponsoring religious or traditional festivals and events, thus creating transnational networks. One of the factors leading to the emergence of transnational networks is the ease and speed of communication and travel, by comparison with earlier dispersions, where immigration often led to isolation from homeland and from kin. Contemporary immigrants can easily sustain their kinship networks globally.

How do transnational immigrants differ from ethnic communities? The transnational community is defined in terms of transnational social space whereas the ethnic community is nation specific. According to theorists of transnational immigration, the distinction is made possible because of technological advances in communication over the past century. Personal computers, telephones, reduced cost air travel and other forms of modern telecommunications have made it relatively easy for immigrants to maintain personal contact with people in the homeland and other Diaspora communities. Essentially contemporary immigrants are different from their predecessors insofar as modern technology has strengthened the rate and extent of circulation between homeland and host country. Furthermore, not only does cheap, high speed travel allow frequent physical contact but it also accelerates the movement of goods, services and ideas.[78]

The classic anthropological example of this diasporic process is Rouse's study of the movement of labour migrants from Aguililla. Aguililla appears to be an isolated community dedicated to small-scale farming and manifestly part of the Mexican periphery. Appearances can be deceptive, however, and Aguililla's growing involvement in transnational migration has profoundly changed both its economic orientation and its socio-spatial relationships. By the early eighties, Aguililla was functioning largely as a nursery and a nursing home for Mexican wage labourers in the United States. Almost every family had members who were or had been abroad; the local economy depended heavily on the flow of dollars; and many of the farms operated only because they were sustained by migrant remittances. Aguililla had become part of a transnational network of settlements and, in doing so, significantly changed its status as a marginal site within a purely national hierarchy of places. Over the years, since the early 1940's United States-bound migration began, migrants have established numerous communities in the United States, the largest being a rapidly growing Latino neighbourhood in Redwood City, on the Northern edge of California's Silicon Valley.[79]

Aguilillans have formed socio-spatial alignments that seriously challenge the dominant ways of understanding migration. In other words, Mexican immigrants have conventionally been viewed as persons who uproot themselves, leave behind country, community and family, and endure the painful process of integration into a new society and culture.[80] Aguililians, however, find that their most important family and friends are as likely to be living hundreds or thousands of miles away as immediately around them. Those living in Aguililla are as much affected by events in Redwood City and the same is true in reverse. Moreover, they are able to maintain these extended relationships as effectively as the ties that link them to their neighbours. Increased access to the telephone has been particularly important, allowing people not just to keep in touch periodically but to participate actively in familial events from a considerable distance. Furthermore, through the continuous circulation of people, money, goods and information the various communities have become so closely interconnected, that they have come to constitute a single community spread across several sites, to which Rouse refers to as a "transnational migrant circuit".[81] Put simply, the Aguilillan migrants who have settled in Redwood City have not severed their ties to home, but have instead maintained connections so intense that Aguililla and Redwood City can no longer be perceived as separate communities.[82]

Aguilillan migrants have not abandoned one national space for another, but have formed, through the continuous circulation of people, capital, goods, images and ideas, a community that stretches across national boundaries. Aguilillan migrants thus occupy no singular national space, but live their lives transnationally. The Aguilillan case undoubtedly has its local peculiarities however there is evidence that such arrangements are becoming increasingly important in the organisation of Mexican migration to and from the United States. Throughout this fractured territory polarised economies are reshaping traditional images of community. What all this illustrates is that we are witnessing a world in which social relations and the parameters of community are no longer confined within a single territorial space. In other words we live in a world which has become scattered with migrants who inhabit communities that cut across and encompass multiple national terrains.[83]

Most transnational writing has addressed the experience of post-colonial groups including African origin peoples, South Asians and Latin Americans who have worked to develop fields of social membership that transcend the limited options available either in ancestral countries of origin or diasporic settings where they are subject to cultural isolation, and economic exploitation. Armenians have not commonly been included in the post-colonial discourse of the transnational immigrant community nor have they seen themselves as part of it. Nevertheless, given the Armenian legacy of dispersion, oppression, marginality and indeed cosmopolitanism, their experience clearly corresponds to this position. By way of example, Armenians identify not only with being Armenian—a strong loyalty to the Old World from which they or their ancestors originally came, as well as a product of their host country but also as a product of their particular home countries from which they emigrated. The experience of Armenian migrants emphasises their ability to combine resources, networks and identities available from multiple locations in order to maximise their freedom and independence from the confines of any one nation state and to minimise obligations and limitations connected with patriotism, citizenship, military service and gender restrictions etc.,

Clearly developments in the field of transportation and communication technology have made tremendous changes in transnational linkages, enabling immigrants to communicate far more effectively with each other. Media provide ways for audiences to traverse great distances without physically moving from local sites, thus they are crucial components of transnationalism. Marie Gillespie has produced a valuable ethnographic study of the role of transnational television and film in the formation of identity among young Punjabi Londoners. Gillespie looks at, among other things, the transformational ties such media creates between India and persons throughout the Diaspora. She argues that the transnational media is being used for the purposes of reformulating and translating cultural practices in the Indian Diaspora.[84] Indeed such technological innovations have established new forms of communication unimaginable only two decades ago.

ArmeniaDiaspora.com is a comprehensive web site developed in the United States in conjunction with the Republic of Armenia, which deals with Armenian news and current affairs both at home and globally, business and economic developments, job vacancies in Armenia, Church and cultural issues, chat rooms in many languages, as well as an email directory of Diaspora members throughout the world.[85] Indeed at the opening of the Second Armenia Diaspora Conference held in Yerevan in May 2002, President Kocharian's opening speech focused on the creation of an all-Armenian internet network, the implementation of pan-Armenian initiatives and active involvement of the Diaspora on equal rights with Armenia. Such initiatives included festivals, events, conferences and competitions under the title of 'One Nation, One Culture' as well as a pan-Armenian youth centre and the establishment of an Armenian Development Agency whose board would include representatives from the Diaspora. These emerging communication networks and economy air travel to the Republic of Armenia, as well as the processes of globalisation, and the flow of capital may have accelerated the transnational social formation of the Armenian Diaspora.

Toloyan states 'within Diaspora studies the discourse of transnationalism has helped to dislodge the study of Diasporas and other minorities from the analytical strait jacket of the prevailing orientation towards the nation-state'.[86] The implication of these developments, however, is disturbing for nation states. According to Appadurai, the nation state has historically functioned 'as a compact and isomorphic organisation of territory, ethnos (or people), and governmental apparatus'.[87] In other words, the nation state has traditionally been constructed as a territorially and culturally homogenous political space. It has achieved this through systematically subjecting the people who live within its borders to a wide range of nationalising technologies. By way of example, border control, linguistic conformity, citizenship rights, rules on nationality, political obedience, invention of symbols of nationhood, observance of national holidays, social welfare policies and conscription. Nation states historically vary in their ability to penetrate the every day lives of the people under their domain. They are not always, and have not always been, successful in defining and containing the lives of their citizens. On the whole, however, nation states have been effective, not only for those born within its borders, but the many migrants who settle within its boundaries.[88]

There are two strongly divergent arguments about the future of nation states. The more radical view is that nation states are in the process of dissolution in the face of global pressures and are no longer able to adequately shape all the citizens under its domain, defined by residence in a common territory, a shared cultural heritage and undivided loyalty to a common government. Rosenau (1990) identifies five sources of this dissolution. They are the development of micro-electronic technologies that reduce global distances by enabling the rapid movement of people, ideas and resources across the planet; the emergence of planetary problems that are beyond the scope of states to resolve them; a decline in the ability of states to solve problems on a national basis; the emergence of new and more powerful collectivities within nation states; and an increasing level of expertise, education and reflexive empowerment in the adult citizenry that makes them less susceptible to state authority.[89] In other words, the penetration of civil society by transnational forces has altered the form and dynamics of the nation state and the exclusive link between territory and political power has been broken. What we have is a chain of cosmopolitan cities and an increasing proliferation of Diasporas and ethnic minorities that cannot easily be contained within the nation state. There are many migrants who live their lives across national boundaries, because they are intimately linked to more than one place, and to not one place in particular. These migrants are able to circumvent, to some degree, the nationalising or assimilating tendencies of the nation state, since their experience is not limited to one single space. Thus, the inability to construct a monolithic national community has resulted in Western nation states becoming the host of diverse and sometimes incommensurable peoples and cultures.[90]

The more conservative view is that nation states are adapting to the new pressures by changing their functions. By way of example, according to Held and McGrew it can be argued that the nation state no longer crystallizes and organises domestic capital, but that it continues to police inward labour flows and seeks to encourage, although with diminishing capacity a single identity around a national leadership and common citizenship. However limited the actual control most states possess over their territories, they generally fiercely protect their sovereignty and their capacity to choose appropriate forms of political, economic and social development. The choices, benefits and welfare policies of states vary considerably according to their location in the hierarchy of states but the independence bestowed by sovereignty still matters significantly to all states. Although national political choices are constrained, they still count and remain the focus of public reflection and debate. The business of national politics is as important as, if not more important than it was during the period in which modern states were first formed.[91]

Should we express sympathy with contemporary nation states and the difficult challenges they encounter due to the growing number and efficiency of Diasporas. It could be argued that the bonds of language, religion, customs and a common sense of history embody a transnational relationship and endow it with an intimate quality that formal citizenship and long term settlement often lack. Nevertheless Western liberal democracies can construct an egalitarian multicultural society where it is possible to recognize that minorities have a right to their own language and customs, the right to practice their own religion, and organise family relations in their own way, without threatening the overall unity of the nation. The alternative argument claims that certain values and ways of life that are imported are incompatible with the way in which Western liberal democracies have evolved. Essentially the outcome of these contrasting views will depend on the capacity of nation states to manage diversity whilst allowing free expression and the degree of social cohesion sufficient to guarantee legitimacy for the nation state and its principal institutions.[92]

Conclusion

For the ancient Greeks Diaspora signified migration and colonization. For the Jews, Armenians and the Africans who later adopted the term, the concept implied more painful meanings of loss. As the history of migration and settlement of these populations and for other populations that have moved across the world has changed, so did the concept of Diaspora. Diaspora has made a dynamic return in the debates around ethnicity, nationality, boundaries and identity. A concept that has transformed in time has returned to address the understanding of migration and people's multiple sense of belonging and loyalties beyond national boundaries. In the final analysis, therefore, Diaspora forces us to re-examine the role of the nation state and its citizens. Throughout the last century, under the pressure of transnationalist and global shifts, economically, politically and geographically, the nation as a political ideal has undergone significant changes. Diaspora has become 'an intermediate concept between the local and the global that nevertheless transcends the national perspective'[93] and highlights the existence of transnational networks of people and their sense of belonging in communities beyond spatial boundaries. Diaspora illustrates the hybrid and ever-changing nature of identities and cultures that reflect the different starting points, histories and journeys. Diaspora implies multiple points of departure and multiple destinations. It implies instabilities and inequalities not only in the meeting of different cultures but within specific cultures characterised by internal diversity, especially generational.

Diaspora communities include people who have experienced migration and others who have been born and brought up in a new country of settlement. Diaspora implies that a sense of ethnic belonging is not only attached to the experience of migration but is significant for younger generations who have not experienced the migratory process. Diaspora implies that specific cultures survive, transform and maintain their identity even when members of an ethnic community have not lived in the original homeland. Diaspora, however, is a concept with its limitations. Its meaning is not always clear and the way people have been associated and attached to Diaspora often varies. Nevertheless it is a useful concept that helps us to understand the complexities of the contemporary world. It demonstrates that ethnicity can persist as a reference for generations and it emphasises that communities can extend beyond national boundaries.

Furthermore Diaspora has been loosely associated with other terms, particularly transnationalism, to describe the fractured condition of the contemporary world. Transnationalism may be interpreted as the flow of people, ideas, trade and capital across national borders in a way that undermines the nation state as a category of identification, economic organisation and political constitution. With this in mind, if a convincing case is to be made that transnationlism is a qualitatively different form of immigration from the immigration of ethnics, it is essential to find ways to measure and assess comparatively circulatory rates. In doing so, it is necessary to avoid the inadvertent tendency of many scholars of transnationalism to embrace a notion of technological determinism. Certainly while raising important issues and generating insight, some versions of transnationalism are marked by problems as well. Much work on transnationalism emphasizes abstract motives as the major forces of migration. As suggested by the following quote, some texts are plagued by hyperbole:

By means of strategies of transnational mobility, Chinese have eluded, taken tactical advantage of, temporized before, redefined, and overcome the disciplining of modern regimes of colonial empires. These mobile practices have intersected with the imposition of modern regimes of truth and knowledge to take the form of a guerrilla transnationalism.[94]

In what way, one may ask, do such esoteric motives or enigmatic practices actually enter the minds of migrants planning their lives? As Kivisto suggests, among the things we know too little about at the moment are the actual travel patterns of immigrants. How much travel actually takes place? How much travel to the homeland involves flying or, like the Mexicans in the United States, do they drive or take the bus? What role does distance play? How different are immigrants, whose homeland adjoins the borders of the host country compared to immigrants who must make transoceanic journeys to visit their homeland? What roles do social class and gender play in defining travel? With regard to communication, we need to examine ownership or access to such technology. The fact that someone has access to such technology does not necessarily equate with transnational linkages. It should be borne in mind that differences exist between the communication and informational needs or interests of Armenians of the Homeland and those of the Diaspora as well as significant differences among the various Diaspora communities. These differences are the result of the varying developmental processes these communities have undergone, as they are influenced by their social and economic environment. By way of example access to the internet and the virtues it brings may be a foregone conclusion to an American or British Armenian however elsewhere Armenians may not have the same freedom of access. Therefore, it is vital to explore not simply access to communication technology but the ways in which different groups employ them.[95] Perhaps much more practical issues are important to migrants when they decide where to live, such as getting an education, earning a living, maintaining family relationships or avoiding maltreatment. Most importantly, while Diaspora exists in conjunction with transnationalism, and it can be argued that immigrants may use transnational strategies, Diaspora cannot be reduced to macro economic or technological forces. The Armenian Diaspora essentially remains above all else a distinctly human lived and experienced phenomenon.

CHAPTER TWO

SITUATING ETHNICITY

What do we mean when we talk about ethnicity? The term ethnicity has become central to the everyday language of political difference, therefore, it is important to be clear about what ethnicity is and what it is not. Firstly, this chapter begins by situating ethnicity conceptually, by distinguishing our subject from other central concepts widely in use in political discourse. Words like ethnic group, ethnicity and ethnic conflict have become common terms in the English language. The same can be said for nation and nationalism and the major source of confusion is the tendency to conflate ethnicity and nationality. Secondly, why do people identify themselves as members of a particular ethnic group? Here, attention is given to the various theories of ethnicity. The existing approaches tend to fall into two broad categories, the primordialists and the constructivists, those theorists who emphasize the socially constructed nature of ethnicity. The socially constructed nature of ethnicity is particularly useful in the study of Diasporas as such scholarship emphasises the ability of individuals to cut and mix from a variety of cultural traditions and to forge their individual identities. The aim here is to provide an overview and systematic assessment of the main theoretical issues involved.

There is a Socratic parable, known in some quarters, about a teacher who gives his students two magnifying glasses and invites them to look at the one through the other. When each has told of all he has learned, the teacher delivers his lesson in the form of a question: "Of what have you told me," he asks, "the thing you have seen or the thing through which you have seen it?" The same problem lies behind the study of ethnicity. Is the latter an object of analysis, something to be explained? Or is it an explanatory principle capable of illustrating significant aspects of human existence? It has certainly been treated in both ways and as a result, there is still a notable lack of agreement on even the most fundamental of issues. What is ethnicity? Has ethnicity the capacity to determine social activity, or is it a product of other forces and structures? Does ethnicity lie in primordial consciousness or in response to specific historical circumstances?[1]

In addressing these questions this chapter focuses on the theoretical terms by which ethnicity may be comprehended.

Ethnicity is a concept in wide currency in contemporary social science and yet it remains an ambiguous concept. The term ethnicity is a derivative of the older adjective 'ethnic', which in the English language dates back to the Middle Ages. This term derives from the ancient Greek term ethnos, and was used in a variety of ways. In Homer we hear of 'ethnos hetairon', meaning a band of friends or 'ethnos Lukion', a tribe of Lycians. Pinder refers to 'ethnos aneron' or 'gunaikon', meaning a race of men or women, and in Plato, we hear of 'ethnos kenukikon', a caste of heralds. What these terms have in common is the idea of a number of people who share some cultural or biological characteristics, but they also imply 'other' peoples who belong to some group unlike one's own. Indeed, we could go as far as to say that ethnocentricity is the natural condition of humanity. It is probably a truism that all peoples are ethnocentric. It is also more than likely that ethnocentric constructions of 'the other' always follow a process through which the alien is reduced to a familiar form that is easily accessible to self. All systems of otherness are structures of identity and difference that have more to do with the establishment of self identity than with the empirical reality of 'the other'. This is one of the most widespread ways in which people declare and affirm their identity, by saying who they are not. Furthermore, the dichotomy between a non-ethnic 'us' and ethnic 'others' is implicit in concepts used within the fields of ethnicity and nationalism.[2]

The term 'ethnicity' first appeared in the Oxford English Dictionary in 1953 and it was defined to mean 'the essence of an ethnic group' or the 'quality of belonging to an ethnic community or group'. Alternatively it may refer to a field of study; classification of peoples and relations between groups, in a context of 'self-other' distinctions. The English language reserves the term 'nation' for themselves, namely white Anglo-Saxon Protestants, and 'ethnic' for immigrant peoples, as in the frequently used term 'ethnic minorities'. Until recently, however, in the United Kingdom, in a strange popular usage, Black and Asian peoples were regarded as immigrants, whereas actual immigrants from Europe, Ireland and the White Commonwealth were not. As more positive attitudes towards the Blacks and Asian were adopted, they were referred to as ethnic minorities, along with other visible groups like Jews and Cypriots. In the United States the term 'ethnics' became popular following the Second World War as a polite term referring to Jews, Italians, Irish and other peoples considered inferior to the dominant population of largely British descent. Thus, in everyday language, the word ethnicity still has a ring of 'minority issues' and 'race relations', however, in social anthropology it refers to aspects of relationships between groups who consider themselves, and are regarded by others, as being culturally distinctive.[3]

Ethnicity is a concept of which different accounts have been given. Every society in the modern world contains sub-sections, groups of people, more or less distinct from the rest of the population. The most suitable generic term to describe these sub-sections is an ethnic group. The term ethnic group has come to mean something like 'a people' but what is 'a people'. Is the population of Britain a people or does it constitute several peoples?[4] Peoples, however they are classified, are bounded communities, in the sense that no one individual can be a member of two distinct peoples within the same classificatory system. In different social and historical contexts, however, a process of re-classification may occur. For example, immigrants from South Asia can be defined as ethnic, racial or religious groups, using the terms Pakistani, Black or Muslim; Jews in different contexts can be classified as ethnic or national. Therefore groups that have been called, or have called themselves national at one point, or in one territory, have become ethnic or racial in other contexts.[5]

While all these classifications are difficult to ground, what is common to all, in their diversity, is that they involve the social construction of an origin as a basis for community. This origin, real or mythical, can be territorially, culturally, historically or physiognomically based. It can be internally created by the group or externally imposed, or both. Furthermore, whilst all peoples are generally systemically bounded, it is not always clear what this assumption rests upon. By way of example, geographical location does not always give rise to bounded communities of people, since not everyone is located somewhere in a permanent way. Similarly linguistic categories are not bounded in this sense, since people may speak more than one language, so that language speaking per se cannot mark out distinct ethnic groups.

An ethnic group has a proper name for itself, which expresses the essence of the ethnic group, and this is often believed to be the necessary condition for its existence. It would be implausible to suppose that people simply notice some feature that they share, a common culture perhaps, and on that basis apply a name to themselves quite independently of it forming part of some socially motivated practice of classification. Furthermore, there must always be two of something to create a difference. It would be absurd to suggest the idea of an isolated ethnic group. It is through contact with others that we discover who we are. Thus, ethnic groups involve the positing of boundaries in relation to who can and cannot belong, according to certain criterion which are heterogeneous, ranging from the credentials of birth, being born in the right place, language or conforming to cultural or other symbolic practices. In other words, the way in which membership of an ethnic group is demarcated is socially motivated and depends upon the preferences of its members.

The critical feature of an ethnic group for Barth is the characteristic of self ascription and ascription by others, in terms of general identity, determined by origin and background. Individuals use ethnic identities to categorise themselves for purposes of interaction and organisation. Ethnic groups take cultural differences into account but those features are not 'the sum of objective differences', but only those regarded as significant. Environmental variations may exaggerate difference: some cultural features are used as markers of difference, whilst others are ignored and in some cases radical differences are denied. By way of example, in one research study of ethnic relations carried out in Thailand on The Lue, Michael Moerman[6] discovered, that their cultural traits were in fact shared with other neighbouring groups, they had no exclusive language, no exclusive customs and no exclusive religion. Does this imply that ethnic groups do not necessarily have a distinctive culture? Can two groups be culturally identical and yet constitute different ethnic groups? Moerman was forced to conclude that someone is Lue purely by virtue of believing and calling himself Lue, and of acting in such a way that validates his 'Lueness'. Being unable to define Lueness using objective anthropological criteria such as language, religion or culture, Moerman defined the essence of an ethnic group as emic category of ascription.[7] Essentially, belonging to an ethnic group implies possessing certain characteristics judged by others and oneself relevant to that identity, none of which can be categorised within a descriptive list of objective cultural features or differences. Accordingly, the emphasis is ascription by oneself and others as the fundamental feature of ethnic groups and as such the nature of continuity depends on the maintenance of a boundary that defines the group, not the cultural stuff that it encloses.[8]

Barth's main contribution to the study of ethnicity is to urge a shift away from analysis of the cultural content of ethnic identity (ethnic markers such as language, dress, food etc) towards an examination of the boundaries that mark the limits of such contents. Ethnic boundary maintenance requires complex organisation of behaviour and social interaction. The identification of another person as a fellow member of an ethnic group implies sharing the criteria for judgement— 'two people playing the same game'. This relationship permits the possibility of development of their social relationship to include practically all areas of activity. Conversely, a 'dichotomization' of others as not belonging, strangers, limiting understanding and restriction of interaction to areas of assumed common understanding and mutual interest. By way of example, Armenian Diaspora communities tend to view excessive social and cultural relations with non-Armenians as being inimical to their survival as a close-knit community. Centuries of persecution have deepened this sense of paranoia towards 'outsiders', who they call 'odars'. On the other hand, however, 'odars', if they marry an Armenian, are welcomed into the community should they show readiness to integrate themselves into the Armenian cultural milieu.[9]

Thus, ethnic boundary maintenance necessitates contact with individuals and groups of other cultures. Distinct ethnic groups only survive as significant communities if they imply marked difference in behaviour and distinct cultural diversity. Therefore, the boundary is the invisible dividing line between them and us. Boundaries are two way, both groups in the relationship demarcate their identity and distinctiveness vis-à-vis the other. With regard to such boundaries, Barth makes two very important points. Firstly, boundaries persist despite a flow of people and information across them. Secondly, and as a natural consequence of the first point, such groups cannot exist in isolation but only in contrast to other such groups. Indeed, Barth constantly emphasises the importance of interaction between ethnic groups and the ways in which actions across the boundary served merely to strengthen it.

Barth, however, does not ignore the cultural content of an ethnic group but he considers this to be of two types: diacritical markers such as language and dress and 'value orientations' such as moral principles and other social norms and customs. Barth argues it is sheer folly to try and typologize ethnic groups on the basis of objective lists. Such lists would be endless and individuals will choose, or detail features, which legitimate their location and status in any given situation. This idea of choice or variation, in the manifestation of ethnic identity is one that is generally regarded as situational ethnicity. Situational ethnicity becomes a vehicle of class in macro-structures and functions primarily as a resource. Ethnicity can be used to reinforce social organisation for the attainment of goals when it is needed, but it can also be ignored. Such negotiation over identity may be regarded as a struggle between different world views. For instance, some groups who may be the victims of damaging ethnic stereotypes may try to argue the irrelevance of ethnic distinctions or challenge the prevailing stereotypes. Thus, ethnicity might not simply be a useful resource it could be appealed to by other groups as a basis for denying rights. In other words, it could become a stigma or liability, which actually stands in the way of the members of an ethnic group attaining their goals. For Barth, however, ethnicity is an identity, which transcends or is at least equivalent to all other social identities, such as class or gender, and as such his position is much closer to primordialism.[10]

Nevertheless, Barth has been criticized for delimiting ethnic groups as fixed categories, with borders permanently guarded by linguistic and cultural symbols. A much more instrumentalist approach, that of Abner Cohen, argues that ethnicity should be regarded as a type of political resource for competing interest groups, and therefore, unlike Barth, he refuses to take the ethnic boundary for granted.[11] Cohen argues that ethnicity is instrumental, that is there are reasons for a group asserting and maintaining an ethnic identity, which are economical and political rather than psychological. Cohen emphasises the continuous dialectical relationship between the symbols, which mark different cultures, and the way these symbols are used to further the political and economic interests of the bearers of those cultures. He argues that many groups in both traditional and modern societies find their interests better served through invisible organisations such as membership of common social clubs, religious affiliations and informal networks, rather than through highly visible formally recognized institutions. Ethnic groups may wish to increase their visibility as strangers to maintain their interests, or they may prefer to lower their profile and manifest to be an integral part of society.[12]

Cohen's empirical study of the Ibadan Hausa trading Diaspora, which until recently maintained the long distance trade of kola nuts and cattle in West Africa, depicts ethnicity as an instrument for competition over scarce resources. Cohen identifies two interacting causes that have brought about the strong sense of ethnicity of the Hausa. Firstly, internal causes relating to the need to maintain a monopoly of the trade. Secondly, there are external causes. Cohen notes that during the colonial period, small ethnic groups, such as the Hausa, were granted a degree of autonomy and developed corporate, political and economic interests. As indirect rule subsided, prior to independence, and Nigerian politics became more developed, the autonomy for the Hausa began to be eroded. Simultaneously, the Yoruba, a neighbouring community, who had previously been non-Islamic, in contrast to the Islamic Hausa, turned to Islam rapidly. There was little the Hausa could do to retain their political autonomy, however, they quickly changed their religious adherence, rapidly becoming members of the Tijaniya Order. Cohen argues they re-defined their ethnic identity in order to maintain control of the kola nut and cattle trade. Both trades depend on a high degree of mutual trust and careful organisation between parties. Thus, if the Hausa became indistinguishable from the Yoruba, what would prevent the Yoruba from being able to infiltrate their trade.[13] Thus, trade was the principal function of ethnicity and had it not been profitable to be a Hausa, they may well have disappeared as a distinct ethnic group.

Cohen's analysis stresses the ways in which ethnic groups are useful and effective for the achievements of individuals and collective ambitions. Indeed, Cohen's perspective defines ethnicity as goal-directed, formed by internal organisation and stimulated by external pressures, and held not for its own sake, but to defend an economic or political interest. Social interaction and organisation are dual phenomenon comprising aspects of utility and aspects of meaning. Ethnicity exploits this duality for particular ends, which may or may not be acknowledged by the members themselves. Essentially ethnicity must have a function in order for it to be viable, and by focusing on the functional aspects of ethnic identity, it is possible to explain why some ethnic groups thrive while others disappear.[14] Interestingly, Abner Cohen has taken an extreme position in arguing that London Stockbrokers may constitute an ethnic group as they are largely endogamous, marrying within their class, and possess a shared identity. Arguably, however, ethnic status should be delimited to groups with a more obvious permanence in time and a coherent cultural identity based on a belief in common descent and kinship, perhaps underscoring the belief that ethnic identity is something that binds itself to the individual and one cannot entirely rid oneself of it.[15]

Ethnicity is thus something that the analyst uses as a tool to describe and understand processes of which those involved may not have any clear understanding, namely the Hausa acting as an 'interest group' and using their ethnicity to defend an economic interest. Clearly, whilst this analysis may hold true for the particular ethnic group Cohen encountered, it cannot explain all expressions of ethnicity to be found in the modern world. Epstein[16] notes that among American Jews, there were periods in which corporate interests were more readily apparent than in others and yet an identifiable Jewish community persisted in both types of situation. Constantinides[17] in a study of London Cypriots also found that the concept of an interest group was not easily applicable to this community. Although Cypriots were more numerous in certain boroughs of London, they were also scattered residentially, and although they did tend to specialise in catering and dressmaking, they did not monopolise these sectors. Similarly Werbner[18] in a study of Manchester Pakistanis, also found the concept of the interest group less than immediately applicable to this community. Economic competition was as readily apparent, perhaps even more accentuated, among Pakistani traders as it was between them and non-Pakistanis.[19]

Moreover, whilst Armenians generally abstain from involvement in host country political affairs, the internal life of Diaspora communities is often marked by vigorous competition between the various societies and groups. These conflicts are often exacerbated by generational differences and cultural and gender cleavages between groups of immigrants from different countries, but a strong sense of Armenian identity persists. According to Werbner[20] the public sphere of the Manchester Pakistani Diaspora is a place of intense local micro politics, debated in the globalized language of world affairs, and dramatically enacted through public performance. Werbner reveals a multi-centred world among Manchester Pakistanis, a locally created diasporic public space that appropriates and combines travelling ideas and images from a variety of sources into meaningful moral allegories. By way of example British South Asian Muslims became visible in the protests mobilized against The Satanic Verses, during which Pakistani immigrants abandoned the role of a silent, well behaved minority in the public defence of their religious imagination and group honour. In opening up a new realm of activist citizenship politics, the Rushdie affairs also provided the opportunity for the Pakistani Diaspora to liberate themselves from the intimidation of their own religious extremists. This has resulted in the flourishing of cultural and religious societies, festivals and public celebrations, often with women taking more visible and vocal roles, thus challenging the hegemony of male elders within the community. Werbner illustrates that ultimately living in the Diaspora is a matter of continually negotiating the parameters of minority citizenship. Therefore, if the cultural content of a group's ethnic identity is constantly shifting, which Barth claims, and yet the presence of an ethnic identity persists, it will persist both in times of economic need and instability as well as in times of stability. Therefore, Cohen's instrumental theory would need to be at least more widely applicable than just the case study of the Hausa in order for the concept of 'ethnic interest group' to be unproblematic. [21]

Some older theorists such as Rex[22] distinguish ethnicity from race, purely on the grounds that ethnicity involves cultural rather than physical difference. In neither race, nor ethnicity, is group identification required. Most recent theorists, however, in common with Max Weber view group identification to be the essential prerequisite of ethnic groups. The serious study of ethnicity owes much to the reflections of Weber, whose insight illustrates the definition of ethnic groups as mass status groups. Weber defines ethnic groups as 'human groups that entertain a subjective belief in their common descent because of similarities of physical type or customs or both, or because of memories of colonization and migration. He further states 'this belief must be important for the propagation of group formation; conversely, it does not matter whether or not an objective blood relationship exists'.[23] Weber is concerned to combine their subjective and objective aspects, and balance their cultural and political bases. He fluctuates between according primacy to political factors and historical memories in the shaping of a sense of common ethnicity, and the prevailing preoccupation with cultural and biological differences in limiting ethnic alliance.[24] There does not necessarily have to be common kinship or blood ties between the members, only a belief in common ancestry.

According to Gilbert[25] race is a way of classifying people based on perceived physiognomic differences. 'Racial description is a form of social categorisation that embodies a mode of classification arrived at by classifiers acting as observers of those they classify and classifying them in terms independent of any of those classified might use to classify themselves.'[26] In other words it classifies people by reproductively transmitted physical characteristics. In Africa, the term ethnic group has replaced 'tribe' which has recently come to be considered pejorative. The switch from tribe to ethnic group may also mitigate an ethnocentric or Eurocentric bias, which social scientists have often been accused of promoting. If we talk about tribes, we implicitly draw a distinction between ourselves and the people we wish to study, a distinction which generally correlates to the difference between modern and traditional, Western and non-Western peoples. If we talk of ethnic groups, however, such a sharp distinction becomes difficult to maintain as virtually every human being belongs to an ethnic group. Nevertheless, there is a need to distinguish between race and ethnicity. Ethnicity, understood as membership of a significant social group, provides a different standard for the survival of a people as opposed to race, because an ethnic group, unlike race classification, has to be a people according to its own members, not just to outside observers.[27] Therefore, perhaps it is possible to agree that ethnic identity is maintained through a subjective belief in a common culture, and because ethnicity, unlike race, requires group association and self ascription by its members, it is preferable to distinguish them as an ethnic group rather than racial.

If an ethnic group is a cultural community, so too is a nation. Therefore, one needs to locate the differentia specifica of nation and ethnie. Weber describes the nation as a 'prestige community' bestowed with a cultural agenda. Nations are too complex to be defined in terms of any one criterion, but he associates nations to ethnic communities as people unified by common myths of descent, but what distinguishes the nation is the fundamental commitment to a political programme.[28] Deutsch's socio-demographic analysis proposes a functional definition of the nation, which also negates single factor criterion and suggests 'the presence of sufficient communication facilities with enough complementarity to produce the overall results'.[29] Deutsch claims that nationalist objectives aim to broaden and consolidate the channels of communication to enable popular agreement with national symbols and standards. Geertz, from an anthropological perspective, expresses the notion of 'two competing yet complementary components—'ethnic and civic' in the nationalism of post-colonial states. The ethnic factor is highlighted as a commitment to 'primordial' loyalties, which bestow individuals with a distinct identity; the civic factor aspires to citizenship in a modern state.[30] This civic ideal can be most strikingly illustrated in the attitudes of the French revolutionaries, as Clermont-Tonnerre put it to the French Assembly in 1791: "To the Jews as a nation we give nothing; to the Jews as individuals we give everything".[31]

More importantly, with the advent of the modern bureaucratic state and capitalism, ethnic communities take on a new political importance. In the older empires, ethnic groups remained unassertive but recognised ethnic communities, like the Christian millets of the Ottoman Empire. In the modern rational state, however, ethnic autonomy interfered with the prerequisite for all citizens to integrate into the new ideal of the nation state. One of the most important features of modernity was that leaders of powerful hegemonizing nation states sought to make exclusive citizenship a sine qua non.[32] The ideological claims of political nationalism required all the peoples of a nation state to be united and homogenous. Nationalism was predominantly a doctrine of popular freedom and sovereignty, and has been the most powerful political force in the world for two centuries. The people must be liberated, free from any external constraint; they must determine their own destiny and be masters in their own house; they must control their own resources; they must obey only their own 'inner' voice. All this required fraternity. The idea that the will of the people and not the monarch is law was given potent, indeed violent, expression by the French Revolution. And by defining 'the people' as 'the nation', the will of the nation became the supreme fact of political life. The people must be united; they must dissolve all internal divisions; they must be gathered together in a single historic territory, a homeland; and they must have legal equality and share a single public culture. But which culture and which territory? Only a homeland that was 'theirs' by historic right, the land of their ancestors; only a culture that was 'theirs' ancestrally, passed down the generations, and therefore an expression of their authentic identity. These sentiments were idealised and pursued by nationalists everywhere since Rousseau, Herder, Fichte and Mazzini popularised them in Western and Central Europe.[33]

The parallel between nationalism and ethnicity is obvious in that most nationalisms are based on ethnic ideologies. A fundamental difference, however, between ethnic ideology and nationalism is that the latter predicates the existence of an abstract community, one that is loyal to a legislative system and a state which represents one's 'people', not loyalty to individuals one knows personally. The nation, therefore, only exists if one is capable of imagining its existence. Benedict Anderson[34] refers to an imagined community, in his account of nationalism when he stresses the development of mass media, particularly print capitalism. The nation is imagined because the community defined by 'nationhood' necessarily extends beyond the normal world of face to face interaction between individuals. Thus to conceive of any community on such a large scale involves either the creation or awakening of a new kind of world view or consciousness. This new national identity is fostered through the media of mass communication and the educational system. Print capitalism enables a large number of people to gain the same knowledge through the standardization of language. New historical myths, usually based upon military achievements, and symbols of national solidarity are reconstructed.[35]

By imagination, however, Anderson does not mean that the nation is a total fabrication of modern ideology. He is referring to the adaptation of pre-modern forms of ethnic expression to the exigencies of modern life, however, he does not provide a clear explanation of what this means. Moreover, he appears to attribute the phenomenon of nationality to a modern process, placing strong emphasis on economic and technological features. By failing to recognise the importance of territory, language and religion, Anderson does not fully appreciate the historical continuities that motivate the modern phenomenon of nationalism. Despite the limitation of Anderson's theory, the notion of imagination and re-imagination describe accurately the process of reformulation, redefinition and adaptation that an ideology such as nationalism experiences throughout the course of its history. As Anthony Smith[36] suggests the formation of nations is by definition an on-going process which involve ceaseless reinterpretations, rediscoveries and reconstructions. Thus re-imagination embodies how ethnic identifiers are continually reshaped by different sectors of the nation to suit the political and socio-cultural milieu of the moment. More importantly, it carries the possibility of further reconstructions in the future.

Such re-imagination, however, operates within certain limits because the processes of imagination and re-imagination generally draw upon pre-existent ethnic assumptions which set the boundaries for nation building. Consequently, re-imagination occurs within the confines of definite emotional and intellectual matrices. Ethnies, a term coined by Smith to refer to pre-modern ethnic based communities are clearly but flexibly demarcated; their boundaries persist even though their meanings and even their forms change to suit their circumstances. Thus, although certain changes take place in the form of nationalism, this does not necessarily imply the radical alteration of the ethnic essence. Smith's argument is valuable because an appreciation of the fluidity of boundaries is crucial to an understanding of the nation, one which focuses on the imagination and reimagination of boundaries within which communal consciousness is permitted to operate. At the same time, however, this understanding emphasises the complexities involved in attempting to produce a timeless definition of nationalism. If such a task was indeed possible, it would be necessary to incorporate the concept of re-imagination as an inbuilt dynamic of nationalism. With this in mind, such an understanding of nationalism is perhaps more easily understood in the context of an historical overview of the process of nationality formation.

Like ethnic ideologies, nationalism stresses the cultural similarity of its adherents and, by implication, it draws boundaries vis-à-vis others, who thereby become marginalized or excluded. The distinguishing mark of nationalism, however, is its relationship with the state: a nationalist holds that political boundaries should be coterminous with cultural boundaries, whereas many ethnic groups do not demand control over a state. A successful nationalism implies, in most cases, an intrinsic connection between an ethnic ideology, stressing a common origin, and a state apparatus. A nationalist ideology may therefore be defined as an ethnic ideology, which demands the right to its own state on behalf of the ethnic group. Thus, the difference between nationalism and ethnicity is clear if we adhere to this distinction, however, in practice the distinction can be much more complex.[37]

According to Eriksen such ethnic groups may be located analytically between nationhood and ethnic identity. It is plainly not accurate that ethnic groups have a shared will. Some members may wish for independence, while others are content to have linguistic and other autonomous rights within an existing state. A person may also switch situationally between being a member of an ethnic minority and a member of a nation. An Iranian migrant in France belongs to an ethnic minority but belongs to a nation when they return to Iran. Furthermore nationalism may articulate an ideology which represents and is supported by a majority of ethnic groups. This is clearly the case in Mauritius where no ethnic group openly wishes to make nation building an ethnic project on its own behalf. Nationalist projects in such countries may be seen as polyethnic in that it tries to resolve ethnic differences, but not eradicate them, within a shared framework of a nation.[38]

Confusion also arises because every day language and mass media constantly juxtapose the concepts of nation and ethnic group. Clearly nationalism and ethnicity are related phenomenon but there are many ethnic groups, which are not national, and there are many nations, which do not constitute a single ethnic group. Indeed, today most countries are polyethnic even if they are dominated by one ethnic group, for instance, the English in the United Kingdom and the French in France amongst many others. Thus, nationalist ideology seldom fits the territory. There is rarely, if ever, a perfect correspondence between the state and the ethnic group.[39] Are these polyethnic countries nations in an analytical sense? This is a matter of definition, however, if the concept of nationalism defined as the doctrine of congruence between state and ethnic group is to be cross-culturally applicable, it cannot be limited to mono-ethnic nations and it must be redefined to accommodate the global terrain.

Why should people attach importance to their ethnicity? Why should they not be comfortable with state imposed identities or the identities of other groups? One of the oldest explanations, and one which is popular with the public at large, is that people have been the way they are from time immemorial i.e., defined by language, customs, religion and territory. Ethnic consciousness expresses deeply rooted human sentiments. In other words, ethnicity is primordial: people would favour members of their own group if they had to make a choice between outsiders and their fellow group members. It is useful in discussing the concept of ethnicity in relation to identity by referring to 'primordial theory' associated with Clifford Geertz (1963). According to Geertz, primordial attachment refers to one that results from the 'givens' or more accurately, as culture is involved, the assumed 'givens' of social existence: hereditary kin connections in the main but also the 'givenness' that results from being born into a particular religious community, speaking a particular language, and following particular social customs. These attachments of blood, language and customs are fundamentally coercive. We are bound to our kinsmen, not merely as the result of personal affection and common interest but essentially by virtue of some overwhelming, inexplicable attribute of the tie itself. Such primordial attachments may vary between individuals and communities, but virtually all these attachments stem from a natural, possibly spiritual connection rather than social interaction.[40]

The claim that Geertz makes is important, distinguishing ethnic attachments from those which arise from similar interests, for instance, the attachments which bind members of a political or economic class together. According to Geertz, in modern societies the elevation of such primordial ties to the level of political supremacy has, of course, occurred many times and will continue to do so. By way of example, Nehru, repeatedly proposed primordial ties as the preferred basis of demarcation of political units:

> The reasons why a unilingual state is stable and a multi-lingual state are unstable are quite obvious. A state is built on fellow feeling. What is this fellow feeling? To state briefly, it is a feeling of a corporate sentiment of oneness which makes those who are charged with it feel that they are kith and kin. This feeling is a double-edged feeling. It is at once a feeling of 'consciousness of kind', which, on the one hand, binds together those who have it so strongly that it overrides all differences arising out of economic conflicts or social gradations and, on the other, severs them from those who are not of their kind. It is a longing not to belong to any other group. The existence of this fellow feeling is the foundation of a stable and democratic state.[41]

Increasingly, however, national unity is maintained by allegiance to a civil state, supplemented by differing levels of governmental powers and ideological manipulation. Geertz argues, it is this conflict between primordial and civil sentiments that gives rise to what is commonly referred to as parochialism, tribalism,

and communalism and so on. There are many other competing loyalties in contemporary states such as class, business or professional, but such groups are virtually never considered as self-standing social units. Conflicts may occur among
them but no matter how severe they may become, they do not intentionally
threaten the political integrity of the nation state. It is only when such conflicts
are infused with primordial sentiments or ethnic unity, that the integrity of the
nation state is undermined, resulting in partition, irredentism—a re-drawing of
the very limits of the state. Thus, primordial discontent strives more deeply, is
satisfied less easily, and conflict is inevitable when a country is inhabited by
more than one ethnic group.[42]

Yulian Bromley's position on ethnicity is one of the most strongly primor-
dialist. The expression of ethnicity is so strongly resilient that it persists through
generations and through a variety of social formations.[43] Bromley's Soviet ethnos
theory suggests that a stable core of ethnicity persists through all social formations and historical eras. It is fundamentally affected, however, by the prevailing
economic and political environment of any social formation and is manifested as
an 'ethnosocial organism'. The problem is to determine the most intrinsic features
of this stable core. Bromley defines an ethnos or ethnic community as being 'a
historically formed community of people characterized by common, relatively
stable cultural features, certain distinctive psychological traits, and the consciousness of their unity as distinguished from other similar communities'.[44]

It is clear that Bromley comes close to Barth by not simply working from the
inside out, listing features, but by also observing the boundaries that enclose these
features. In other words, it is in ethnic interaction that ethnic identity is consolidated. Furthermore, the actual origins of ethnic identity are unimportant—to possess it is simply an aspect of being human. Bromley warns of the futility of
searching for such origins and assigning them importance. The prevailing economic environment does, however, bear upon the character of the ethnos, but it
shapes it rather than breaking or distorting it completely. Bromley's term 'ethnosocial organism' defines the interaction of the ethnos with the historical stage
or economic environment. The ethnosocial organism is a historically located
group of people, which is affected by other factors such as the physical and economic environments in which they inhabit. Thus, we begin to come close to
Barth, the boundary of the ethnic community is always in place, but the cultural
contents or distinctive characteristics change. Bromley gives us a theory of ethnicity, which despite its claims to a primordial core of identity, it recognises that
specific historical and economical factors are fundamental in shaping the expression of ethnic identity.[45]

Primordialism presents us with a picture of overpowering consciousness,
coercive yet varying. This sense of ethnicity cannot be removed by social mobility, as for instance social class can, and thus becomes incorporated into the self.
According to this view, ethnic ties cannot become too involved with or dependent
upon class or political factors, they simply cut across it. Ethnicity cannot be
altered in the face of external pressure and has its own dynamic independent of
other elements in the political process. In this sense it is interesting that Tabibian
has argued that Armenians understand history, nationalism and ethnicity as tran-
scendental forces, free from the constraints of structural forces. They are, in a

sense, 'God-given' forces. The fact or myth that Noah's Ark ended upon Mount Ararat has a lot to do with Armenians' convictions that they have a private line with God, through which come, not only God's grace but also his curses. As long as they believe that line to be private it strengthens the need for detached status. Consequently, they believe that neither Armenian history nor culture is subject to structural analysis. [46]

Dekmejian suggests that cultural parochialism has developed a kind of one-dimensional ethnocentrism within the Armenian Diaspora communities. While it may take very little, apart from survival, which is no small achievement for Armenians, to have history, a double consciousness is required, to be part of history and be external to it. This necessitates a level of intellectual activity in which objectivity and subjectivity must collaborate. In other words, Armenian history is full of interpretations of Armenian events, but it has seldom gone further than attempting to give an accurate account of these events. Historians have suggested that the Armenians have been guided at all times and places by a single ideological motivation, that of self-determination or freedom, or after the adoption of Christianity, the preservation of their particular faith. Mythological heroes and villains have been defined in their relation to these fundamental goals. Thus, whilst Armenians have history, they are confined by it, because they are unable to fully understand. Rarely has an ethnic community put as much emphasis on its history as the Armenians and the teaching of history within Diaspora communities has been second only to the teaching of the Armenian language. [47]

It is necessary, however, to qualify Dekmejian's analysis in one final way: this phenomenon is not unique to Armenians. Certainly Armenians may experience this with greater intensity, but the difference is perhaps quantitative rather than qualitative. Ethnocentrism, fatalism, parochialism and conservatism are terms that could be used to describe any ethnic group. In other words, the critics of Armenian political and cultural norms and institutions are themselves falling into a trap of ethnocentrism, by seeing the Armenian experience as unique in a negative sense.

Indeed an essentialist view of Armenians and other ethnic groups, that as a people they have always and everywhere possessed a core of discernible, ethnically determined qualities, has been for political nationalists the basis of their political ideology. The continuous existence of the Armenians as a historic people, their origins in ancient Armenia provides them with the right of self-determination, nationhood and a historically sanctified claim to the territories that constitute Armenia. Because this view of Armenian history plays such an important political role for Armenians, as indeed it does for Georgians, Turks and other peoples, any attempt to dispute it, or revise this single narrative of history must be done with a great deal of care and sensitivity. [48] Certainly ethnic identities may seem invented and arbitrary to the outside observer but they are generally regarded as immutable and age old to those holding them, who will resist challenges to them, including those originating with the well meaning academic!

Post Modern Perspective on Ethnicity

According to Friedman, cultural parochialism and globalisation exist as a Janus type of social organisation in the form of Diaspora. It is an attribute of the contemporary world that groups and individuals become more similar and more different simultaneously. 'Ethnic and cultural fragmentation and modernist homogenization are not two arguments, two opposing views of what is happening in the world today, but two constitutive trends of global reality'.[49] Here it is useful to highlight one aspect of globalisation the notion of deterritorialization with regard to social identities. The world is structured vertically by nation states and region but horizontally by an overlapping multiple system of interaction—communities not of place, but of interest, shared values and beliefs, tastes, cuisine, medicine (both Western and complementary), lifestyles, fashion and music.[50] Contrary to those theorists that argue a single homogenised culture is emerging, this position suggests that multiple cultures are being drawn from a global array but they will mix and match in each location producing new kinds of cultural difference in the interface between the global and the local. In this global arena, ways of life are frequently influencing, dominating, parodying and subverting one another. Thus, there are no traditionally fixed, spatially and temporally bound cultural worlds from which to depart, nor return: all is situated and all is moving.[51]

Anthropological research on globalisation stresses the need to account for the relationship between the global on one hand and the local on the other. Ethnicity as process, micro and macro, allows us to view this contravention as a duality between correspondence and difference, between homogenization and fragmentation. In other words, the central paradox of globalisation is that it has made the world both larger and smaller simultaneously. It has become smaller in the sense that it is possible to travel anywhere in less than twenty four hours, and it is possible to have practically the same life style anywhere in the world. Conversely, it has become larger in the sense that we know more about remote and alien places and therefore more easily recognise our mutual differences. Ethnic differentiation draws upon social, cultural and political resources, which assume an earlier institutionalization of the contacts between the groups and their incorporation into a single system in certain respects.[52]

If we analyse this general statement to the specific, it is apparent that Diasporas are one significant form of horizontal social organisation. As previously discussed, the horizontal relations are manifested in the form of maintaining, reinforcing and extending the relations between the migrant communities by sending remittances to their families and friends, arranging and participating in marriage and other ceremonies as well as sponsoring religious or traditional festivals and events, thus creating transnational networks. One of the factors leading to the emergence of transnational networks is the ease and speed of communication and travel, by comparison with earlier dispersions enabling immigrants to sustain their kinship networks globally.[53] Therefore the scope for multiple affiliations and associations that has been opened up outside and beyond the nation state has allowed members of a Diaspora to become both more open and more acceptable. There is no longer any stability in the points of origin, no finality in the points of destination and no necessary coincidence between social and national identities. What nineteenth century nationalists wanted was a 'space for each race',[54] a territorializing of each ethnic identity, what they have got is a chain of cosmopolitan cities and an increasing proliferation of transnational identities that cannot easily be contained in the nation state.[55]

As Cohen so succinctly illustrates Diasporas are disproportionately advantaged by these transformations and are able to develop them to their own advantage. A world economy is driven by many social and economic actors, including states and transnational organisations but the driving force is the family, kin and ethnic networks that organise trade and allow the flow of economic transactions and family migrants. Furthermore, global cities which are usually the host of Diaspora communities profit from their cosmopolitan character. Deterritorialized, multi-lingual and capable of bridging the gap between global and local propensities, Diasporas are able to take advantage of the economic and cultural opportunities on offer. By working and living productively in the global cities of the world economy, Diasporas strengthen, even if they do not exclusively propel, a further phase of globalisation.[56]

This perspective is the starting point for many post-modernists. The notion of post-modernity refers both to the fulfilment and the ultimate expression of modernity as well as to its dialectical opposite. The latter is the understanding that is most often expressed by the post-modern pioneers themselves, such as Lyotard, Habermas, Foucault and Derrida who regard post-modernism as anti-modern and for who post-modernity supersedes modernity.[57] Moreover, it is in many ways difficult to separate the processes of modernity and post-modernity, partly because of the ambiguity in defining what post-modernity actually is, and partly because the processes of modernity and post-modernity are always occurring simultaneously in varying degrees in different places. With this in mind, it is useful to understand post-modernity as an extension of modernity, in that it defines itself, albeit inadvertently, in a dialectical relationship to modernity. Post-modern scholars argue that traditional sociological and political categories have become too ossified to embrace the fluidity of the contemporary world, thus, the concepts of society and culture have become even more problematic. Networks of communication, migration, trade, capital and politics cross virtually every boundary. Rarely, if ever, are states or local communities clearly prescribed.

Bhabha[58] criticises the concept of the nation and its implied homogeneity, in other words the politics of collective boundaries dividing the world in to us and them usually around myths of common origin. What Bhabha suggests is abolishing the division of space/time and emphasizing the constantly changing boundaries and contested nature of the constructed boundaries of the imagined community and of the narratives which constitute its collective discourse. Bhabha's approach to space reflects the more general division between 'social' and 'real' space that pervades post-colonial theory. It becomes apparent that for Bhabha space is a way of talking about time: thus assumed hierarchical frameworks are temporal rather than spatial. Space is understood as identical with the shifting social world of ideas and identity. In 'The Location of Culture' he announces that through a post-colonnial archaeology he has derived modernity's spatial time and its spatial boundaries.[59] What does he mean by this? He has established a way of reflecting on the assumed hierarchical forms of rationality and universality that are a feature of the modern world.

He highlights the appearance of counter-narratives from the nation's margins, by those cultural hybrids that have lived, because of migration or exile, in more than one culture. He further argues the need to abandon the belief in the exclusiveness of national languages and nation states, as well as the concepts of class and gender as organisational categories. The argument appears to be that the migrant should not be placed in one cultural space, instead we must be aware of the 'multiple subject conditions', including race, gender, generation, institutional location, geo-political position and sexual orientation that form the building blocks of identity in the post-modern world. Bhabha uses the word 'unhomely' to refer to this situation, the plight of all those people—refugees, migrants, the colonized, women, gays, who have no home within the system. By demonstrating to the powerless the unhomely territory which is singularly their own, his aim is to suggest a way through which they could begin the process of self empowerment. By discovering their own voices, their writings could have a significant effect towards the ending of destabilizing traditional relations of cultural dominance, a means of self empowerment.[60] Such hybrids both bring to mind and erase the totalising boundaries of their adoptive nation. Such counter narratives do not, of course, have to come from immigrant minorities, the growing voice of indigenous people is also a counter-narrative which is heard within. Nevertheless such counter-narratives have to be situated within wider negotiations of meaning and power at the same time as recognising local stakes and specifities.[61] As a construct it refers to the state of 'hybridity', being neither here nor there. Diasporas and other ethnic communities, as well as the difference between the two, so he argues, are negotiated in strange, unexplored and fluid 'frontlines' and 'border-posts' of identity. We are asked to examine the overlapping edges, the displacement of difference and the mixing of cultures, religions, languages and ethnicities. Bhabha writes 'hybridity to me is the third space' which enables other positions to emerge. This third space displaces the histories which constitute it and set up new structures of authority.[62] Certainly one can agree that identity is complex but it seems to me that what Bhabha in his tortuous way is trying to endorse has little to do with space beyond its metaphorical function. What he is really considering is that every human problem or social identity should be considered from the perspective of time or history thus the third space is where we contest identities imposed upon us from within and without.

Despite Bhabha's embattled vision of identity, varieties of functionalism and structuralism have come to share anthropological and political approaches which emphasize the extent to which cultural reality is negotiated and contested, its definition contextual and interpretative. They have come to regard social life as turning on the use of symbolic not structural logics. Applying these ideas successfully to the concept of the ethnic community, Anthony Cohen[63] emphasises the ambiguous nature of the symbol. It is precisely this ambiguous nature of symbols that lends them to be simultaneously used as both points of unity, shared symbols and points of division, contested symbols. In other words membership comprises not so much of particular behavioural patterns more of thinking about behaviour in common—attachment to a common body of symbols, a shared vocabulary value.

Armenians do not share a uniform experience of ethnic identity. What they do share is a set of symbols, which provide a framework for their interpretations of their 'Armenianness'. Symbols of the genocide, the exilic Armenian, the Armenian homeland, language, and the Armenian Apostolic Church, gain strength from their ambiguity. These constitute rallying points that even in the symbolic form have prevented assimilation. It is because of the inherent ambiguity of symbols and their partial subjectivity they are 'ideal media' through which people can speak a common language, behave in apparently similar ways and participate in similar rituals without subordinating themselves to a tyranny of orthodoxy. Individuality and commonality are thus reconcilable. It is this very flexibility, this propensity for reimagination that gives a symbol its usefulness, for without this ambiguity a symbol would not properly function to establish continuity over space and time. By contrast any attempt to define terms too precisely would result in social dysfunction in the face of drastic change, thus symbolic ambiguity is a means of cultural preservation.[64] With this kind of approach we would avoid the tendency to treat ethnic boundaries as if they were social phenomena capable of analysis in their own right. A social boundary does not simply happen as a reaction of one system to another. It also reflects a variety of symbolic meanings occurring within ethnic communities, in which the impact of external factors is understood through the varied experiences of its members.

What this means is that external pressures and perceptions are not uniform throughout the membership of an ethnic group. Individual experiences before migration as well as their experiences within the host country will vary. Furthermore, their perceptions of the world vary accordingly and with it their interpretation of the way in which they relate to other groups. Complex historical processes led to the formation of the Armenian Diaspora communities. Therefore, complex material and organisational reasons lead to divisions within the Diaspora. Once groups fragment, they are no longer the same, they have distinct names or representations, and also bear the trace of the common origin. Stuart Hall provides a disclosure of the ontological and phenomenological dimensions of this fragmentary principle. Opposites not only repel but they are attracted to one another.[65] Cultural identities are emerging that are in transition, drawing on different or opposing traditions and synthesizing old and new traditions, echoing, to some extent, Barth's argument that identity is never fixed, it is always shifting and under construction. This does not mean, however, that they have no collectivist spirit. What they do share are the cultural symbols that represent ethnicity, but they do not necessarily attribute common meanings to those symbols.

Stuart Hall's post-modern interpretation of Diaspora peoples is one of the most consistent and well known voices to the debate on hybridity. Hall's theory is grounded, above all, in the Gramscian idea that hegemony or counter-hegemony must necessarily be constituted through alliances across differences. Antonio Gramsci writes about hegemony as not simply political or economic forms of rule but the entire process of dissent and compromise through which a particular group is able to determine the political, cultural and ideological character of a state. Hegemony, however, does not refer exclusively to the process by which a dominant group exercises its influence but refers equally to the process which emerges when other groups organise and contest any specific hegemony. In other words, we may say that hegemony is not the only political process by which a particular group constitutes itself as the dominant or majority group in which minorities are defined and know themselves to be the 'other' but is equally the process by which various positions of 'otherness' may constitute a new majority within a counter hegemony.[66]

Hall argues there is a strong connection between the development of hybridity and the changing character of Diasporas. He emphasises, in common with Friedman, that the late modern world is highlighted by two contradictory trends. Firstly, that globalisation encourages homogenization and assimilation. Secondly, perhaps in reaction to globalisation, is the re-assertion of nationalism, ethnicity and religious fundamentalism. Thus a feature of globalisation at the cultural level is that it has brought about the fragmentation and multiplication of identities. Cultural identities are emerging that are 'in transition', drawing on different traditions and synthesizing old and new traditions, without assimilation or total loss of historical traditions. He describes this development as the 'evolution of cultures of hybridity' and associates the development of these cultures with the 'new Diasporas' created by colonialism and the succeeding post-colonial migrations.[67]

The focus on post-colonial Diasporas is especially important for Hall who identifies 'the end of the innocent black subject' stating that a politics of representation has brought forward an important ongoing debate. Hall suggests that some sectors of the black youth have taken advantage of the enterprise culture of nineties Britain, whilst black cultural politics, related to campaigning, representations and the media 'has had its edge blunted in the nineties'. This trend, which correlates with the general trend of cultural politics in the Western world, is also associated with the issue of multiculturalism that Hall applauds: 'the racial and ethnic pluralization of British culture and social life'. For Hall, identity is a vision for the future and a mobilising call.[68] This process is happening to a greater or lesser extent everywhere, and through television and other media 'the unwelcome message of cultural hybridization' is being brought into the domestic sphere. This same process is evident in youth culture, where black street styles are the cutting edge of the generational style wars.[69] Hall describes Diaspora peoples as:

> Products of cultural hybridity. They bear the traces of particular cultures, traditions, languages, systems of belief, texts and histories which have shaped them. They are not and will never have been unified in the old sense, because they are inevitably the products of several interlocking histories and cultures belonging at the same time to several homes—and thus to no one particular home.[70]

Hall argues the need to recognise and meet the challenge that in the modern world identity is never fixed, it is always shifting and under construction. Essentially Hall is arguing that negotiable, socially constructed identities and cultural diversity are a somewhat new phenomenon—the fate of the modern world. The culture of the nineties, Hall argues, is far less collectivist, and more internally differentiated by location, generation, ethnic background, political outlook, class, gender and sexuality, than the older models allow. The weakness of Hall's argument is to assume a vision of the past as totally homogenous and unified. Indeed Armenians throughout their long history, and other ethnic collectivities, have had contact and interaction with other peoples. Influences of different cultures have always had an impact on the determining and maintenance of identities, just as there has been counter-narratives to the official canon within such communities.

Similarly, Iain Chambers, who is influenced by Hall's work, although he maintains that the creation of new identities is a more universal phenomenon than Hall's emphasis on post colonialism and argues all identities are formed 'on the move', at the unstable juncture where subjectivity meets the narrative of history. Ethnicity is always 'open and incomplete', involving a continuous re-invention and reconstruction in which there is 'no fixed identity or final destination'. Chambers argues to be a stranger in a strange land is typical of the human condition, not just typical of those who suffered forced migrations.[71]

> The migrant's sense of being rootless, of living between worlds, between a lost past and a non-integrated present, is perhaps the most fitting metaphor of this post modern condition. This underlines the theme of Diaspora and draws us into the processes whereby the previous margins now fold in on the centre. As a further supplement, think of migration, movement and the historical harvest of hybridity that characterise diverse historical novels.[72]

The migrant has become a symptom of the post-modern world. What is home? What is exile? Are there any distinctive factors of a national culture left intact? Chambers expresses a militant attitude towards any form of rootedness or any sense of belonging. He refers to the anathema of the former Yugoslavia as an example of irrational thought based on 'authenticity and national identity'. He argues the need to give up roots and embrace the hybridity of the Diaspora. If we could only understand how confused we all are, there would be no inter-ethnic conflict in the world. Furthermore, the genesis of evil is Western nationalism—we need to reject Western ideologies and its language of identity to discover our real identity—the reality of hybridity.[73] Arguably nationalist ideology can foster feelings of xenophobia in its ideal commitment to unifying members of a nation state culturally and linguistically, although in practice this rarely happens. Nevertheless the major flaw in Chamber's analysis is that people do still refer to home, whether that be their place of origin or settlement. This can also be the case for indigenous peoples. They may relocate but more often than not they refer to home as the town or village where they were born. People do not exist in a state of liminality. Identities are complex and always on the move, but people are grounded in the sense that they still refer to home, whether imaginary or real.

One of the most creative scholars of Diaspora identities, in my opinion, is James Clifford, who strongly advocates the importance of a 'discourse that is travelling or hybridising in new global conditions'. He focuses on the ways in which cultures travel. The idea of travelling cultures is explicitly linked to Diasporas, where he distinguishes between borderlands and Diasporas. Borderlands imply a position of dual locality, where an emerging syncretic culture is temporarily divorced by arbitrary territorial controls, but linked by legal and illegal migration. He uses the example of the Rio Grande, the zone separating Mexico and the United States—where do El Paso and San Diego end and Cuidad Juarez and Tijuana begin? He admits there are similarities between borderlands and Diasporas in that they merge into each other but Diasporas have distinctive features. Fundamentally, they are associated with and defined against the nation state. Diasporas, however, can never be exclusively nationalist. The guiding principle of the nation state is about living together in a single territory, and integrating ethnic minorities. Diasporas imply multiple loyalties. Clifford maintains Diasporas are situated between nation states and travelling cultures in the sense that they reside in a nation state in a physical sense but are travelling in a spiritual sense that dwells outside the nation state's space. Diaspora, Clifford concludes is something in between primordial codes of belonging and the wandering installation of alliances envisioned by postmodern theories. 'A 'changing same', something endlessly hybridized and in process but persistently there—memories and practices of collective identity maintained over long stretches of time'.[74] Thus we are territorially bounded in one sense but Diaspora view everything in terms of what has been left behind and what is actually here and now, there is a dual perspective that never views things in isolation.

For post modernists the collective identity of homeland and nation is a vibrant and constantly shifting set of cultural interactions, which fundamentally challenge traditional ideas of home and host. Anthropologists, however, firstly theorized the notion that there were seminal changes in cultural interactions. Geertz argues that provided the communities we study are really there, the task of fieldwork is a practical problem, not a theoretical one. Clearly many scholars have very different methods and theories but what they share is the idea that the 'other' is in a world elsewhere. This world embodies different ways of thinking, reasoning and behaving that is different to our own. What the creation of Diasporas has done is to move the margins to the centre. Marginal groups are suddenly present and co-existent. Geertz, however, warns against the naïve assumption that a reduction in distance automatically means that the gaps between cultures have been overcome. Group identity may remain strong and even strengthen in response to the shrinking of space between peoples. That space remains and its character has to be explored if we are to understand not only how we are alike, but also how our differences remain profound and sometimes insurmountable.[75] This new discourse is the recognition and celebration of difference: as a defence against fundamentalist images of the world; as a declaration of the rights of marginalized minorities to autonomous co-existence; as the encouragement for politics of representation which challenge the homogenization, integration and domination of the nation state. This debate openly acknowledges that the world is a less orderly place than we assumed. Essentially it is a response to the contradictions of relativism but most importantly post modernism is finally a recognition that ethnicity is subjective, inconsistent and definitively socially constructed.[76]

Conclusion

What conclusions can be drawn from all this and what do we mean when we talk about ethnicity? Ethnicity is a concept widely used in academic debate, yet as has been illustrated, it remains an ambiguous concept. Ethnic identity is maintained through a subjective belief in a common culture, and because ethnicity, unlike race, requires group association and self-ascription by its members, it is preferable to distinguish them as an ethnic group rather than racial. Thus, every society in the modern world contains sub-sections, groups of people, who consider themselves more or less distinct from the rest of the population and the most suitable generic term to describe these sub-sections is an ethnic group.

An ethnic group has a proper name for itself, which expresses the essence of the ethnic group, and this is often believed to be the necessary condition for its existence. There must always be two of something to create difference. Difference cannot exist without similarity and vice versa and it is through contact with others that we discover who we are. For difference to be socially marked, it follows that there has to be something to utilise as its marker, no matter how minor or arbitrary. For similarity to be identified there has to be something in common. Furthermore, ethnic groups involve the positing of boundaries in relation to who can and cannot belong, according to certain criteria, ranging from the credentials of birth, language, or conforming to other cultural or symbolic practices. Thus, ethnic demarcation is socially motivated and depends upon the preferences of its members.

Moreover those on the inside and those on the outside may use different criteria for membership. Therefore, the notion of how the boundary is constructed is not only diverse but is also contextual and relational to other groups. If we agree with Weber, however, and acknowledge ethnicity as a principle of collective social organisation, in the context of group identification, there has to be at least mutual understanding of behaviour and the criteria of identification have to possess at least some social importance to the group. In other words the differences that mark cultural differentiation have to make a difference. Thus, there are limits to how arbitrary and fluid the social construction of identity can actually be. Most importantly, ethnicity means something to individuals and that is what really matters.[77]

As discussed the relationship between the terms ethnicity and nationality are complex as discussed above. Nationalism, like ethnic ideologies, emphasises the cultural similarities of its adherents and implicitly draws boundaries against others, who become outsiders. A nation is a group of people who feel that they are ancestrally related, however fictitious that relationship is. The same is true of an ethnic group. All that is irreducibly required for the existence of a nation or ethnic group is that its members share an intuitive conviction of the group's separate origin and evolution. The distinguishing mark of nationalism, however, is its relationship with the state in that a nationalist group stresses political boundaries should coincide with cultural boundaries, whereas many ethnic groups do not demand this.

Frederik Barth and Abner Cohen are largely responsible for shaping current anthropological approaches to the field of ethnicity. Both Barth and Cohen would probably agree that ethnic groups emerge under certain circumstances and can persist even after the initial conditions prompting their mobilisation have changed. The distinction between them is largely through their points of entry into the analysis. Barth focuses his analysis at the level of individual choices within structural constraints. Cohen focuses his analysis at the level of group interaction. Both approaches are complementary rather than opposed; one examines macro issues of the relations between ethnic groups and the other is concerned with micro issues, the grass roots investigation of ethnic communities.

In summary, therefore, the long-standing belief is that the roots of ethnicity lie in the assumption that culturally defined communities everywhere entertain an intrinsic awareness of their own identity, and that the traditional loyalties vested in this identity are the source of ethnic consciousness and community formation, which provides the basis for collective action and inter-group relationships. The counter-argument suggests that the expression of ethnicity is socially constructed and does not arise in any communities, except as a reaction to threats against its integrity. As long as this integrity remains unchallenged, ethnic ties either do not exist or remain dormant. Both these arguments are simultaneously correct and incomplete. On the one hand, the pre-capitalist world where primordial connections and loyalties are presumed to have had their origins, were never so atomistic that communities did not have relations with others. It is absurd to suggest that people could have lacked common identities or a concern for socio-cultural differences. Therefore, it is wrong to assume that primordialism is set in opposition to social constructionism. If an ethnic community is classified only through a socially motivated practice of identification, then this in itself is consistent with that kind of practice being an unchanging aspect of human existence, influenced by the fundamental human desire for group identification. On the other hand this form of awareness is distinctly different from ethnic consciousness suis generis.[78]

Clearly the mutability and variability of an ethnic group's cultural characteristics, demonstrates that it is misleading to view ethnic groups as individuated by their cultures. It is necessary to look at the scope of the group, which may in reality be determined by other factors, so that a common culture serves as a focus for group identification rather than being what generates the boundaries of the group. In other words, two groups being culturally distinctive do not create ethnicity, ethnicity occurs when cultural differences are made relevant through interaction. Thus, we should be concerned with what is socially relevant to an ethnic group, not objective cultural differences. Moreover, an ethnic group is not necessarily a community in the real sense of the word because group identification and membership can be maintained when its members are widely dispersed, as in various Diasporas.

Most importantly, ethnicity is no more fixed than the culture of which it is a component, or the situation in which it is produced and reproduced. A recognition that all contemporary cultures are to some extent hybrid is required to understand the micro politics of local and global interactions. The term ethnicity recognises the place of history, language and culture in the construction of subjectivity and identity, as well as the fact that all discourse is positioned, situated and all knowledge is contextual. What is involved is the splitting of the notion of ethnicity between on the one hand the dominant notion which connects it to race and nation and on the other hand the beginning of a positive conception of the ethnicity of the margins. In other words we are all ethnically located and our ethnic identities are important to our subjective sense of who we are. Diaspora as a lived experience is certainly profoundly shaped by the Armenian experience and the inheritance of systems of representation and aesthetic traditions from other cultures. Thus it seems to me that the concept of Diaspora is much more than an empirical reality widening itself in front of the researcher or a new and more appropriate analytical tool. Rather a dual development that underlines the significance of the nation state and national-culturalist modes of ascription and levels of belonging yet simultaneously rejects being completely subjected to the discursive power of the nation. The discourse of Diaspora pushes dialogue of identity and belonging to their limits.

From this intellectual mire, there has emerged a wider concern for the elements of both ethnic and national identities. The influx of immigrants, asylum seekers, and ex-colonials has decomposed received narratives of 'national identity' into their 'hybridized' cultural components. Multiculturalism has become the buzz word of political expression, incorporating a more pluralistic approach to nationhood in polyethnic states. How can people of different cultures live together in the same state? This is the question that scholars have in mind when they debate the nature of and prospects for multiculturalism. There is, of course, a presumption that there is a problem here with cultural co-existence under the same polity. This arises on the one hand from the need for citizens to be able to communicate together, which their use of different languages may hamper, and, on the other, from the need to live under the same laws, which different ethnic groups' cultural values may find difficult to accommodate.[79]

Nevertheless as we move into the third millennium, the prospects for ethnicity are uncertain. Contemporary states will increasingly face choices between encouraging a single identity and a unitary vision of the nation, and alternatively providing an environment in which different ethnic identities and relationships within and across territorial boundaries may flourish. Most highly developed countries, and indeed many less developed ones, have become more culturally diverse than they were a generation ago. The majority of nation states must acknowledge the reality of ethnic pluralism. Arguably few modern nation states have ever been ethnically homogenous, however, the nationalism of the last two centuries has created myths of homogeneity. Nationalism, in its extreme form, attempts to bring about homogeneity through the expulsion of minorities and ethnic cleansing.[80] Nowhere is this more evident, than in the multi ethnic states of Eastern Europe and the former Soviet Union, where territorial disputes, involving minority Diaspora populations still threaten ethnic conflagration. The revival of ethnic nationalism following events in the former Soviet Union and Eastern Europe re-emphasized the importance of understanding nationalist movements and ethnic groups, like Diaspora communities.[81] Furthermore, the devastating example of ethnic cleansing in the former Yugoslavia clearly reveals that such tendencies exist. The reality, however, for most modern states is that they have to acknowledge ethnic pluralism and even if migration ceased, this will affect countries for generations.

Ethnic diversity affects nation states in many ways, and one of the most important issues is cultural pluralism. The process of marginalization of ethnic groups in many countries has led to the problem that culture has become a marker for exclusion by some sections of the majority population, and simultaneously a mechanism of resistance with minorities. Notwithstanding serious attempts by various governments to end all forms of discrimination and racism, cultural and linguistic difference will persist for generations, especially if new immigration takes place. Consequently majority populations will have to contend with cultural pluralism, even if it means modifying their own expectations of social conformity. This trend towards cultural pluralism corresponds with the emergence of a global culture, which is nurtured by global travel, mass media and the commodification of cultural symbols. This global culture is anything but homogenous but it permits a new understanding of ethnic cultures: difference may no longer be a marker for exclusion, but rather the possibility for ihformed choice among a myriad of opportunities. Therefore this global culture presents new and endless combinations of choices.[82]

Trends towards cultural pluralism, however, can threaten national identity, particularly in countries where nationhood has been constructed in an exclusionary manner. If the ideals of belonging to a nation have focused on historical myths and ethnic purity, ethnic diversity may well result in insecurity and unrest. Indeed the community of the nation as belonging to the 'Volk' as in Germany, or a unitary culture, as in France, requires major political and psychological adjustments to incorporate ethnic diversity. Countries, such as Britain, which has long been a recipient of immigrant flows, whose political structures and models of citizenship are geared towards incorporating newcomers, also has historical traditions of racial exclusion and cultural homogeneity. Indeed, the assimilation of ethnic groups as epitomised in the 'American Dream' appears unattainable in the light of future population shifts and the strong tendency by ethnic communities towards cultural and linguistic insularity.[83]

What all of the above represents is a growing need for countries of immigration to re-examine their understanding of what it means to belong to their society. Assimilationist models of national identity may no longer be adequate and ethnic communities may be able to contribute to the development of new forms of identity. The argument that locates the political good firmly within the terrain of the nation state fails to consider or properly appreciate the diversity of ethnic communities and the fact that individuals can involve themselves coherently in different associations at different levels and for different purposes. The proponents of globalisation conclude that the political good today can only be revealed by reflection on the diversity of the communities living together within the nation state. Contemporary people are subject to an extraordinary diversity of information and communication that can be influenced by images, lifestyles and ideas from well beyond their immediate communities and can come to identify with groupings beyond their borders, thus cultural and political identity is constantly under review and reconstruction.

The inescapable trend, therefore, is the increasing ethnic and cultural diversity of most countries and the emergence of trans-national networks which links the countries of origin and host. The migrant culture is comprised of multiple identities, which are linked to the cultures of both the homeland and the host country and such identities incorporate complex cross-cultural factors. Migrants often develop a consciousness of their dually rooted culture, which is demonstrated in their artistic work and social and political action. Moreover, multi ethnic countries provide grounds for optimism, as multilingual capabilities and transcultural understanding are clearly important economic assets in the context of international trade and investment. Globalisation is helping to create new communications and information patterns linking particular groups through networks of relations to one another, transforming the dynamics of political relations. Increasingly successful political communities have to work with, not against, a multiplicity of identities, cultures and ethnic groupings. Hopefully, new principles of national identity may emerge which will neither be exclusionary or discriminatory, which will pave the way for improved cooperation and communication between ethnic groups, resulting in increased unity throughout the world in dealing with the pressing problems that beset humanity.

CHAPTER THREE

THE ARMENIAN DIASPORA—HISTORICAL ORIGINS

As the Soviet Union began its rapid disintegration, the smallest republic, Armenia, now governed by a democratically elected national movement, assumed the legitimacy of its independence and full statehood on the basis of a confident claim to antiquity as a nation and historic responsibility for the destiny of the Armenian people. Citizenship in the new republic was granted, not only to all living within its territorial boundaries, but also to those Armenians in the Diaspora who wished to exercise that right. With a new state, a new concept of nationhood was being invented for the world's Armenians.[1]

The Republic of Armenia declared its independence in September 1991, having been part of the Soviet Union since December 1922. It is one of three internationally recognised states: Armenia, Azerbaijan and Georgia in Transcaucasia, the southernmost area of the former Soviet Union. Armenia has a population of around four million and is the most ethnically homogenous state of all the former republics of the Soviet Union, with almost ninety per cent of its population being Armenian. It is 11,620 square miles in area, about the size of Albania. This is a fraction, of which Armenians put at one tenth, of the historic land of Armenia. Historic Armenia is not easily identifiable because areas of Armenian settlement and culture do not always coincide with areas of Armenian rule. Further, the extent of Armenian controlled territory has varied considerably. One estimate of what constitutes historic Armenia suggests an area of 239,320 square miles, another considering historical and geographical Armenia suggests approximately 154,440 square miles, whilst the territory actually under Armenian rule (56BC-AD298) was considerably less, around 108,108 square miles.[2] Historic Armenia has also been described as the land of the three major lakes; Van (presently in Turkey), Sevan (in present day Armenia), and Urmia (presently in Iran). Even Mount Ararat, closely identified with Armenia and towering over the Armenian Capital of Yerevan, now stands in Turkey.[3]

Central to the perception of historical legacy among the Armenians is the concept of the Armenian homeland. It is difficult to delineate this concept, however, in historical terms due to the mystery surrounding the origins of the Armenians as a people. The history of the Armenian people is long and complex and scholars have yet to ascertain whether Armenians originated in Western Asia Minor or among the native inhabitants of Eastern Anatolia. Armenian tribes, however, were first identified between 500 and 550 BC with the collapse of the prosperous kingdom of Urartu or biblical Ararat (centred in Van).[4] The earliest known mention of the Armenian people (Armenoi) occurs in the writings of the Greek historian Hecataeus of Miletus, who travelled widely between 515 and 500BC, and of Armenia (Armina) in the trilingual illustrated inscription of Darius I (522-486BC), the Achaemenid King of Persia, carved high on the cliff face at Behistun (Iran). Darius describes them as one of twenty three lands, or more probably peoples, to come under his control and pay tribute to him. These references, however, do not confirm whether Armenians arrived in the highlands of Eastern Anatolia and Transcaucasia at this time or earlier, or from where they arrived, although it is known that their language falls into the Indo-European group of languages along with Farsi.[5]

Lang suggests that 'the modern Armenian nation is in fact the product of a process of ethnic mingling which has been going on for thousands of years in Transcaucasia and the mountains and valleys of the Ararat region'.[6] Lang identifies the ancient 'Hayasa' mentioned in Hittite records with the term 'Hayastan'[7] by which Armenians refer to their country. He also identifies King Arame, the founder of the Urartian Kingdom, which flourished between the ninth and sixth centuries BC with the legendary Armenian King Ara[8], and Urartu itself with the name of Mount Ararat. Burney, however, an archaeologist and specialist in Urartian culture, warns against the insistence on similarities between proper names and geographical names and rejects any direct link between the Armenians and the Urartians. Burney suggests that the Armenians may have been one of a number of peoples who, taking advantage of the fragility of the Urartian Kingdom during its final years and eventual collapse migrated into its territories and established themselves there.[9]

Nevertheless, whether Armenians are direct descendants of Urartians or indeed their successors, this area of Eastern Anatolia and Transcaucasia has been described as the historic land of Armenia. It must be emphasized, however, that it should be described as a geographical region, not a political region. Armenia's political extent fluctuated enormously over a period of some two thousand years, until the fifteenth century AD, subject to the vicissitudes of war and peace. Following this period, in spite of five hundred years of Turkic occupation, this geographical area continues to be referred to as historic Armenia just as, for example, Poland, although occupied in turn by Germans or Russians for centuries, has sustained its geographical and, like Armenia, its ethnic and linguistic identity.[10]

Moreover, this area was not only the scene of competing interests by rival empires but of competing interests between members of the indigenous Armenian ruling class. Walker quotes Cyril Toumanoff's description of this 'class of dynastic princes':

They were older than kingship which derived from them. Their principalities were self-sufficient and self-determined, being territorialized tribes and clans of old. And their rights over these states were fully sovereign, including executive, judiciary, legislative and fiscal independence, control of their own armed forces, and, from the princes' point of view at least, the right to negotiate with foreign powers.'[11]

It was not uncommon, therefore, to find Armenian noble families aligning themselves with different imperial powers. During each succeeding empire, the power of these dynastic princes and the territories governed by them expanded and contracted, with areas being partitioned, recaptured and lost again.[12]

Following the Urartian period, Armenia was subsumed into the Achaemenid Persian Empire, only achieving effective independence under a native dynasty, the Ortonids, following the conquest of Alexander the Great (345-323BC). After the turn of the millennium, Armenians were caught up in Roman-Parthian rivalry and became subject to the rule of relatives of the Parthian kings, the Arsacids. With the Arsacids came an intensification of Persian influence upon Armenian culture until Tiridates the Great was appointed king in the early fourth century. Tiridates established Christianity as the state religion, trying under Roman protection, to stave off the threat to the very existence of the Armenian kingdom posed by the Sassanians, who had conquered the Arsacids in Parthia in the early third century. The Arsacid dynasty ruled Armenia until 428 when the Sassanians eventually conquered it. With the rise of the second Persian Empire (Sassanid 226-651), Eastern Armenia was drawn more deeply into the Persian domain, while Western Armenia remained chiefly under Roman and then Byzantine influence. Two great empires, Rome and Persia struggled for centuries to establish dominance over Armenia, making Armenia the scene of almost constant warfare. Partition between the East Roman (or Byzantine), and Sassanian Persian Empire was ended by Arab conquest in the seventh century.[13]

In 301, the Armenian King, Tiridates, responded positively to the mission of St Gregory the Illuminator and embraced Christianity, as did his people. Armenian merchants and travellers frequented Antioch, one of the earliest sites of Christian teachings and practice and had relations with other Christian centres in Northern Mesopotamia, where Christianity flourished. Thus, Christianity must have had many adherents and a formal structure in Armenia by the time of the official conversion. Furthermore, the Armenians have the distinction of being the first political community to adopt Christianity, despite sustained pressure to convert to Zoroastrianism and indeed Islam from the eighth century onwards. In these circumstances of adversity, the Armenians viewed themselves as the 'flock of New Israel' committed to the Christian faith, which eventually became the ideological foundation of a peculiar religio-cultural nationhood centred in the Armenian Apostolic Church.[14] Therefore, the establishment of Christianity is a crucial landmark in Armenian history, not merely for its importance in the fourth century, but because to contemporary Armenians, church and faith appear to have been the fundamental instruments, shaping and preserving the Armenians as a people. The creation and dissemination of the belief that 'we are a chosen people' has been crucial for ensuring long term ethnic survival.[15]

In no sense, however, should ancient Armenia be seen as a nation state in the modern sense. A cluster of principalities often fighting each other fiercely and often allied with non-Armenian powers against their fellow Armenians. Political solidarity was weak among Armenians but there was a commonality of language, an attachment to territory and fierce devotion to the national religion, firstly pagan, the amalgamation of Iranian and Greek deities that formed Armenian paganism or later Armenian Christian. Christianity that the Armenian Church adopted was the primary identification of this people, coinciding roughly with the linguistic and territorial community. Thus, Armenians can be said to have formed what Smith refers to as an ethnie, a unique identifiable ethno-religious community. Their community was distinguished from those of their neighbours by a collective name; they shared a common myth of descent and sense of solidarity and kinship and the boundaries of their church coincided with the linguistic cultural community.[16]

A common theme in Armenian historiography has been a connection not only between national identity and Christianity but also between national identity and Christology. The idea that Christianity ultimately unified Armenians and hindered foreign assimilation or elimination is convincing. Indeed Tiridates' conversion was due, in part, to hopes of unifying his people. Persian and Arab attempts to eradicate Christianity failed. The impression of a Christian link with Armenian identity was promoted in the fifth and sixth centuries by Agathangelos and Elishe, whose works became classics depicting Gregory the Illuminator as the role model for the church leaders within Armenian society after the abolition of the monarchy. The significance of the Armenian Church's renunciation of the Council of Chalcedon, the Christological doctrine that Christ has two natures, thus rejecting church union with Rome and Byzantium, is debatable. It has been argued that anti-Chalcedonianism and national identity are inter-related, suggesting ancient heresies were camouflaging national movements. Armenian scholars, however, have concluded that the rejection of Chalcedon was not nationalist sentiment but due to a genuine theological dispute. What is not disputed, however, is that Christianity did play an important role in the construction of a sense of Armenian identity, and continued to reinforce it and sustain through its turbulent history.[17]

The Armenians had weathered Persian persecution and warfare, Roman-Persian relations were stable and Roman-Armenian relations close. Unfortunately this was all to change when the Prophet Muhammed died in 632 and his followers emerged from Arabia. With startling rapidity Arab forces conquered Persia, Byzantine Syria, Mesopotamia and Egypt. In Armenia, however, the establishment of Arab rule took several decades. During the eighth century this rule was oppressive but its gradual relaxation in the ninth century culminated in the re-establishment of the Armenian monarchy. The rise of the Arabs demonstrated how the Armenians were dramatically affected by a major political change in the area. Armenia suffered or prospered depending on who held the Caliphate and the condition of public order. In 885 after much effort, Ashot Bagratuni secured appointment by the Caliph in Baghdad, and in 886 by the Emperor in Constantinople, as King of Armenia. The royal house of Bagratids was divided into two branches, the Georgian Bagratunis (who passed into the Russian nobility as

Bagrations) and the Armenian branch, which ruled the medieval Armenian kingdom of Ani (885-1045).[18]

Throughout the latter part of the eleventh century, Byzantium gradually annexed Armenian territories and it was during this period that a new force burst upon the scene, the Seljuk Turks. The defeat of the Byzantines by the Seljuks at the battle of Manzikert in Armenia in 1071 brought all Armenians under Turkic rule. During this period many Armenian noblemen, their armies and their people fled southwest to Cilicia to take refuge in this mountainous region. These immigrants grew numerous and powerful establishing an independent principality which eventually became a kingdom, under Prince Ruben I. The Armenian kingdom of Cilicia (1080-1375) existed, under the Rubenids, among the Taurus and Amanus mountains and along the Mediterranean coast to Alexandretta. Cilicia became an Armenian Diaspora kingdom, thus, the epicentre of Armenian political, cultural, economic and religious activity shifted away from the traditional homeland. The kingdom of Cilicia acted as a Diaspora repository for the Armenian heritage, particularly through its monasteries and libraries. The legacy of Cilicia was significant in that it provided a strong link with Europe through the Cilician monarchy's intermarriage with the French monarchy, and through contact with the Crusaders who passed through the country. Following the collapse of the kingdom, a large number of Armenians made their way to France where they established a small but significant community. Cilicia enjoyed great prosperity at a time when the Armenian homeland was falling into ruin. The Cicilian period was productive of great wealth, substantial learning, and is noted for its ecclesiastical manuscripts. This last Armenian kingdom fell in 1375, and the last Armenian King, Levon VI, died in exile in 1393 in France, however, Armenian communities continued to live in this area until 1915.[19] The three hundred years of the Cilicia Kingdom is considered to be the golden age of Armenian enlightenment, and produced a wealth of exquisite manuscripts. In fact, apart from an interlude in 1918-21, no Armenian state existed again until the Republic of Armenia was established in 1991.

According to the historian Amanda Redgate, what is most striking about Armenian historiography is Armenian ethnic, political and cultural longevity, a factor practically unequalled in European history. By the late eleventh century, there had been an independent Armenia, albeit in varying form, for almost thirteen centuries since 189BC, despite having been both buffer and theatre of war between neighbouring powers, and suffering temporary subservience and oppression. Politically, Armenia comprised feuding dynastic principalities, a societal pattern that persisted throughout the medieval period, making Armenia easy prey to its neighbouring larger empires. At the same time, it is argued, that this societal pattern probably maintained a distinct ethnic identity, as some parts of Armenia remained autonomous, thus avoiding pressure to assimilate.[20]

Other factors contributed to the sense of Armenian identity. The geographical location of Armenia helped resistance to conquerors, and also hindered their consolidation, as much as it did Armenia's political unity. The sharing of a language may well have emphasized both internal and external perceptions of national identity. The Armenian language, like Greek and Iranian, is part of the Indo-European family that is spoken from North India, through Afghanistan, Iran,

Armenia and Greece into Europe and European Russia. The Armenian alphabet of thirty six characters, devised early in the fifth century by St Mesrop, who also produced a script for the Christian Georgians and Albanians, is unique. In later periods, however, the sacral language of Armenians was often reduced to symbols of religious identity, and Armenians adopted languages like Farsi or Turkish. Throughout these processes of linguistic shift, Scriptures and liturgy remained in the original sacral language. Indeed strong resistance against using foreign linguistic elements, however beneficial they might be, suggested deviation in the direction of a hostile faith. By way of example, Armenian children were forbidden to learn Latin, which was identified with the dreaded Latin Church 'better the Armenian faith in Hell than to get to Heaven with Latin'.[21]

A further factor, which complicates the discussion of the historic homeland are the numerous population movements, which unsurprisingly, occurred in the process of conflicts over this region. The Armenian 'spiurk', scattered peoples, is an ancient phenomenon. Indeed since the Middle Ages and the fall of the Bagratid Kingdom the Armenians have been in large measure a dispersed people. The rise of Cilicia was the most eloquent expression of such dispersion. Armenian merchants have for centuries sought better economic opportunities in other lands, however, the majority of Armenians did not leave their country voluntarily, resulting in a belt of Armenian communities, old and new, stretching from South East Asia to Western Europe. Invasion by Turkic tribes in the eleventh century, followed by the Mongol invasions, and occupation of Armenia, in the thirteenth and fourteenth centuries, provoked Armenian migration to cities in Europe, Russia and the Middle East. As the Mongols declined in power Armenia was devastated by raiding bands of nomadic tribes, culminating with the barbaric invasion of the hordes of Timurlane in 1400. By the end of the fifteenth century, the Ottomans had consolidated their power throughout Anatolia, and following a treaty in the sixteenth century with the Persian Empire, Armenia was divided between the Ottoman and Persian Empires.[22]

Historians of the Ottoman Empire tend to paint a rosy picture of the Christian minority peoples within its borders. By contrast historians of the subject peoples, Serbs, Bulgarians, Greeks or Armenians tend to do the opposite, emphasizing the brutality of Ottoman rule. The disagreement pivots on different assessments of the unique millet (religious community) system, by which the Ottoman Christian minorities enjoyed relative autonomy. The Prophet Muhammed (570-632) first instituted the 'dhimma' or treaty, which defined the relationship between the 'people of the book' (Jews and Christians), defeated in a jihad or holy war as 'dhimmi' or tolerated people. This treaty usually specified that the conquered people of the book, in return for submission and the payment of a tax, would have protection for their lives, religion and property. This was, of course denied to pagans. Thus the non-Muslim subjects were grouped by religion into self-governing units, millets. The Ottoman Empire at its zenith was well governed and religious minorities enjoyed freedom of conscience and relative autonomy within their religious communities. The unique millet system of self-government for the non-Muslim minorities of the Ottoman Empire apparently satisfied the Armenians to the degree that they were known as the 'millet-i-sadika' or 'loyal community', because of their deference to official authority and their remarkable achievements under the Ottomans in trade and commerce. These millets were internally largely self governing and retained their own laws in those areas which were connected with the Muslim concept of societal responsibilities, such as contracts within the community, family life, marriage, public instruction, charities, worship and ecclesiastical administration, with the head of the millet being responsible to the Ottoman authorities.[23]

Indeed, compared with what preceded and succeeded the Ottomans, the Byzantine Empire and modern Turkey respectively, there is no doubt that the minorities lived relatively well under the Ottomans, enjoying greater religious tolerance and communal autonomy, than minorities in contemporary Western and Central European societies. It would be anachronistic, however, to suggest that the Ottomans demonstrated racial and ethnic tolerance. Islamic ideology unambiguously proclaimed the inferiority of non-Muslim peoples. Christians did not enjoy equal rights with Muslims in the judicial system, the most important of which was the inadmissibility of their evidence in the Muslim religious courts. The tax system openly discriminated against them; they were not allowed to serve in the higher ranks of the government or the military; and they were forced to pay a heavy tax for their exemptions from military service. The Armenians alone had the obligation of providing free winter quarters to the nomadic Kurds, which could amount to considerable expense in the provision of food for both the Kurds and their animals. Furthermore, the Kurds, as Muslims, were entitled to bear arms, which left the Armenians almost defenceless. As long as the Christian communities were prepared to accept these strictures, they were able to prosper in their communities. Moreover, because Islamic law discouraged Muslims from participation in banking and commerce, Armenians and Jews increasingly dominated the economic life of the Ottoman Empire.[24]

The next major political development for the Armenians was the extension of Russian authority. In 1722 Persian Armenia suffered invasion by Peter the Great (1682-1725) and rebellion followed, led by David Bek, an Armenian from Georgia. Bek used the fort of Tatew as his base and established a principality. The result was Ottoman invasion and the division of Persia's Armenian territory between Russians and the Ottomans in 1724. Bek's principality subsequently fell to Ottoman forces in 1730.[25] By the beginning of the nineteenth century, however, Persian Armenia was annexed to Russia. The Russians annexed the kingdom of Georgia in 1800 and in wars against the Persian and Ottoman Empires from 1804 to 1829, they took the regions that today are Azerbaijan and the Republic of Armenia. When conditions of peace treaties forced the Russians to leave some of their conquests, tens of thousands of Armenians followed them out of the Ottoman domain. These Armenians were replaced by even larger numbers of Muslims forced out of the New Russian conquests. A forced exchange of population was transpiring. In each war and each forced movement of peoples, hatred and fear of the other increased.[26]

It was during this period that distinctions such as 'Eastern' or 'Russian' and 'Western' or 'Turkish' Armenia came into sharp focus. When Russia annexed the Khanate of Yerevan in 1828, a process of separation or polarization, that had been noticeable for some time, accelerated to an unprecedented degree. Two urban communities, those of Constantinople and Tiflis emerged as focal centres for the Eastern and Western Armenians respectively. Thus the overwhelming majority of Armenians were now subjects of either the Ottoman or Russian Empire, two implacable rivals, with different civilizations and different political systems. There were then about 1.5 million Armenians in Russian Armenia but the number in Ottoman Armenia is harder to establish. Ottoman government statistics acknowledge only 1,295,000 Armenians but the figures compiled in 1912 by the Armenian Patriarchate in Constantinople were 2,100,000.[27]

Apart from the geographical divide, the wars and antagonism between the two empires precluded direct and active contact between the two halves of the Armenian people. The legal basis of recognition extended to both Eastern and Western Armenians was religious affiliation, thus membership of the Armenian Apostolic Church promoted and enhanced a sense of belonging to a distinct religious community. The church followed the immigrants wherever they went, and church buildings functioned as the centres of Armenian cultural life. According to Armstrong, it is important to emphasize that even when effective communication with the church hierarchy was impracticable, the Armenian Apostolic Church seems to have been able to maintain uniformity almost entirely through tribunals and informal pressures. Ethnoreligious identity remained central to Armenian identity and complete adherence to boundary mechanisms, in matters like endogamy were strongly enforced by the same system of community tribunals that adjudicated commercial disagreements.[28]

In contrast to the Armenian homeland, a wealthy commercial bourgeoisie developed in the urban Armenian migrant communities. It was in the cities that these Armenians were influenced by the pervasive revolutionary and nationalist ideas that were sweeping Europe during the eighteenth and nineteenth centuries. Two currents of thought had a marked influence on Armenian avant-garde circles. The first brought home from Western European intellectuals who studied there, was democratic liberalism, the concept of the rights of man, a legacy of the French Revolution of 1789. It was prevalent especially among the Armenians of Constantinople and the intellectuals in the provinces. The second, again imported from Europe, but essentially filtered through Russian revolutionary thought was socialism, specifically its Marxist variant. Arguably theories of historical materialism and class struggle did not directly apply to the realities of Ottoman Armenian reality, however, socialist ideology was adopted by the Armenian intelligentsia. Furthermore, always present but inflamed as a reaction to the growing persecution under Ottoman rule, was reawakened pride in historic Armenia, a national consciousness. These ideas formed the genesis of an Armenian cultural awakening.

A significant factor in this cultural awakening was the rediscovery and publication of classical texts, which originated in the Armenian Benedictine Order of Mekhitarists, founded in Venice in the eighteenth century by a young priest, Mekhitar (1676-1749).[29] Mythological Armenian heroic figures, which had battled against foreign domination, were offered as icons of Armenian honour. Nationalistic literature became the agency in which appeals were made to Armenians in the Ottoman Empire "wake up . . . from your death-inviting slumber of ignorance, remember your past glory, mourn your present state of wretchedness and heed the example of other enlightened nations."[30] Arguably, there existed a growing sense of national self-awareness and nationalistic tendencies and these attitudes and feelings were present in varying proportions amongst both Western and Eastern Armenians towards the end of the nineteenth century. This represented a fundamental shift in Armenian consciousness and the development of a political programme for Armenian liberation.

Although the majority of Armenians in the Ottoman Empire were semi-literate Turkish speaking, a new middle-class of doctors, teachers and lawyers in the provinces began to challenge elite social and political control. Prior to the nineteenth century, the literacy of the Armenian clergy contrasted sharply with other sections of Armenians, including the aristocracy who were mostly illiterate. This new educated class therefore turned its attention to improving literacy and educating the masses, emphasizing nationalist sentiment and love of the mother-land, thus defining the nation as linked to a particular historic territory. An extensive network of schools was set up teaching Armenian language and history, often supported by cultural societies that also engaged in charitable and social work. Western Armenian literature flourished acquiring its distinct features and very own canon.[31]

Numerous printing presses and libraries attended to the needs of a cultivated readership, disseminating information throughout the provinces. The printing press also helped to synthesise the national experience through time by connecting the past with the present and the experiences of one section of people with another. Thus creating historical continuities and commonalities where these did not necessarily exist. Therefore, by the 1870's the consolidation of Western Armenian identity was well established. Religion and education were significant factors, shaping national identity, together with new ideas flowing from Europe, and the recovery of the Armenian past through old Armenian historical texts. More importantly this new national identity is fostered through the media of mass communication and the educational system. Print capitalism enables a large number of people to gain the same knowledge through the standardization of language. New historical myths, usually based upon military achievements, and symbols of national solidarity are reconstructed. Thus to conceive of any community on such a large scale involves either the creation or awakening of a new kind of world view or consciousness.

In addition in Eastern Armenia, as in Western Armenia, a new generation of intellectuals emerged, whose revolutionary politics asserted considerable influence on the Armenian political parties. The Eastern Armenians set up institutions and societies similar to those established by the Western Armenians but developed more secular and liberal tendencies. The Eastern Armenian mind was shaped primarily in Russian and northern European universities, and under the heavy impact of social, economic and political turmoil in Russia. This, together with the leading role the Eastern Armenians came to play in the liberation movements, gave rise to more radical traditions in Armenian political thought. The Eastern Armenians, however, considered Western Armenia an indivisible part of Armenia and, until the rise of the parties, had a simple solution to the Armenian Question: the annexation of Western Armenia by Russia. By contrast, most probably due to the cautious approach dictated by political circumstances, the Western Armenians focused on reform in the provinces.[32]

Thus during the late nineteenth century a new generation of intellectuals emerged. Armenian revolutionary groups began to appear in Eastern Armenia and in Western Armenia, particularly Constantinople. While unsuccessful in their primary goal, they did raise the revolutionary consciousness of Armenians. Attempts were made to gain Russian financial and military support for Armenian communities, particularly in Van and Zeytun. With the exception of Zeytun, however, where the Armenians held off an Ottoman army sent to assert state authority, nationalist activities before 1878 had little effect. In 1878 the Balkans were granted liberty from Ottoman rule in the Treaty of Berlin. The Armenians, who had sent a delegation to the conference petitioning for some form of local self-government, but not independence, found their hopes dashed with the promise of reforms, but with no provisions made for their enforcement.[33]

These events had two important effects on Ottoman perceptions of the Armenians and the development of Armenian movements for autonomy respectively. Firstly, it increased the Ottoman authority's suspicion and distrust of the Armenians, who had turned to the European Christian powers, in particular Russia, with their demands for self-government and reform. The Ottoman Empire's most loyal millet had become in their eyes the most treacherous. This was no doubt exacerbated by Turkey's loss of administrative control over the Balkan territories. Secondly, it encouraged the development of nationalist movements among the Armenians, who inspired by the Balkan example, increasingly adopted policies of direct action to achieve reform. Consequently tension increased between the Ottoman authorities and the Armenians, which reached its peak under Sultan Abdul Hamid II in 1895-6.[34] The Armenians had broken the informal social contract, by crossing the boundaries of the millet, and as such had given up their rights to protection from the Islamic state.

During the latter half of the nineteenth century and the first quarter of the twentieth the relationship between the Armenians and the Ottomans was to change dramatically. With the rise of revolutionary nationalism and the decline of the multi-ethnic Ottoman Empire, one by one, the various Christian nations on the Ottoman frontiers in the west broke away.[35] Furthermore, the Ottoman government became increasingly dependent on European bank loans. Indebtedness increased to the point that in 1881 it was forced to surrender the revenues from its salt and tobacco monopolies, silk tithes, as well as stamp, spirits and fish taxes. A Public Debt Administration (PDA) was created with a board dominated by European bond-holders. Turkey was essentially reduced to a state of economic vassalage. As a consequence of this new economic dependence, the European powers, which had considerable investments at stake in the Ottoman Empire, became committed to its preservation, while the Ottoman authorities became increasingly hostile to and defensive about European interference in their internal affairs.[36]

More effective revolutionary organisations appeared after the Armenians disappointment of 1878. Two of these parties, the Hunchakian Revolutionary Party, Hunchaks, (Geneva 1887)[37] and the Dashnaksuthian Party, Dashnaks or ARF, Armenian Revolutionary Federation (Tbilisi 1890)[38], although founded outside Armenia, were to take the lead in organising revolution. The Hunchaks followed a proven method of organisation, creating an organisation among students and exiles in Europe, then exporting the revolution to Anatolia. The founders of the Hunchak party were all Russian Armenians and had never lived in the Ottoman Empire. The Hunchak programme called for the assassination of anyone, including Armenians who stood against the nationalist cause, as well as terrorist acts that would weaken Ottoman control. The Hunchaks, however, distrusted the Russians and warned against Russian imperialism. This was unique among Armenian revolutionary movements and, naturally, it cost them Russian support. The Hunchak party essentially was Marxist and strongly influenced by Russian revolutionaries, thus, its aim was a democratic and socialist Armenia.[39]

The most successful of the revolutionary parties, the Dashnaks, was organised firstly among the Russian Armenian intelligentsia, in Moscow, St Petersburg and cities in Transcaucasia. The Dashnak programme was dedicated to the import of arms and men into the Ottoman Empire, and to the use of terror and destruction of Ottoman government organisations to further the revolution. Indeed, the Dashnak's manifesto issued in 1891, sounded like a declaration of war against the Ottoman authorities "to attain its aims by means of revolution, the Armenian Revolutionary Federation shall organise revolutionary bands which shall wage an incessant fight against the Government", wrote Simon Vratzian, the Dashnak leader who briefly became the Premier of the independent Republic of Armenia after the First World War.[40] More importantly, the Dashnak revolutionaries were strongly affected by recent events in Bulgaria, where a small group of revolutionaries had killed large numbers of Muslims, drawing retaliation and an even larger number of Bulgarians dead. Russia had finally intervened, causing mass expulsion and the creation of a new Bulgarian state. The Dashnaks viewed this as an effective plan, even if it necessitated the loss of Armenians. The demographic and geographic differences between Bulgaria and Anatolia do not seem to have been considered.[41]

The Armenian nationalists encountered problems unknown to other national revolutionaries. Despite the presence of sizeable minorities, the majority in Bulgaria were Bulgarians, the majority in Serbia Serbs, and the majority in Greece Greeks. This was not true of Armenians in Armenia. It is known that Armenians had been migrating for centuries even before the Turks appeared on the scene in the eleventh century. In 1911, in Bitlis, one province of the southeast, Armenians accounted for thirty per cent of the population, in Van slightly more than twenty five per cent. All other provinces had considerably lower proportions of Armenians. Muslims were a large majority in every Anatolian province; some were Kurdish, most were Turkish, but none were Armenian.[42] Thus, the self government, which began to work for the Christian nations of the Balkans, did not prove appropriate for the Armenians because unlike the other nations, the Armenians were concentrated in Anatolia, the very heart of the Ottoman Empire. In addition, they constituted a minority in the very land they sought as their own autonomous or even independent state. Careful analysis of the official Ottoman census, incorporating into it the necessary adjustments to correct for undercounting and other problems, concluded "one fact is obvious . . . all Anatolian provinces had overwhelming Muslim majorities, not simply pluralities. . . . In the centuries of Turkic rule, Asia Minor had become thoroughly Islamicised".[43] To the Turks, therefore,

Armenian independence was a logical absurdity and a threat to their very existence.[44]

In 1894 Armenian revolutionaries began attacking Ottoman tax collectors and other officials. The Ottomans retaliated with the army, which pursued the revolutionaries. In 1895 an Armenian rebellion in Zeytun spread throughout the region. The Ottoman army defeated the rebels, killing numerous civilians and rebels. In a further revolt in Van in 1896, an estimated 400 Muslims and 1700 Armenians died. An Armenian bombing campaign in the capital and subsequent riots resulted in more Armenian deaths than Muslim. On 26 August 1896, a group of young Armenians occupied Constantinople's Ottoman Bank and threatened to blow it up together with the bank's 160 employees. This desperate terrorist act was intended to prompt the European powers to offer protection to Turkey's Armenian provinces and to extort reforms. After sixteen hours the hostages were released and the Ottoman authorities allowed the Armenian terrorists safe passage to France. This act of Armenian terrorism, however, was used as a pretext for reprisals against Constantinople's innocent Armenian community. During the following week, uniformed policemen, religious fanatics and Kurdish tribesmen massacred the Armenian population of Constantinople. The massacres of 1895-1896 claimed approximately 300,000 Armenian lives. A further 20,000 Armenians were forcibly deported from Constantinople to central and eastern Anatolia and many Armenians now saw emigration as their best option, despite its expense and difficulty. Some 20,000 went to Russia in 1892-3; 12,500 to the United States between 1891 and 1898; and 51,950 (some from Russia) to the United States between 1899 and 1914.[45] Thus the formation of the contemporary dispersion of the Armenian people can be traced to the great massacres of 1895-96 perpetrated under Sultan Abdul Hamid II.

All had gone to the revolutionary plan for the Armenian revolutionaries except for European intervention. The British and Russians had both protested at Muslim actions against the Armenians, neglecting as always the deaths of Muslims. Most of Europe damned "the unspeakable Turk" for what ensued. Lord Bryce, the great friend and admirer of the Armenians, declared that what occurred "were massacres such as no Christian people has ever suffered before."[46] Other scholars, while not condoning the massacres, suggested that the Hunchaks and Dashnaks began deliberately to use terror against the Turks to incite reprisals and massacres which would then encourage broad Armenian support for revolution and finally great power intervention. Historian, William Langer, claimed "Europeans in Ottoman Turkey were agreed that the immediate aim of the Armenian agitators was to incite disorder, bring about inhuman reprisals, and so provoke the intervention of the powers."[47] Walter Laqueur, a noted authority on terrorism concurred "since the Armenian terrorists could not possibly hope to overthrow the government, their strategy had to be based on provocation. They assumed, in all probability, that their attacks on the Turks would provoke savage retaliation, and that as a result the Armenian population would be radicalised; more decisive yet, the Western powers, appalled by the massacres, would intervene on their behalf as they did for the Bulgarians two decades earlier."[48]

The European powers were in general agreement that Sultan Abdul Hamid II should be forced from the throne, and the Ottoman Empire should be divided.

Nonetheless, their protests remained diplomatic—they simply did not trust each other. The British planned to send their navy through the Dardanelles, depose the Sultan and accede to Armenian demands. Russia felt it had great influence with the Ottomans and did not wish to see it replaced with British, French, Austrian or international control. Russia might have been willing to agree to an occupation of Istanbul, provided the Russians gained control of the Straits, something the British would not agree upon. France was afraid that a British-Russian division of the Ottoman Empire would leave nothing for France, and Austria, anticipating strengthened enemies was opposed to any action. Ultimately none of the European powers was willing to go to war with the Ottoman Empire or each other.[49]

The great mistake of the Armenian revolutionaries had been to believe the rhetoric of the European powers. The Armenians believed that the European powers sincerely cared about the predicament of the Armenians and were committed to Armenian independence. Indeed, public opinion in Europe was greatly concerned about the plight of the Armenians. Throughout the nineteenth and early twentieth centuries, Christian missionaries and their supporters flooded the English speaking countries with pro-Armenian and anti-Turkish propaganda. This contributed significantly to hostile feelings against the Ottomans in the West. The Western governments, however, were far more concerned with the balance of power and their own interests. In human terms, this proved disastrous.

Hopes for the peaceful coexistence of Armenians and Turks in the Ottoman Empire were raised in 1908, when the 'Young Turk' revolution swept away the conservative Islamic autocracy of Sultan Abdul Hamid II, and supported the institution of a liberal constitutional government. Initially Armenian political groups supported the Young Turks, 'Ittihadists', (1908-1917), and signed an agreement of cooperation, but the rule of the Young Turks rapidly degenerated as the Committee of Union and Progress (CUP), 'Ittihad ve Teraki', became increasingly dominated by men of ultra-nationalist thinking driven by the ideological force of Pan-Turkism. Pan-Turkism was inspired by ancient Turkic tradition and Islam, but in Pan-Turkism emphasis shifted radically away from classical Islam towards Turkic tradition. Islam as a spiritual and cultural force remained an integral aspect of Turkish life but the political and social aspects of Islamic law were expendable. More importantly, Pan-Turkism was influenced by Western elements; modern, scientific and technological means to material progress, and the concept of national statehood based on a common language.[50]

Turkish Nationalism

Muslim peoples were the last to be touched by nationalism. Nationalism thrives when groups of people feel they are not empowered, however, the Ottoman Muslims were the last in a long line of powerful religious states extending back to the Umayyads. Bulgarian, Serbian or Armenian nationalists did not wish to be ruled by the Ottomans, this was not a problem for Ottoman Turks. The Ottoman Empire was known as Turkey in Europe and America long before the Ottomans referred to themselves as Turkish. The Ottoman Empire, however, was not Turkish in the way France was French or Germany was German, the Ottomans comprised a variety of ethnic groups, Turks, Arabs, Albanians and Kurds etc, all of them Muslim.[51] Recognising the benefits of nationalism in organising a state and claiming the loyalty of its peoples, the CUP made attempts to create a Turkish identity. As the nationalism of the Christian groups of the Ottoman Empire began with literary revivals and the study of historical myths and folk customs, Turkish nationalism arose slowly amongst the intelligentsia, particularly those who had European contacts. They began to write of a Turanian[52] people, which included Ottoman Turks, Central Asian Turks, and Azeri Turks spreading the idea that Turks were one people, separated only by politics and history.[53] This ideology was Pan-Turkism.

The principle aim of Pan-Turkism was the Turkification of the non Turkic nationalities of Ottoman Turkey. The Young Turks who came to power in 1908 believed this could be achieved within the constitutional framework. They advocated the Turkification of language, using Turkish words, not Arabic or Persian, and the culture of the Turks of Anatolia, not the high culture of Istanbul. This translated into a great deal of real reform, real democracy and political participation, completely secular courts, equality for women, including an end to polygamy and a nationalised Islam reduced to basic principles and then merged with Turkish customs and language. In 1912 Turkish Hearth Societies began to appear and greatly multiplied thereafter in schools and government agencies. These taught the purified Turkish and Turkish values of the nationalists, bringing to the masses what had essentially been an ideology of the intelligentsia.[54]

When it became evident, however, that the non-Turkic peoples would not willingly submit to assimilation policies, nationalist initiatives were expanded. A boycott of Greek business in Western Anatolia was accompanied by threats and coercion that forced the emigration of the Greeks, and Arab nationalists were hung. The Turkish Minister of War, Committee of Union and Progress (CUP), or 'Ittihad ve Teraki (the political party of the Young Turks), Dr Nazim openly declared on the eve of the First World War "our state must be purely Turkish, because the existence of other nationalities inside our borders gives only an excuse to foreign powers for intervention on their behalf. We must Turkify non Turkish nationalities by force".[55]

Many Armenian political activists might have accepted a piecemeal approach with the Young Turks, if they introduced some form of autonomy, but sentiment was hardening within the disparate components of the CUP, and they were agreeable on one point, that their base would be ethnocentric. The Armenians had no recourse but to appeal to powerful foreigners, even though this had the effect of inflaming the hatred of the Turkish authorities. The Armenian leaders in the millets kept the foreign diplomatic establishment informed of all crimes against Armenians, and the plight of the Armenian population and its struggle for civil rights and administrative reforms became known to western commentators as the Armenian Question. Armenian ecclesiastics and activists kept a running tally of all the offences committed and details were methodically circulated to consulates of foreign powers in the vain hope that this would stimulate foreign sponsorship of the Armenian cause. By way of example on 30 January 1913, the Austrian Consul at Trebizond informed Vienna "the question of Anatolian reform is on everyone's mind. . . . I consulted with Armenian activists asking what they wanted. All agreed they needed a guarantee for their lives and property, something which does not exist . . . and in this connection they demand first and fore-most, the subjection of Armenian areas to foreign control."[56]

When the war finally broke out, Russian Armenians formed volunteer corps fighting alongside the Russians, while Turkish Armenians were enlisted into the Ottoman army. The first Armenian rebellions in Zeytun and elsewhere often began in opposition to conscription. The Ottomans believed that the Armenian revolts and their unwillingness to serve in the Ottoman army proved that the Armenians were disloyal. Perhaps most Armenians, like most Muslims simply did not wish to be soldiers at all. Nevertheless once the Armenians of military age fled the Ottoman draft boards, they had made a political decision to become rebels, and many of them enrolled in the greater rebellion of Armenian revolutionaries. Between 4,000 and 6,000 went across the border to train in Russian territory. These Anatolian Armenians were trained and armed, and many were sent back across the border, and were joined by others who had stayed behind in Anatolia. Turkish estimates suggest that 30,000 had formed into guerrilla and partisan bands in the Sivas Province alone, probably an exaggeration. Neverthe-less, when the war began, these rebels revolted across the Ottoman east, acting as agents of the Russians in the vain hope that Russia would favour Armenian inde-pendence. Russian history should have indicated to them that this was unlikely, however, Russia was their only hope. Russia as a Christian power was preferred to the Muslim Turks.[57]

The outbreak of the war diverted the attention of the European powers from Turkey's domestic affairs and the Young Turks were now in a position to treat the Armenians and other non Turkic minorities as they wished without fear of reprisals. Furthermore, Turkey's alliance with Germany in the war against Rus-sia, held the promise of union with the Azeri Turks and Central Asia, which was under Russian rule. In February 1915, while the British were assembling their fleet off the Island of Lemnos, a speech was being delivered at a closed session of the CUP. The speaker, Dr Nazim, expressed himself as follows:[58]

If we remain satisfied with the sort of local massacres. . . . If this purge is not general and final, it will inevitably lead to problems. Therefore, it is absolutely necessary to eliminate the Armenian people in its entirety, so that there is no further Armenian on this earth and the very concept of Armenia is extin-guished. We are now at war. We shall never have a more suitable opportunity than this. We need pay no attention to protests from the press or fear the inter-vention of the Powers. And even if we were to pay attention, it will make no difference because it will be an accomplished fact for all time. This time the action will produce total annihilation and it is essential that no single Armenian survives it. Perhaps there are those among you who feel it is bestial to go so far. You may ask, for instance, what harm can children, the elderly or the sick do to us that we feel compelled to work for their elimination. Or you may feel that only those guilty should be punished. . . . *I beg you, gentlemen, don't be weak. Control your feelings of pity. Otherwise these very feelings will bring about our own demise.*[59]

The Armenian Genocide

The first move of the Turkish authorities was to deny the Armenians the possibility of defending themselves. In February 1915, Armenians were purged from state administration and military combat positions. Armenians officers in the Turkish army and tens of thousands of able-bodied men were taken as hostages. Armenian communities were searched by special Turkish militias 'cete', and these searches were accompanied by barbaric atrocities such as rape, the roasting of women and children to death, the Turkish' falaka'—hanging the victim upside down while beating the soles of their feet, and crucifixion. On April 24 1915[60], 235 Armenian intellectuals were arrested in Constantinople. These arrests sparked the order for the deportation of the entire Armenian population of Turkey and resulted in the massacres that left an estimated 1.5 million Armenian dead.[61]

The deportations had a defined pattern. All able bodied Armenian men were ordered to report to their local government office, where they were arrested and executed. The old men, women and children were forced to make the long death march across the desert of northern Syria to Aleppo from where they were sent east into the Mesopotamian desert or south in the direction of Damascus. The trail was littered with corpses and the survivors were placed in camps. These camps were filled with emaciated women and children, ravaged by starvation, dysentery and typhus. The Turkish authorities obstructed efforts to provide relief and Western diplomats and missionaries were prevented from offering assistance. There is evidence of Turks and Kurds also being sickened by these horrors but all help offered to members of the Armenian community by members of the Muslim community was punishable by death. The Governor of Van issued an order declaring "The Armenians must be exterminated. If any Muslim protects a Christian, first his house shall be burnt, then the Christian killed before his eyes, then his family and himself."[62]

The Turkish authorities sought to justify such atrocities by claiming that the Armenians were in rebellion but the German liaison officer in Erzerum, General Posselt, informed his embassy on 26 April 1914, that "the Armenians will stay calm if they are not pressured or molested by the Turks" and that "the behaviour of the Armenians has been perfect."[63] In some locations, such as in Van and Sivas the Armenians managed to put up some armed resistance, but greatly outnumbered and outgunned, they were overcome. Estimates of the Armenians killed in the deportations and massacres of 1915 range from a few hundred to 1,500,000. The number of Armenians in the Ottoman Empire is hard to establish. Ottoman government statistics and some modern Turkish scholars acknowledge only 1,295,000 Armenians including 660,000 in the six provinces which lay in historic Armenia, comprising seventeen per cent of those provinces' people. But the figures compiled in 1912 by the Armenian Patriarchate in Constantinople were 2,100,000 and 1,018,000 respectively, suggesting that the Armenian population of the six provinces was 38.9 per cent as against 25.4 per cent Turks and 16.3 per cent Kurds.[64] Whatever the actual number killed, the result was the physical annihilation of Armenians in the greater part of historic Armenia, the final breaking of a continuous inhabitation of that region by people who called themselves Armenian.[65] The precise death toll in the Armenian Genocide is less important than the fact that the Ittihadists had achieved their reprehensible goal of the fact that the Ittihadists had achieved their reprehensible goal of eliminating the Armenians as a serious factor in Anatolian politics and society. The Ottoman empire was ethnically cleansed of the Armenians; the demographic and cultural links between the Armenian people and their Anatolian homeland were permanently severed.[66]

The plight of the Armenians of Turkey was known in Europe and North America. Western public opinion was powerfully moved but the action of government was determined by Realpolitik. On 23 May 1915, the allied governments declared that "for about the last month Kurds and the Turkish population of Armenia have been engaged in massacring Armenians with the help and often connivance of the authorities" and promised to hold implicated Turkish government officials personally responsible. Turkey's opponents in war, Britain, France and after 1917, the United States, were in no position to fulfil these aims before the end of the war but Turkey's allies, Germany, were in a position to influence the government of the Young Turks. Winning the war, however, had far greater priority with the Central powers than stopping the genocide. After the war, the victorious allies stopped short of the liberation of the oppressed non Turkic peoples of Anatolia, preferring to strengthen Turkey against Europe's new menace, the Bolsheviks in Russia.[67]

Successive Turkish governments, as well as Turkish academics, have denied that the Young Turk government intended these deaths, despite definitive proof that there was nothing less than a centrally organised government attempt to systematically eliminate the Armenians, shifting the blame to uncontrolled attacks by Kurdish villagers. Reports of eye witnesses, however, not only Armenian, but German, American and Danish missionaries, foreign residents, European and American consular officials (compiled in the volume presented to the British Parliament by Viscount Bryce in 1916 and a subsequent addition to this Blue Book published by the British foreign office in 1917); the reports of German diplomats whose country was an ally of Turkey during the war; published accounts of eye witnesses like the Bedouin Faiz El-Ghusein; and the detailed accounts of Armenians who survived the deportations, leave little doubt that the massacres were part of a centrally organised and coherent plan devised at the highest level of officialdom.[68]

The genocide of the Armenian community in Turkey provided the twentieth century with its first example of ethnic cleansing on a massive scale. Indeed, there is now consensus among scholars that the Armenian genocide, which was the first large-scale genocide in the twentieth century, is the prototype of much genocide that has occurred since 1945. There is a divided or plural society in which one ethnic group strives to dominate other distinct groups. This can lead to the desire for autonomy, even independence, and the challenge, real or imagined, to the control of government by the ruling party, or dominant ethnic group. Such demands are most likely to be made at a time of political crisis, whether due to internal and/or external causes, and in the process there is often an escalating emphasis on nationalism. If civil or international war breaks out, the likelihood of genocide is greatly increased as genocide can now proceed under the cover of war, and the victims can be blamed for their own elimination.[69]

There are, however, many different means in which ethnic groups can be eliminated. By way of example, in Rwanda, 800,000 people were killed in the space of two months by machetes and clubs; in Bosnia, it was a combination of artillery and concentration camps. The distinctive feature of the Armenian genocide, which sets it apart from the post 1945 examples, is deportation. When the Turkish authorities gave the orders for these deportations, they were essentially giving the death warrant to the Armenians. Henry Morgenthau, the American Ambassador to the Ottoman empire, reported that from April to October 1915 the 'caravans of death' could be seen moving on and on and those deported scarcely knew where to, except that every road led to death:

> In a few days, what had been a procession of normal human beings became a stumbling horde of dust-covered skeletons, ravenously looking for scraps of food, eating any offal that came their way, crazed by the hideous sights that filled every hour of their existence, sick with all the diseases that accompany such hardships and privations, but still prodded on and on by the whips, clubs and bayonets of their executioners. And thus, as the exiles moved, they left behind them another caravan—that of the dead and unburied bodies, of old men and women dying in the last stages of typhus, dysentery and cholera, of little children lying on their backs and setting up their last piteous wails for food and water. There were women who held up their babies to strangers, begging them to take them and save them from their tormentors. [70]

It is impossible to over-emphasize the significance of the 1915 genocide both in Armenia and in the Diaspora. The new dispersion was not only large in number and more globalised, it was also the result of unique circumstances: genocide. The massacres and deportations virtually eliminated the Armenians from nine tenths of the historic land of Armenia. The Armenians who survived the atrocities joined earlier communities in Russian Armenia, the Middle East, particularly Lebanon, Syria, Palestine and Iran. Deportation and massacre stripped this region of its Armenian inhabitants. Essentially, to be a Western or Turkish Armenian was, with few exceptions either to be dead or in exile. Throughout Europe, North America and the Middle East it produced vast Armenian communities where historical memory of the Genocide serves as a significant marker of ethnic identity amongst Armenian families, who have repeatedly sought an official acknowledgement by Turkey of the Genocide.[71] Contemporary Armenians have to live not only with the fact that their descendents were mercilessly slain, but they also have to swallow the bitter pill of decades of denial that these events ever happened.

The Post Genocide Dispersion

On the whole the post-genocide dispersion consisted of impoverished, traumatised people whose overall purpose during the first decades of the twentieth century was survival. The massive influx of the twentieth century, however, was unprecedented both in scope and character. Those able to survive the Ottoman deportations poured across the Middle East in thousands, in fact well over 250,000 by 1925. The Middle Eastern communities of Egypt, Iran, Syria and

Lebanon provided an appropriate setting for re-orientation. Firstly, these countries were most familiar with the millet system and so the Armenians were able to transplant many of their old world structures directly into their new environment, which also made it easier to retain their cultural traditions and the Armenian language.

As Marienstras emphasises time has to pass before we can know that an ethnic community has become a Diaspora.[72] Diasporas do not quickly assimilate into the receiving country. Long term ethnic survival depends in the first place on the active advancement by the leaders of the community and others of a heightened sense of collective distinctiveness. Such a community is made to feel that their historic community is unique and myths of ethnic election have helped to ensure their survival over long periods of time. For the Armenians a sense of religious and moral superiority is gained through pride in the fact that they were the first nation to adopt Christianity. Through a combination of preference and social exclusion, they maintain their identities and solidarity over extended periods. Institutionally, this involved the strengthening of party structures and the proliferation of Armenian social centres to provide an Armenian environment for the Armenian youth. Along with internal cohesion migrant groups tend to maintain links with their country of origin. Thus the Armenian Diaspora did not only retain their group identity and their institutions over extended periods, they also maintained continuing links both material and sentimental with their country of origin.[73]

Lebanon in particular became the new nucleus of Armenian life. Lebanon was originally populated by Armenian descendants from the Cilician period and an Armenian Revolutionary Federation local party committee had been established in Beirut in 1904. These Armenian communities came to occupy a distinctive position within the Diaspora in at least three ways. Firstly, the Armenians living in the Middle East remained in close proximity to the ancestral home in the Caucasus and Anatolia and were active in voicing the political concerns of the Armenians. Secondly, they harboured an intense national spirit and maintained a vibrant Armenian culture in exile, whilst other communities around the world succumbed to the inevitable forces of assimilation. Indeed there was an inverse relationship between the rate of assimilation and the incompatibility of the religious and cultural environment, thus the rate of assimilation was much lower in Muslim countries than in Christian countries.[74] The Middle Eastern communities intentionally became known as the non-Soviet cultural centre for all Armenians, with publishers, music studios, schools and other cultural, social and political institutions. Thirdly, these communities were, by far, the most unstable ones in the Diaspora and the unrest during the latter part of the twentieth century had a dramatic effect on the Armenians.[75]

Various twentieth century political conflicts and wars caused many Armenians to leave the Middle East. Since the 1950s, a number of forces—Arab nationalism, Islamic fundamentalism and socialism, to name a few, have displaced countless tens of thousands of Armenians from these affluent yet precarious communities. The period following World War II saw increasing instability in the Middle East as the nations of that region sought to reassert their indigenous identity. By way of example, approximately 50,000 Armenians lived in Egypt in 1952 when Gamal Nasser's revolution toppled the monarchy, however, following the 1958-61 collapse of Nasser's attempted United Arab Republic with Syria, government economic control became draconian; banks and businesses were confiscated and the Armenian community was hit by severe tax changes. Armenian schools came under state control and the Arabic language became mandatory. As a result Armenians fled to Canada, the United States, or other more stable Middle Eastern countries. In Syria the number dropped from 150,000 to less than half that figure. With the rise of Arab nationalism in the fifties and sixties, however, Syria closely followed Nasser's lead, and the socialist pan-Arab Ba'arth party seized control in 1963. Consequently, Armenian participation in government was curbed, the Armenian Church was closely scrutinized, and in 1967 Armenian private schools were forced under government control. Thus, an Armenian exodus began around 1960, with an estimated 60,000 Syrian Armenians moving to Lebanon alone.[76]

Lebanon, more than any other country in the Middle East, with its improbable nation of Muslim and Christian minorities, was a growing and prosperous Armenian centre. During the First World War approximately 50,000 Armenian refugees entered Lebanon, and this number swelled as Armenians from Palestine, Egypt, Syria, and elsewhere sought safe haven. Armenians became fully integrated into Lebanon's bustling high finance, politics and culture, however, they managed to successfully maintain their separate Armenian institutions. Nevertheless, the steady tension between Syria, Israel and refugee Palestinians, which erupted into the Lebanese civil war in 1975, was a further catalyst for migration. Although the Armenian community survived intact, its numbers sharply declined. This was a major cultural, political and economic set back for the Armenian Diaspora, which had looked upon that community as the bastion of Armenianness, symbolising the best hopes of the Armenian Diapora with its flourishing intelligentsia. The civil war forced the emigration of about half of Lebanon's Armenian population and wound down the community's infrastructure to its bare minimum. It also compelled the reconsideration of the premises on which the Diaspora had developed, being the final catalyst in the shift of the epicentre of the Diaspora from the Middle East to the West. This number declined further with the 1982 Israeli invasion into Lebanon and the intensification of the internal conflict there. Thus, over the past fifty years, virtually every Middle Eastern Armenian community has been dislocated by outside events. Further troubles in Iran, Israel, Jordan and Iraq have all stimulated Armenian migration from the Middle East, gravitating by the thousands towards Europe and, more so North America.[77]

Today, there are many Armenians in England, France, Canada and South American countries, and in the United States where there are more Armenians than anywhere else, outside the former Soviet republic. In England, Armenians are concentrated in Manchester and Greater London, where there are approximately 15,000. In France, Armenians are concentrated in Paris and Lyon. Paris, where a number of periodicals are published and Armenian Studies taught at university level, is the centre for intellectuals. France was the destination for many Armenian intellectuals, and during the inter-war years France emerged as a Mecca for the Armenian Diaspora intelligentsia. Politically, too, France functioned as a major Diaspora centre. Between 1920 and 1965 Paris was host to the

Patvirakutiun (Delegation), the Armenian government's delegation to the Paris Peace Conference which continued its operations after the Sovietization of Armenia as a 'government-in-exile'. The Land and Culture Organisation (LCO) was also created in Paris in the 1970's to preserve Armenian monuments in the historic Armenian areas of the Middle East. In carrying out such work, this transnational organisation has also helped to preserve an Armenian identity and pride in places where it otherwise might have disappeared.[78]

In the United States it is estimated that there are over one and a half million Armenians. The history of significant Armenian immigration to the United States dates back to the nineteenth century. By 1894 there were an estimated 3-5,000 Armenians in America. This trickle was later boosted by two major waves of arrivals: 1894-1924; and 1965 onwards. The estimated 100,000 migrants of the first phase consisted mainly of refugees fleeing the Hamidian massacres and deteriorating economic conditions of the Ottoman Empire. Following World War One, another wave arrived, this time consisting of survivors of the Genocide. The migrants throughout this period arrived alongside other European and Middle Eastern immigrants leaving their homes for economic reasons, and their immigration to the United States must be understood in the context of the global movement of peoples.[79] The political parties also established their presence in the growing American-Armenian community. Branches of the Hunchak party were first opened in Boston and Worcester in 1890, though with the split in the party in 1896 it came to be dominated by the Reform Hunchak Party. In 1899 the ARF established its presence in Boston. The ARF in America received a boost with the second split within the Hunchak party in 1906-7, and then with the collapse of the Republic of Armenia in 1920 when many of the Dashnak leaders found their way to the United States. Many of these arrivals took up leadership within the American branch of the party. The first American branch of the Armenian General Benevolent Union (AGBU) was set up in Boston in 1910. Despite the emergence of the political parties, however, the community life of the majority of American Armenians continued to centre on the Church. This pattern was reinforced by the central role played by churches in defining group identity in the United States, and meant that the Armenian churches quickly flourished and gained a greater significance in American Armenian life than elsewhere in the Diaspora. Up until the 1960's, American ethnic groups were defined primarily by their denomination. This further strengthened the position of the Armenian Apostolic Church, while also reinforcing its political role and its central place in American Armenian partisan rivalry.[80]

Finally, the psychological attachment, and to a greater extent the cultural traditions of Western Armenia continue in the contemporary Armenian communities concentrated in various cities throughout the world. Today the modern descendants of Western Armenians live in cosmopolitan cities and many, but by no means all, manage to maintain a sense of continuity with their historical traditions, and devotion to their motherland which is now lost to them. Indeed, to a great extent, these modern Armenians are both biologically and culturally Armenian. Historically, their communities have maintained a strong tradition of marrying within themselves, therefore reinforcing a strong sense of Armenian identity. As a result of these historical events, many Armenians see themselves as a uniquely martyred Christian nation ignored by the West and crucified by the Ottoman Turks. The political and symbolic expressions of genocide remembrance have flourished through ethnic education, annual commemorations, preaching of the church and the erection of monuments to name but a few. In view of these events, it is not surprising that in answer to the question: 'What is an Armenian'? Armenians are unlikely to confine their answer to the contemporary composition and nature of their particular community. Rather, this community would form but one instance of a general phenomenon spanning not only the contemporary international structure of the dispersion and settlement of the Armenian population as a whole, but an interpretation of the historical factors which led to the formation of the dispersed Armenian communities.

CHAPTER FOUR

THE CONTEMPORARY ARMENIAN DIASPORA

The period 1915-20 marked a significant stage in the demographic territorial configuration of the Armenians. The genocide effectively emptied those very lands on which the Armenian revolutionaries had placed their hopes for self-determination. At the same time, the concentration of Armenians within the Russian Armenian provinces increased, due to the migration of Genocide survivors and the general chaos of the post war Middle East. A new epicentre of Armenian political life was established in Russian Armenia, marking the first time in centuries when Armenian affairs were conducted from within the homeland, at least as much as they were from without. For the first time also, the Armenians were responsible for the establishment of their own state infrastructures. The short lived Republic of Armenia was significant in that the Armenians were no longer just a nationality but also a nation state.

Nevertheless, the much longed for self determination was short lived and quickly followed by a new political separation of the homeland and Diaspora. The creation of Soviet Armenia challenged the Diaspora's self appointed role as custodian of the Armenian heritage. At the same time, Sovietization created a new role for the Diaspora, since the Soviet homeland was limited in its ability to make territorial and legal demands against Turkey. Thus, within the Diaspora, the question of territories produced a unifying point. At the same time the Armenians of the Diaspora slowly adjusted to the increasingly obvious reality that returning to their ancestral lands was not an option in the near future. The exiled Diaspora organisations, in particular the political parties, functioned as governments in exile, acting as service providers for the Diaspora and unofficial representatives of the interests of the Armenians in the homeland.[1]

The First Armenian Republic 1918-20

Initially, the Transcaucasian socialist parties (with the exception of the local Bolsheviks) separated the region from the rest of Russia, by first declaring autonomy, and later independence for the whole of Transcaucasia, and finally establishing three separate individual republics.[2] Soviet Armenia was the smallest Soviet Republic in area and also the most ethnically homogenous. Furthermore, some twenty five per cent of the Armenian population in the Soviet Union lived outside its republic. Thus, effectively, there was a second Armenian Diaspora within the borders of the Soviet Union itself that is larger than any single one abroad. Karabagh (an enclave within Soviet Azerbaijan that had a population of approximately seventy five per cent Armenians) became the most famous example of this second Diaspora. The totally unprecedented demonstrations in Soviet Armenia concerning Karabagh in 1988, followed by escalating violence that led to what has been termed a "civil war" in January 1990, made it an issue for Armenian activists throughout the world, surpassing in immediacy that of Turkey. By way of example, to protest at Azeri clashes with Armenians over the Nagorno Karabagh, the Armenian community in New York City was unable to stage a unified rally for the arrival of Soviet leader Mikhail Gorbachev in December 1988. The Diocese and the Prelacy, amid mutual recriminations, sponsored two completely separate rallies. As sadly reported by a leading Armenian newspaper "as in past years, the split in the Armenian Church emerged as the principal reason the two sides could not come together at this critical juncture in Armenian history".[3] Although it is too early to project the final outcome, it is clear that Karabagh issues have permanently altered and enlarged the agenda for Armenian activism, and it has major ramifications for the very future of the Republic of Armenia, but this is beyond the scope of this present analysis.[4]

Following the collapse of the Tsarist regime in February 1917, the stated aim of the Russian Provisional Government was to continue the war and fulfil its aim of annexing the Turkish Armenian territories, by placing such territories under the authority of a general commissar. Initially, none of the Armenian political parties had considered declaring independence, for instance, the Armenian Revolutionary Federation favoured an ethnic based division of the Transcaucasus with guarantees of basic civil and ethnic rights. This policy was predicated on the continuing positive attitude of the Central Government to Armenian interests; however, with the overthrow of the Provisional Government by Lenin's Bolshevik faction in October 1917, such hopes were dashed. With the Bolsheviks now in power, anti-imperialism meant an anti-British alliance including Muslims which led to a Soviet-Turkish rapprochement. The Soviet government did not oppose the creation of an independent Armenian homeland in Eastern Turkey and the Caucasus, however, such realizations were futile when the Armenians were in no position to defend these territories. Moreover, Turkish troops had already begun their advance across the Russo-Turkish border, and in the humiliating Treaty of Brest-Litovsk in March 1918, the Russians ceded all their annexed territories including the occupied Turkish Armenian districts.[5]

In April 1918 the three Transcaucasian countries: Georgia, Azerbaijan and Armenia declared the establishment of an independent Transcaucasian Federative Soviet Socialist Republic. During this time Turkish troops continued to advance into Armenia and they quickly approached the province of Yerevan where the Armenians were left to defend themselves. Armenia was the weakest of the three new republics and lacked a powerful overlord as possessed by Georgia in Germany, and by Azerbaijan in Turkey. Furthermore, Yerevan, was an impoverished backward minor province based on the old Tsarist government and had no resources to manage an independent republic. Nevertheless, at this point the Dashnak leaders in Tiflis had no choice but to declare Armenian independence on 28 May 1918. Unlike the Georgians, however, the Armenian Revolutionary Party, the Dashnaks, chose not to work with other revolutionary parties within the Russian empire and the new Armenian republic began its existence in July 1918 under the leadership of the nationalist and socialist Dashnak party.[6]

The republic had severe problems: it had to deal with the needs of thousands of refugees from Anatolia, food shortages and epidemics. As well as these basic problems facing the young republic, the situation was exacerbated because the new republic was landlocked. Prior to 1914, Armenia had imported its food from Russia, but following the revolution, the supply was cut off and the new Armenian republic had neither the resources nor lines of communication to open up alternatives. Almost twenty per cent of the population died of famine or disease during the first year of the republic's existence. As if domestic problems were not bad enough, the new republic was born into a state of war with Turkey. This rapidly came to an end with the humiliating treaty of 4 June 1918, but Armenia soon became involved in ethnic conflict and territorial disputes with Georgia and Azerbaijan. Following British intervention in the autumn of 1918, these were mostly suspended, but as soon as the British departed in 1920, the conflicts re-emerged and Armenia was again at war with Turkey. By the end of 1920, the Dashnak government surrendered without opposition to the Bolsheviks, choosing Soviet takeover to annihilation by Kemalist Turkey. The Dashnaks ceased to operate in Soviet Armenia, but continued to operate within the Diaspora communities, as did the Hunchaks and Ramgavars.[7]

Soviet Republic of Armenia

The Sovietization of Armenia formalized the duality in the life of the Armenian people between those living under semi-indigenous authority and those in dispersion. Despite the loss of independence, however, the establishment of Soviet power over a legally designated territory called Armenia was significant in that Armenians were guaranteed a physical space of their own to which those who had been dispersed could return. The Armenians had an autonomous Republic, with fixed borders and its own government, protected from any threat from Turkey. Torossian[8] argues that many Armenians perceived Soviet Armenia as 'the seed for a future strong, united and independent Armenia', which provided inspiration for the Armenian nationalist movement in the Diaspora. There was also a new safe haven where a new 'ingathering' of Armenians, including many leading intellectuals and literati immigrated from all over the world. The population of Soviet Armenia estimated at 720,000 in 1920 had grown to 1.2 million by the eve of World War II.[9]

Furthermore, Sovietization introduced important elements of stability into Armenian life. The main element of stability was the promise of physical security for the Armenians living in the Republic and those throughout other parts of the Soviet Union. Armenia was devastated and with starvation claiming thousands of lives, the Soviet priority was to provide food and shelter. Within six years agricultural output had increased from thirty to ninety per cent of gross domestic product. Irrigation projects were well under development as well as transport networks. During the first ten years of Soviet rule, economic and industrial reconstruction took priority but the radical change came after 1929 when Armenia was forced through collectivization and industrialization. The human costs were immense, but the achievements considerable. In 1929, 3.7% of peasant households were in collectives, by 1936 the figure was eighty per cent. Armenian industry significantly increased and unemployment was officially eradicated by 1931.[10]

Throughout the 1930's, the Soviet state promoted education in the non-Russian languages to bring the less developed peoples up to the level of the more developed, and the new Stalinist formula of 'national in form, socialist in content' could be circulated. This formula proposed that ethnic-national sentiments, loyalties and energies were to be harnessed for the interests of the socialist state and the greater ideology of communism. Education was conducted in 70 different languages and the Soviet authorities worked hard to recruit non-Russian teachers. In Armenia, seventy per cent of the teachers were Armenian. Furthermore, educated Armenians who sought to rise in the party and state learned Russian, for that language was necessary for upward mobility, and ambitious parents sent their children to Russian language schools. It is estimated that between 1926 and 1939 some 10 million non-Russians, including Armenians, adopted the Russian nationality. For Stalin and the Soviet leaders, nationality was an objective reality and internal passports were introduced in 1932, each adult Soviet citizen had a fixed nationality. Ethnicity was usually inherited from one's parents and, therefore, had a biological rather than a linguistic or cultural origin. In the case of mixed marriages, however, a person could choose the nationality of either parent. There was a Soviet people but no Soviet nation. By the end of the 1930's, an empire of republics had been created in the Soviet Union, and the state promoted a new Soviet patriotism as the binding cement to hold the union together. Furthermore, Soviet   nationality policy was closely tied to foreign policy. The Soviet Union was to be a model for a future world political order in which the rights of all nationalities would be respected. The party believed that fair treatment of non-Russians would attract Armenians, and other peoples with dispersed populations beyond the   Soviet Union, to support their compatriots within the union.[11]

In the period after the Second World War, social and economic progress continued, but not at the same accelerated pace. Education, health care and standards of living, however, improved markedly. For many Armenians, this economic development took on a "patriotic and quasi-mystical value" as the exemplification of the Armenian people's resurrection, and thereby, as a justification for the Soviet system. They had jobs, food, and were enthusiastic about getting ahead through hard work. Though the official ideology of the Soviet state was atheistic, religion was tolerated, and approximately 8,000 churches, 1,200 mosques and 60 synagogues operated in the Soviet Union. For Armenians, religious feeling remained ultimately connected to their culture. Armenians revered the Catholicos, the supreme head of the Armenian Apostolic Church, more as a leader of the nation, than a religious figure.[12] More importantly, the Armenian language and culture survived in Soviet Armenia, it even flourished. When these factors are considered against the historical memories of massacre and desolation, the average Armenian's pride in Soviet Armenia becomes understandable. The sheer existence of a geographical unit in the name of the Soviet Socialist Republic of Armenia, no matter what its political system or degree of independence and sovereignty, had a unique significance for the Armenians, primarily because it was a novel phenomenon in the life of a people which had been deprived of its own state for several centuries. Moreover, with the establishment of an autonomous Armenian state, Armenian nationalism found its long delayed and natural focus. At the same time, amongst the various Diaspora communities, the popular longing for ethnic Armenian survival and the conservation of cultural characteristics, found its strongest justification. In identifying the heart of their nation some Armenians looked to the Armenian SSR, so poignantly described in Michael J Arlen's 'Passage to Ararat'.[13] One social worker recalls that ANCHA (American National Committee to Aid Homeless Armenians), in 1947 asked a wealthy philanthropic society for funds to bring to the United States thousands of Armenian refugees displaced by World War II; after some delay ANCHA was reportedly told yes, but only if the refugees were transported to the Soviet Armenian homeland rather than to the United State's melting pot.[14] Undoubtedly many Armenians in the Diaspora viewed the Armenian SSR as the heartland, therefore, it was only natural for Diaspora organisations, political and otherwise, to quickly develop dissimilar attitudes to their host countries, and take uncompromising stands for Armenia and its political system. Furthermore, Diaspora communities in Europe and North America, where there were many Communist and left wing literary, educational and cultural societies, felt a special affinity not only to Soviet Armenia but also to Soviet ideology and its system of government.[15]

The Armenians in the Diaspora had to think about the ultimate role and significance of Armenia in their own lives, and assess the nature of possible or desirable relationships. Throughout the life of the Soviet Union, Armenia's relations with the Diaspora were governed by politics and ideology and evolved through a number of phases. One factor, however, that did remain constant was the sensitive issue of repatriation of Diaspora Armenians to their homeland. From 1828 to 1917, an estimated 750,000 Armenians, mainly from Turkish Armenia and Persia moved to Transcaucasia. The repatriation of Diaspora Armenians continued after 1920; in the first decade of Soviet rule, a total of 28,000 refugees settled in Armenia, most of these poor peasants and artisans, who had survived the 1915 massacres and assembled in refugee camps in Greece and Iraq. From 1929 to 1937, 16,000 more Diaspora Armenians moved to Soviet Armenia and unlike those before them, most of these emigrants were intellectuals, professionals and prominent artists, responding to the appeals made by the authorities to return to Armenia and participate in the rebuilding of the country. Communism justified the immigration of Armenians purely on the basis of class grounds, defending repatriation as the right step in realizing the socialist liberation of the Armenian masses. Throughout the thirties, many Armenians from the Diaspora generously responded to appeals made to help the Red Army war effort, but the emigration movement halted abruptly after 1937 and was not resumed until after World War II. Some 300,000 Armenians served in the Red Army in the Second World War, many with considerable distinctions. The period from the late 1930's to the late 1950's, however, was the bleakest era in Armenia's relations with the Diaspora.[16]

In the 1930's under Stalin's politically and culturally repressive policies, there had been persecution and purges, the Catholicos murdered in 1938. During this period, the Armenian Soviet regime and the political parties of the Diaspora played leading roles in the bifurcation of the community. In keeping with its revolutionary creed, the Armenian Communist government sought to maximize its support among Diaspora Armenians through propaganda and the neutralization of the Armenian Revolutionary Federation, the ARF or Dashnaks. As the dominant party in the government of the short lived independent republic, the ARF sought to consolidate its hold on the Diaspora communities after its displacement by the Soviets in 1920. A meeting between representatives of the ARF, the Soviet Armenian government and the Soviet Ambassador took place in July 1921. An agreement was reached but this was never ratified by either party. Over the next seventy years the relationship between the Soviet government and the ARF was consistently hostile. Much of the conflict was over the claim of both sides to control over Armenian affairs in both the homeland and the Diaspora. The ARF viewed themselves as a government in exile, and thus the enemy of Soviet Armenia, hence Soviet involvement in Diaspora affairs was not welcomed.[17]

The sustained efforts of the ARF, however, were diametrically opposed by the pro-Soviet Hunchak Party, and the Ramgavars or Armenian Democratic Liberal Party, (ADL)[18], who viewed the ARF as poor losers and obstructionist. Throughout the Soviet period the name of the ARF was consistently vilified, Dashnaks were arrested, the party blamed for all of Armenia's misfortunes, and its mention removed from successful episodes in Armenian history. Indeed, during the Stalinist period, communists with nationalistic tendencies were often labelled 'Dashnaks'. Consequently, in response, the Dashnak press was equally virulent with its denunciations of the communist regime. This inter-party confrontation culminated in the assassination of Archbishop Levon Tourian, in the full presence of his congregation, in New York City in December 1933, for which several ARF members were inculpated. The motive was the Archbishop's support of Soviet Armenia, a concept the anti-Soviet Dashnaks did not accept. This tragic episode marked a deep cleavage in the American Armenian community, and indeed other Diaspora communities.[19] The fortunes and policies of the Armenian political parties continued to be connected with the Diaspora communities. The period between the two world wars saw the emergence of new cleavages essentially based on the issue of how to relate to the homeland. Different institutions staked their claim to legitimacy on whether they were pro or anti-Soviet.

Throughout the Soviet period, the Armenian Church became a political arena. The key centres of conflict were Lebanon and the United States where the issue was one of Soviet control of the Diaspora church versus control of the church by Diaspora forces, namely the ARF. The Dashnaks succeeded in 1957 to gain control of the Cilician See, in Antelias, Lebanon, appointing Zareh I as their Catholicos, apparently with the backing of the United States Central Intelligence Agency, and began to extend its jurisdiction over various churches in Iran, Greece, and the United States. These Churches traditionally had owed allegiance to the Mother See in Echmiadzin, Yerevan, which was controlled by the Soviet Union. The Dashnaks argued that the Echmiadzin See had become a puppet of the Soviets and the Diaspora church needed to be rescued. In turn the Hunchaks and other pro-Soviet elements of the Diaspora accused the ARF and the Cilician Catholicosate of becoming the tool of the CIA. Indeed the repercussions of this split were strongly felt throughout the Diaspora. By way of example, in Lebanon these cleavages expressed themselves in fratricidal warfare within the Armenian community during the Civil War of 1958. In 1963, following the death of Zareh I, a half-hearted rapprochement was begun, focusing mainly around the mutual recognition of both Holy See's jurisdiction and the need to be united with regard to the genocide and Turkey as their common enemy, however, the split in the church exists to this day. Indeed as Sarkissian has argued the Armenian Church has both a spiritual and national mission, therefore since 'the church is deeply involved in the life of the nation as such, it is not always so easy to stay aloof and remain unaffected'.[20]

Despite numerous half-hearted attempts to achieve an end to this embarrassing disunity, the situation remains because it is really a question of who will possess ultimate power in the Diaspora. As the Supreme Catholicos of All Armenians in Etchmiadzin declared "The real reason for the division is Antelias and the Dashnak political party which in 1957 decided to do it this way to separate the Diaspora churches from Etchmiadzin because of political and other reasons".[21] Moreover, some of the churches within the jurisdiction of the Cilician See have maintained strong support for Armenian activism. By way of example, the Dashnak press reported that a political memorial was held in St Vartanantz Church in New Jersey on 29 January 1984 for the martyrs of the Armenian cause. One of the speakers concluded: "we should not shy away from negative public opinion and harassment from government authorities... We must carry on the struggle". Churches under the authority of the Mother See, however, have not been as outspoken in their support of Armenian activism. Nevertheless, in response to a query concerning his views on the role of Armenian boys engaged in violence, Vazken I declared that "with my whole heart and soul, I defend the justice of their cause", the Catholicos then added "however it is not the right way".[22] In the final analysis, therefore, the split in the church was essentially over Diaspora-homeland relations.

Soviet repression ceased during the Second World War to encourage the effort against Germany and these positive trends continued, one example being the creation of the Armenian Academy of Sciences in 1943. At the same time, pro-Soviet feeling in the Diaspora reached its peak, especially since the denunciation of communism was softened in the West. The Soviet Armenian government was able to rally not just its own people but also the Diaspora. During World War II the Armenians fought on all fronts against the Axis powers. In view of the tacit alignment of Turkey with Nazi Germany in the early war years, the Armenians feared the consequences of an Axis victory. Armenians also fought in the American and French armies as well as in the French resistance against the German occupation. After the war Armenians came 'home' in considerable numbers from Persia and Lebanon, some 100,000 from the Middle East alone.[23] Furthermore, perhaps the clearest indication of well-being was the dramatically increasing population of Soviet Armenia. Some of this is accounted for by increasing longevity (officially measured at 73 years in 1985) and better health care, but most of the increase has to be attributed to voluntary return migration. If the Soviet population censuses are to be believed, the population of Soviet Armenia increased by two and a half times from 1,320,000 inhabitants in 1940 to 3,317,000 people in 1985.[24]

The Cold War from 1947 caused both Soviet and Western powers to be uncooperative towards Armenian ambitions which complicated relations between Armenians inside and outside the republic. The ensuing ideological and military confrontation seriously affected the Armenian Diaspora. By way of example, it hindered the Armenian Republic and Soviet authorities' attempt to repatriate the Diaspora after the Second World War. The death of Stalin in March 1953 and Khrushchev's de-Stalinization campaign contributed to the gradual relaxation of Soviet-American relations. Significantly, de-Stalinization had found vocal support in Anastas Mikoyan, the Politburo's sole Armenian member. One consequence of the Soviet liberalization drive was the establishment of close cultural relations between the Armenian homeland and the Diaspora. Thus further repatriation became possible and many Soviet-Armenian writers, musicians, composers, scientists, and dance ensembles toured the Diaspora communities.[25] The first sightseeing tour of Armenia was organised by the Jeunesse Armenienne de France (Young Armenians of France) formed in 1945. The journal Sovetakan Hayastan, aimed at informing the Diaspora about the homeland was first published in the same year. Throughout the next two decades more such projects were initiated which had a powerful effect on the ethnic life and regeneration of the cultural ethos of Diaspora Armenians. Equally important was the growing spiritual impact of the Holy See of Echmiadzin, which had been accorded considerable latitude by the Soviet authorities to minister to the religious needs of the Diaspora. For the first time in modern history, the Supreme Catholicos of the Armenian Apostolic Church was able to pay visits to his people in dispersion.[26]

A further consequence of de-Stalinization was the progressive remission of the Cold War amid efforts by the super powers to forge a modus vivendi. The mid sixties saw a considerable decline in internecine political conflict together with enthusiastic attempts for communal harmony. Indeed there was some degree of rapprochement in the post-Stalinist period between the ARF and the Soviet government, however, the relationship between the parties remained tense and the ARF was generally excluded from the cultural and educational activities outlined above. Coexisting with the decline of ideological fervour, however, was a general increase in the economic security of Armenian Diaspora communities throughout the world. Having suffered the ravages of massacre and deportation during World War I, most Armenians were now achieving a significant degree of economic prosperity in virtually every host country. Economic well being, however, did not coincide with a sense of contentment and happiness.[27] According to Dekmejian, several factors were responsible:-

1. The gradual realization of the permanence of diasporic existence, in view of the prevailing socio-political conditions of the homeland.
2. The persistent concern with the threat of assimilation and loss of identity.
3. The pervasive feeling of political impotence in the world community of nation states, because of lack of national independence.
4. The deep sense of loss and moral outrage against Turkey for the massacres, which had gone unacknowledged by the world community and denied by the Turkish government.[28]

These factors produced an idiosyncratic personality type in Diaspora communities: the confident, ambitious, good natured member of Western society aspiring to conformity and success combined with the persistent rebel and alien scarred by the tragic past, who viewed the world with deep cynicism, despair and anguish. According to Robin Cohen, these characteristics were in part a reflection of psychosocial trauma, known in more general terms as 'survivor syndrome'. Many Diaspora Armenians felt guilty and undeserving of their material success. They were laden with unresolved anger and found it more and more difficult to enjoy their freedom. It was as if their contentment would provoke further misfortune, or was an insult to the dead. Reports of acute psychological states—reactive depression, hyperaesthesia and nightmares were widely reported. If we ignore these extreme reactions, however, it is noticeable that first and much of the second generation Diaspora Armenians adopted a solitary, inward-looking world of apparent conformity to the assimilationist ethnic, combined with a distinct sense of difference, which was rarely displayed in public.[29]

Some of these confused feelings of acceptance emerge in an apparently autobiographical account provided by the Californian born writer of Armenian descent, William Saroyan. Saroyan recalls his school days in Fresno and a conversation with his teacher who had reprimanded him for speaking Armenian to others in the classroom and making them laugh.[30]

"No, we just like to talk Armenian once in a while, that's all"
"But why? This is America, now"
"The Americans don't like us, so we don't like them"
"So that's it, which Americans don't like you?"
"All of them"
"Me?"
"Yes, you—Americans always stick together"
"Well maybe we do, but then this is America after all"
"But we're here too, now, and if you can't stand the only way we can be American, too, we'll go right on being Armenian".[31]

Significantly, this emotional dichotomy, surfaced during the sixties and seventies with a dramatic increase in militancy in every community from the Armenian Republic to the Middle East, Europe and the United States. The first occurrence of this nationalist fervour occurred on 24 April 1965, the 50th anniversary of the 1915 massacres, when mass demonstrations broke out in the streets of Yerevan. These demonstrations, unprecedented in Soviet history, were directed against Soviet policies of rapprochement with Turkey. During this period, there was a rapid resurgence of nationalistic sentiments, characterised by a revival of historic Armenian revolutionary figures, discussion of the Armenian genocide and attempts to reverse the Russification of the Armenian language[32], as well as a strong emphasis on territorial restoration. Mount Ararat was often used as a symbol of this longing. Dekmejian argues that the intensity of the territorial demands was increasing in direct proportion to the developing Soviet-Turkish rapprochement, thus Soviet policy unwittingly fuelled Armenian nationalism. The predictable Soviet response included the arrest of bourgeois nationalists and an extensive party purge. The authorities, however, made some concessions, sanctioning the public commemoration of the massacres and building a memorial outside Yerevan for the victims of the Genocide.[33]

In 1965, the Committee for Cultural Relations with Armenians Abroad, (commonly referred to as the Spiurk or Diaspora Committee) was created in Soviet Armenia, and it was given the function of developing ties between the Armenian homeland and the Diaspora. At the same time, it provided an opportunity for the dissemination of Soviet propaganda, emphasising the idea that the Diaspora could not have survived without the Armenian homeland, and the Armenian homeland could not have survived without Mother Russia. In its early years it was relatively successful, and previously non-existent relations were initiated, exchange of guests from the Diaspora and cultural groups were arranged, and a new era of relations between the two entities ensued. Diaspora Armenians invited to visit the homeland, however, were often completely out of touch with the main groups of the communities from which they came. It has been suggested that the only reason for their invitation was because they would lavish praise upon the homeland when they returned to their homes. During the latter years of the Soviet Republic, perhaps in the spirit of glasnost, Karlen Dallakian, the new chairman of the Spiurk Committee implied in a speech in Beirut in December 1987 that even contacts with the anti-Soviet Dashnaks were now possible: "all of the organisations of the Diaspora, without any exceptions, are dear to us ... Our hands, our arms are wide open. We are ready to work with everyone".[34]

The continuing links between Diasporas and their homeland can be politicized and this is their major significance in the study of international relations. Diaspora solidarities can be mobilized and focused to influence political outcomes in the homeland. There are countless examples of a homeland government or an aspiring homeland government seeking the political, economic or military support of its Diaspora. In the Armenian case, the segment of the Diaspora living in the United States has provided a useful lobby on behalf of the homeland against Turkish interests. When Diasporas are involved in issues that extend beyond the borders of their host country, the significant actors apart from the Diaspora communities are the host government and to a lesser degree, transnational institutions. The scope and intensity of Diaspora activities including those that affect international relations are determined by the material, cultural and organisational resources available to them. Opportunities in some countries are not equally available to all migrant groups. Some minorities experience severe constraints while others are free to pursue their interests. More importantly Diaspora activity depends on their inclination and motivation—a call to unity—to maintain their solidarity and exert group influence.[35] The point to be made is that activities by Diaspora communities including those that relate to international affairs vary as much with the opportunities available to them as with their skills as much with the opportunities available to them as with their skills and resources.

The outburst of nationalism in the homeland coincided with a new bolder era of ethnic mobilization throughout the Diaspora and the Soviet-American rapprochement of the same decade. On April 24 1965 services in commemoration of the genocide were conducted throughout the Diaspora in many cases organised by joint committees of the three political parties. Articles and pamphlets were published by various groups within the Diaspora communities coupling the demand for genocide recognition with the demand for the restoration of the Turkish-Armenian lands. Such articles were regularly published from 1965 onwards and in each case strong appeals were made to the governments of the Armenians' host countries, particularly the United States. For instance, in 1975 a joint memorandum presented to the United Nations called for 'the return of Turkish held Armenian territories to their rightful owner—the Armenian people'. More importantly during this decade, the lines of conflict began to blur between the antithetical sectors in the Diaspora. By way of example, the ARF was willing to soften its anti-Soviet rhetoric and to cooperate with the pro-Soviet elements in the Diaspora over issues of common interest, namely the genocide and the Turkish Armenian lands. Conversely the Hunchaks recognised that there were nationalistic goals beyond what Soviet Armenia had to offer. There was now a common enemy, Turkey, and there emerged a new discourse within the Diaspora communities, involving increased academic interest and annual commemorations.[36]

Furthermore the three Armenian political parties managed to cooperate with each other on behalf of an activist agenda. In April 1987, they issued a "Joint Communique"[37] which made the following demands:

1. that the Turkish Government, as the heirs of the Ottoman Governments, recognise the Armenian Genocide;
2. that Turkey return the historic homeland to the Armenian people;
3. that the Turkish Government make material reparations for their heinous and unspeakable crime to the victims of the Armenian Genocide;
4. that all world governments, and especially the Superpowers, officially recognise the Armenian Genocide and Armenian territorial rights and refuse to succumb to all Turkish political pressure;
5. that the US Government free itself from the friendly position it has adopted towards its unreliable ally, Turkey, and officially recognise the historical fact of the Armenian Genocide as well as be supportive of the pursuit of Armenia territorial demands; and
6. that the Soviet Armenian government use effective means to have the Armenian Case (including the internal territorial demands) recognised by the Soviet Central Government.[38]

The "Joint Communique" closed with a claim that a new generation has risen—equipped with a deep sense of Armenianism, politically mature and militant, who determinedly pursues the Armenian Cause, through all necessary means, ranging from the political and diplomatic to the armed struggle. As a display of their inter-party cooperation, the three parties jointly sponsored a Martyrs Day rally on the campus of the City College of Los Angeles, to which over

10,000 Armenians came. The Ramgavar speaker "called on the civilised world to help the Armenian people recover its lost territory and see justice done". The Dashnak representative discussed Karabagh and "scorned those Armenians who were abandoning Soviet Armenia and were moving to this country for permanent residence", while the Hunchak official appealed to "the Armenian people for continued struggle till such time as its claims are fulfilled". Political harmony at the rally, however, soon deteriorated over a dispute over the Armenian flag, when the Dashnaks displayed their tricoloured banner of independent Armenia, while the supporters of the other two parties carried the colours of Soviet Armenia. Worse still, in the evening approximately 500 young members of the Dashnaks marched on the Turkish Consulate where they threw a rock through its window and burned the Turkish flag.[39]

A number of other Armenian organisations promote an activist agenda. On the transnational level, the Armenian General Benevolent Union (AGBU), which is affiliated with the Ramgavars and was established in Cairo on 15 April 1906 by Boghos Nubar Pasha (1851-1930), the Armenian son of a former Prime Minister of Egypt, together with some influential friends, has served as an important charitable function, a sort of 'Armenian Red Cross'. Alex Manoogian, president of the AGBU from 1955 until his retirement in 1989, announced at the 75th annual Assembly of the AGBU in Toronto, that the AGBU's assets had surpassed 95 million dollars. Manoogian, a leading member and financial backer of the Ramgavar Party, openly criticised US Secretary of State George Shultz for his role in defeating a Congressional resolution in the summer of 1987 that would have designated 24 April as a 'National Day of Remembrance of the Armenian Genocide from 1915-1923'. Manoogian wrote: "Your policies vis-à-vis the military regime in Turkey and your statement outlined in your letter . . . disturb me to no end".[40]

Reverend Haroutioun Hevadjian, a retired Protestant minister living in Marseilles, has headed the Committee for the Defence of Armenian Political Prisoners (CDAPP). This organisation is closely associated with the anti-Dashnak and Marxist terrorist movement known as ASALA (Armenian Secret Army for the Liberation of Armenia), however, Helvadjian raises funds to defend all Armenian activists who have been accused of assassinating Turkish diplomats. He has also visited them in prisons in England, France, Switzerland and Yugoslavia. Helvadjian declared "all Armenian prisoners are sons of Armenians who defend the Armenian Cause . . . and all those prisoners belong to the entire Armenian nation. . . . They are devoted warriors, not professional killers or criminals." He further stated that "Turkey is our enemy. It has been our enemy for centuries. . . . Those who slaughtered us, massacred thirteen other nations as well." When they were released from a French prison, the three surviving members of ASALA's 'Van Operation' expressed their sincere thanks to Rev Helvadjian and the CDAPP "who with great devotion always visited us. . . . For five years they were our parents and family and somehow alleviated the burden of our imprisonment".[41]

ASALA was born in January 1975 as an alternative to the traditional Armenian political parties, especially the Dashnaks. ASALA's birth was announced by a bombing attack against the Beirut office of the World Council of

Churches on 20 January 1975. Hagop Hagopian, the founder and leader of ASALA, later claimed "I chose it because . . . was conspiring with the United States, with the Dashnak's cooperation to send the Armenian youth away from the Middle East and socialist countries."[42] ASALA was therefore challenging the existing Armenian elites led by the Dashnaks who were allowing emigration, which could only result in assimilation. It is thus critical of its political predecessors, accusing them of failing to deal with the problems of the Armenian people and of dependence on, and collaboration with, the powers which betrayed the Armenians in the past. They represented themselves as the logical and necessary political alternative to the political parties. Its aims were the liberation of Eastern Anatolia from Turkish control and the establishment of an independent Armenia State, which would eventually unify the historic land of Armenia, including the lands in the Soviet Union, Iran as well as in Eastern Turkey.[43]

ASALA was engaged in what can only be called an armed struggle, believing that only by the use of force can Armenians achieve their liberation. It has, since its launch in 1975, been involved in a number of attacks on Turkish companies and tourist organisations, diplomats and officials inside and outside Turkey. On 24 September 1981, four ASALA agents seized the Turkish Consulate in Paris in the so called Van Operation. According to Monte Melkonian, a member of ASALA at that time, "this operation marked ASALA's historic peak. . . . It became the greatest single military/propaganda success ever achieved in the history of the Diaspora . . . a tremendous achievement . . . which created previously unequalled patriotic enthusiasm . . . for the realization of our national aspirations."[44] The deadly attacks on the Ankara and Paris Orly airports in 1982 and 1983 respectively, and the Istanbul Bazaar in 1983 are three egregious examples. As Melkonian explained in an interview "Orly claimed innocent lives. It debases our struggle". ASALA's programme to become the leader of a broad, united front of all Armenian groups, however, was hindered by the general Armenian tendency towards divisive factionalism. Furthermore, the Israeli invasion of Lebanon in June 1982, and the resulting expulsion of ASALA from its base in West Beirut to the isolation of the Bekaa Valley, where the organisation fell under increasing Syrian control, also helped lead to the subsequent splintering of ASALA. It has thus, been reduced to an insignificant group of maybe a dozen or so people in Damascus who appear in public on certain occasions. As an active organisation it is dormant, if not extinct.[45]

Levon Maraslian, a Glendale College professor of history said Armenian terrorists are "patriots who have been waiting for 70 years".[46] Richard Hovannisian, a professor of history at the University of California/Los Angeles (UCLA), and the most prominent Armenian historian and scholar in the United States, addressed the Armenian Assembly and declared that the academic world is not "an ivory tower" but a "battleground, very vicious, brutal and devastating. And we have to be aware of the battle". One of the best examples of this academic "battleground" in the United States involves Hovannisian's colleague in the department of history, Professor Stanford Shaw. In January 1982, Armenian extremists broke up a Turkish history class he was teaching at the university. In addition Shaw's office was broken into and frequent verbal and written threats of violence hurled at him. After his home was bombed and his death prematurely announced, he was forced to cancel his regularly scheduled classes and go into hiding. The reason for this harassment was the pro-Turkish views he expressed in History of the Ottoman Empire and Modern Turkey 1977. When Shaw resumed teaching his course again in 1987, the Armenian Students Association of UCLA once more held a protest rally against him and denounced his views as "scholastic terrorism".[47]

At the present time there are also at least twenty one day schools functioning in the United States and twenty eight different periodicals, of which ten are in English. Armenian Studies are taught in several universities, where Armenian émigrés have endowed eight university professorships.[48] In California alone, there are over 200 separate Armenian organisations such as churches, political parties, athletic organisations, cultural associations, social groups and professional societies, which are constantly sponsoring events. Greater Los Angeles County has the largest Armenian community outside of Armenia. In East Hollywood alone, approximately 30,000 Armenians live and run businesses. In October 2000 the City of Los Angeles designated this ethnic enclave as 'Little Armenia'. As one source put it, "there are probably 10 different Armenian activities during any one weekend night in Los Angeles[49]". The vast majority of these Armenian organisations and activities, of course, have nothing to do with terrorism. A number of them sometimes, and a few of them often, however, pursue the Armenian cause in a manner that overtly supports hatred of Turkey and at times even implicitly condones violence. There are many American Armenians in California who feel great sympathy and support for the Armenian terrorists.[50]

Many Armenian writers and scholars gave their approval ranging from caution to the raising of the terrorists to the level of heroes. The Hunchak party argued that such acts should be limited to inside Turkey itself. By the 1980's the ARF had recognised the need to take a stand on the question of terrorism and began to give its cautious, tacit support to the activities of the various terrorist groups, as evidenced by the increasing number of favourable articles appearing in the Dashnak press. Moreover, according to Torossian a large percentage of the Armenian youth were supportive of the extremist groups. The Armenian Apostolic Church on the whole neither condemned nor supported the terrorist acts, however, for a number of reasons many clergymen felt compelled to take a stand on the matter, particularly in the Middle East. By way of example, most of the churches in the Middle East were under the jurisdiction of the Cilician See where the influence of Dashnak lay members was strongly felt. Thus, the Church was on the whole not pro-active in its response to these events, but rather was moved and shaped by them.[51]

One exception to this was provided by Archbishop Aram Keshishian of the Cilician See, who is currently the Catholicos of that See. In his book 'The Witness of the Armenian Church in a Diaspora Situation' published in 1978, he discusses at length both the political role and nature of the church. His argument is significant in that he suggests that the Church has a vital role to play in 'the process of conscientization', that is 'the revolutionization and politicization of the Armenian Diaspora in its very foundations and structures'. In doing so he walks a fine line between liberation theology and radical nationalism. He appropriates the revolutionary rhetoric of the ARF and, more importantly, of the terrorists by staking a claim for a legitimate role for the Church in Diaspora life.[52] Keshishian states:

> the people should be responsibly and cautiously aware that they are not just religious communities in the strict sense of the term, scattered here and there, but a distinct nation deprived of its national sovereignty and self-determination. The Church should become the avant-garde of this process of self discovery and self assessment, and mobilise the Armenian Diaspora with this end in view.[53]

Thus, overall terrorism mobilised the Diaspora on the one hand by radicalising some segments of the population, and on the other by encouraging those who disapproved of terrorist tactics to lobby their host governments with regard to the Armenian Question. Consequently the late seventies saw the mushrooming of professionalism and a project-orientated ethnic expression. There are a number of factors, however, that help to determine the success or failure of Armenian activism. Armenians tend to be very close communities, who in their own language distinguish themselves from the odar or non-Armenian, which has enabled the Diaspora to provide a unique, transnational system of contact and support. Armenians tend to be more successful in the professions than many others, thus they often possess political influence that belies their relatively small numbers. The most important of which has been the growth of a powerful Armenian political lobby in Washington. Armenian organizers in the United States have sponsored a Bill in Congress to declare 24 April, a National Day of Remembrance of 'man's inhumanity to man'. They have learned from, and made common cause with the Jewish American lobby, sponsoring joint exhibitions, conferences and publications.[54] The strategic importance of Turkey, however, to the NATO alliance prevents the United States from taking as strong a stand on behalf of the Armenians as they would desire. The failure of the Armenian activists in the United States to pass a "Genocide Resolution" in the US Congress and the hesitancy in acceding to the Armenian demands on the Karabagh issue illustrates this point.[55]

Armenian activism against Turkey tends to elicit a vast amount of public and private support and sympathy around the world from non-Armenians because of the widespread knowledge of the Ottoman Turkic massacres of the late nineteenth century and the Genocide that followed. Moreover the Islamic Ottoman Empire was one of the leading historical enemies of Christian Europe. By way of example, Greek sympathy for Armenian activism, results largely from the traditional Hellenic hatred of the Turks.[56] When the Yugoslav authorities released Harutium Levonian from prison in 1987, the Greeks quickly allowed him entry and medical attention. Levonian had been seriously injured when he and Raffi Elbekian assassinated the Turkish Ambassador to Yugoslavia in 1983. The Turks asserted that "this action on the part of Greece clearly indicates that the country openly supports Armenian radicals." The situation regarding France is similar, although to a lesser extent, as the Turks did not conquer and rule that country for 400 years as they did Greece. Indeed, on Thursday 18 January 2001, the French National Assembly adopted a Law recognising the killings of some 1.5 million Armenians as part of the Ottoman Empire's campaign to force them out of Eastern Turkey between 1915 and 1923 as Genocide. Syrian support for Armenian activism stems also from traditional animosities and more specifically contemporary political ambitions. By way of example, the Turkish annexation of Alexandretta in 1939 and current problems dealing with the water of the Euphrates River all encourage the Syrians to support anti-Turkish ends.[57]

Furthermore, despite their passive acceptance of the Soviet authorities, Armenian criticism became public and outspoken after the eruption in 1988 of Armenian Azerbaijani violence in the Nagorno enclave. The contested territory of Nagorno Karabagh, is a fertile, mountainous land overlooking Azerbaijan to the east. To the west lies Armenia, less than five miles away at the nearest point, and the Islamic Republic of Iran is less than fifteen miles to the south. The name Nagorno Karabagh, meaning mountainous black garden, which came into use in the nineteenth century, reflects linguistically the major imperial powers that ruled the region in the last 1000 years. Nagorno means mountainous in Russian, while Karabagh is a compound of the Turkish word for black (kara) and the Persian word for garden (bakh). It is believed that Nagorno Karabagh constituted part of the Armenian kingdom from at least the second century BC, until the partition of Armenia by the Romans and Persians at the beginning of the fifth century. Thereafter, Nagorno Karabagh was no longer in political union with the Armenian lands to the west and fell under the rule of the Seljuk and Ottoman Turks, the Mongols and Persians, before being conquered by the Russian empire in 1805. Russian rule lasted unbroken until the collapse of Tsarist Russia in 1917. Ottoman Turkey attempted in 1918 to conquer this region, but was unsuccessful due to its defeat in World War I. Turkey's failure was followed by attempts by the newly independent Republic of Azerbaijan, which was obstructed by the occupation of the Red Army in 1920. In 1923, however, most of Nagorno Karabagh was granted the status of an Autonomous Region of Azerbaijan but the Bolshevik authorities severed the northern tip of the enclave, known as the Shaumyan district, from the new Autonomous Region, which effectively enabled this district to be integrated administratively with the Socialist Republic of Azerbaijan.[58]

Armenia wanted the Nagorno Karabagh to be reinstated as part of Armenia, and the Armenians who inhabited the Nagorno Karabagh pushed for separation from Azerbaijan and incorporation into Armenia. The Armenians of Nagorno Karabagh claimed the Azeris discriminated against them; that Baku prevented them from attaining higher education, blocked their attempts to travel to Armenia in order to obtain university training, and made insufficient investment in the region. Therefore, union with Armenia would end discrimination by the Azeris and allow Armenians in Nagorno Karabagh to enjoy more educational and economic opportunities.

This autonomous territory was always largely populated by Armenians but was ceded to Azerbaijan by Stalin 1921, and had been subject to a great deal of discrimination by the Azeri authorities ever since. The Azeris, on the other hand, refused to give it up. Armenian campaigners sent petitions to Moscow and linked the integral issue of glasnost and perestroika, by claiming that the demands of the Karabagh were essentially in accordance with the process of democratization. This local dispute was transformed into a major national crisis after 20 February 1988, when the Karabagh Soviet Peoples' Deputies passed a resolution demanding to be transferred to Armenian jurisdiction. Armenians' expressed support by taking to the streets of Yerevan. Western broadcasts of the scene were unbelievable, approximately one million Armenian men and women standing and chanting "Karabagh" in unison, listening to a succession of speakers. Consequently, the cry was soon taken up in the Diaspora: telethons and political fund raising drives were organised, and individual donations poured in. In one Californian telethon in February 1994, the Dashnaks raised $1.5 million.[59] The donations financed not only food and clothing, but also arms and ammunition. Furthermore, the political lobby sprang into action, successfully pressing the United States government to impose sanctions on Azerbaijan. The demonstrations, however, were peaceful and they emphasized their Soviet loyalty by carrying placards of Gorbachev and the flag of Armenia.[60]

The Soviet Central Committee ruled against Armenian jurisdiction of Nagorno Karabagh, but did agree to form a special commission to investigate this serious problem and to determine popular opinion. The Armenian Party Secretary and the head of the Armenian Church made a televised appeal for calm to the demonstrators and on 25 February troops were despatched to Yerevan, though not used against the demonstrators. The demonstration only subsided after assurance that the question would be investigated at the highest level, and on the strength of this, called for a month's suspension of all demonstrations. The proposed breathing space, however, was shattered two days later by the outbreak of violence in Azerbaijan and the murder of Armenians in Sumgait, near Baku. The official version of events was thirty two killed, one hundred injured and Armenian homes burnt. These shocking events provided additional impetus for political organisation in Armenia. Further violence against Armenians followed in Baku and this set off a two-way flood of refugees as Armenians fled from Azerbaijan, and the Azeri rural population in Armenia fled to Azerbaijan for fear of reprisals. In an atmosphere of escalating racial hostility, the movement for both Armenian and Karabagh self-determination grew and tensions between Armenia and Azerbaijan increased.[61] Before negotiations took place, however, something happened which suddenly pushed the whole question of the Nagorno Karabagh to one side.

On 7 December 1988 Armenia was devastated by an earthquake which killed over 40,000, completely destroying the town of Spitak, and leaving 500,000 homeless. Gorbachev dramatically cut short a US-USSR summit in Washington to rush to the scene of the disaster. When he arrived, he succeeded only in making a tense situation worse, when he expressed his irritation at finding unresponsive and angry Armenians still insistent on raising the Nagorno Karabagh issue at this moment of tragedy. The Soviet authorities immediately appealed for international aid and an international relief operation was set in motion. The damage estimated to the Republic's agro-industrial complex was estimated at two billion dollars and the cost of reconstruction at 6.5 billion dollars.[62] The Nagorno Karabagh crisis and the earthquake inflicted enormous damage on Armenia's economy, and thus far outweighed any possible economic benefit of Gorbachev's reforms.

While the political developments in the homeland ultimately sharpened the cleavages in the Diaspora, the Diaspora's response to the 1988 earthquake manifested itself fundamentally as unity around a common cause. Countless articles and editorials called on Armenians world wide to help the homeland. By way of example, one such article pleaded for Armenians to 'put aside all individual and collective rivalries and to unite in a single purpose—the salvation of Armenia'.[63] The future of Armenia was seen as dependent on the efforts of the Diaspora. Furthermore, the three parties contributed to the reconstruction effort in a number of ways. The political arm of the ARF, the Armenian National Committee lobbied the United States government on issues such as aid and trade concessions, and the imposition of conditions on humanitarian aid sent to Azerbaijan. The humanitarian arm of the ARF, the Armenian Relief Society shifted a large portion of its resources from the Diaspora to Armenia and was actively involved in providing emergency relief and self-sufficiency programmes for earthquake victims, and established an Orphans' Fund. Similarly the Ramgavars and Hunchaks contributed culturally through their educational, sporting and cultural associations, and also channelled financial assistance to the homeland through the Pan-Armenian fund.[64]

The Armenian Apostolic Church was involved in spearheading the fund raising drive for Armenia throughout the Diaspora. The Diocese in particular took advantage of its institutional presence in Armenia, facilitating the administration of funds and materials. Within the first five years after the earthquake the Eastern Diocese had raised more than five million US dollars both from the Armenian communities and other organisations, as well as securing six million US dollars as donations in kind. Similar projects were undertaken by the Prelacy which also allocated one million dollars. The AGBU under the leadership of President Louise Manoogian Simone 1988-93 also played a key role in the reconstruction efforts. The AGBU helped establish the American University of Armenia, a hospital, several schools and an emergency relief fund. It also coordinated a medical programme with Yale University as well as soup kitchens and children's centres. Critics within the Diaspora argued that the AGBU unnecessarily undercut its Diaspora projects for the sake of Armenia, claiming that a number of Armenian day schools throughout the Diaspora were closed down. The reality, however, was that only one school was closed down and that was due to the declining population of that particular Armenian community.[65] Manoogian responded to such criticism by stating:

> We think Armenia is a priority which upsets certain traditional groups who feel that there should be just as much attention to the home because their institutions needs support. Personally my support goes more to Armenia than anywhere else . . . people living in America or Europe should be self sufficient and should not have to be subsidised.[66]

It is also worth mentioning the role played by the Land and Culture Organisation (LCO). This organisation formerly concentrated its efforts on the restoration of Armenian style homes and churches in and around the Syrian village of Kessab, as well as the renovation of Armenian monasteries in Iran, nevertheless, the LCO embarked on a number of similar projects. By way of example, in the summer of 1992 just under a hundred volunteers, the majority from France and the United States of America went to Armenia to help construct houses for Armenian refugees, plant fruit trees, and reconstruct a church. Involvement in the work of the LCO carries great symbolic significance for those involved, since it is an act of preserving the architectural and other visible aspects of the national heritage. By working on the land, the participants develop a stronger sense of their ethnicity and a sentimental attachment to the homeland. At the same time, working on the land is an activity with practical benefit for those living in Armenia, thus appealing to the functional component of American-Armenian ethnicity. Ultimately, this kind of activity carries appeal to Armenians of different types of ethnic expression, traditional through to symbolic.[67] The mushrooming of such organisations indicated that many Armenians were seeking alternative channels of involvement through which to assist the homeland. Evidently it was felt that the traditional organisations were not sufficiently tapping the grassroots. Though not all of these organisations were established for the express purpose of helping the homeland, it seems that their establishment was encouraged by the flurry of fundraising activity and the general shift of attention towards the homeland. In particular, the renewed homeland orientation had two effects on the more assimilated American Armenians. Firstly, the images of earthquake ravaged Armenia in the media struck a chord with even the most marginalised Armenians. Secondly, it gave them an opportunity to be Armenian in a practical way. In doing so, it allowed for Armenian involvement that could in large part bypass the traditional organisations. Clearly, while there are many Armenians that continue to be attracted to the more traditional forms of community involvement, American born Armenians were typically attracted to the indigenous, professional organisations that require little commitment and do not have a strong ethnic flavour. Thus the events in Armenia awakened a large number of previously uninvolved, marginalised Diaspora Armenians and drew them into Armenian community life, and yet in doing so were able to sidestep traditional modes of involvement and participate in Western forms of professional activism.[68]

The Armenian Assembly was created in 1971 and engages in public and governmental affairs concerning Armenian issues, and also supports and sponsors academic and educational activities, as well as a host of other projects. In 1972 a national convention was held in Virginia drawing eighty individuals from most Armenian communities, representing many different professions in the United States. The Armenian Assembly's aim was to focus on the enormous untouched resources within the American Armenian community, particularly among the American born and those who had no community involvement and whom demanded professionalism and tangible goals. Thus, the target group of the Assembly was the American, not the Armenian community which was reflected in the overwhelming consensus among the panellists that language was not to be considered a 'key element' in any attempts to ensure ethnic survival in the United States. As one panellist stated 'our young people will learn the language if they want to—language is over-emphasized, more important is culture, history and civilization'.[69]

In November 1988, the Assembly released for the first time a resource guide for secondary school history and social studies teachers on the Armenian Genocide. Dr Rouben Adalian, the Director of Academic Affairs at the Assembly, and the editor of the publication, stated that "this guide is a must for all teachers because it can help instructors effectively communicate the horror of the Armenian Genocide."[70] Moreover, the Assembly was crucial in mediating links between Yerevan and Washington, which it viewed as its primary role, as well as lobbying the United States government on a number of important issues such as humanitarian aid and the Nagorno Karabagh. It has also been pivotal in bringing about Armenia's membership in several international organisations and organised President Ter-Petrossian's trip to the United States in 1990. The Assembly clearly exemplifies the new professionalism within the Diaspora in contrast to the old world behaviour of the parties. Needless to say, the Armenian political parties have accused the Armenian government of showing favouritism towards the Assembly in particular the Dashnaks argued that such a policy is merely a continuation of the Soviet's divisive approach towards the Diaspora communities.

The Zoryan Institute in Cambridge, Massachusetts, has been yet another challenger of the intellectual and organisational status quo. Like the Assembly it offered an opportunity for American-Armenians to by-pass traditional community structures and drew together a number of leading intellectuals into a kind of Diaspora 'think tank' largely free from partisan influence. The institute posed an intellectual challenge to the Diaspora leadership in that it proposed a self-critical approach to the study of Armenian issues which would take place in the context of broader developments in the world. In 1988 it published the Karabagh file, a compilation of historical documents and essays on the Karabagh issue and the Karabagh Movement in Armenia. It has also carried out a long term project of "Genocide Documentation" by videotaping interviews with survivors. The institute has drawn a large proportion of its support from American Armenians for whom it offers a low-cost professional form of involvement in Armenian affairs. Interestingly it has also drawn a large number of foreign born Armenians, primarily intellectuals. This is perhaps due to the mobile and cosmopolitan nature of the Armenian intellectual elite throughout the Diaspora. Moreover, the Zoryan Institute offers a viable alternative to the traditional organisations, in particular for those for whom the traditional cleavages are irrelevant. [71]

Armenian Independence

Following national elections in 1990, the Armenian National Movement formed the government of the republic. It renamed the Armenian Soviet Socialist Republic, the Republic of Armenia and announced a Declaration establishing independence as an objective. It also affirmed the goal of an independent foreign policy, administration of its own economic system, declared a multi-party political system and, following much discussion, advocated the aim of achieving international acknowledgement of the 1915 massacres as an act of Genocide. The Armenian Parliament also declared its intention of extending citizenship to the Diaspora, however a policy on citizenship was not enacted for several years, and in the end this did not include automatic citizenship for Diaspora Armenians.[72]

Following the Declaration, Armenia exchanged trade representatives with Turkey and had high level discussions with Turkish officials, without asserting the acknowledgement of the 1915 act of Genocide as a pre-condition or demanding the return of Armenian territory. The fundamental principle behind these negotiations was to tailor policy according to Armenia's own political and economic resources, rather than pursue unattainable goals. Understandably, many Armenians have disagreed with the ANM's attitude towards Turkey. There remains a lingering distaste for Turkey and the underlying conviction that Armenia needs protection from the perceived continuing Turkish threat, and possible Iranian threat, due to the ongoing violence between Armenians and Azeris over the Nagorno Karabagh. It was during this period that many Armenian Diaspora activists returned from abroad, including many American Armenians, to take advantage of the new political climate.[73]

This prompted talks of Armenian sovereignty and independence from the Soviet Union. In March 1991 the Soviet Union issued its first national referendum. The question asked of the electorate was 'Do you consider it necessary to preserve the Union of Soviet Socialist Republics as a renewed federation of equal sovereign republics, in which human rights and the freedom of all nationalities will be guaranteed?' Two thirds of those taking part voted in favour but Armenia together with Georgia and Moldova, refused to hold the referendum. Indeed the way in which the question had been worded made it difficult to vote 'no' as it could be implied that you were voting against human rights, or against freedom for all the nationalities of the Soviet Union. In September 1991, Armenia held a referendum on independence and ninety five per cent of all eligible voters voted for independence. Two days later the Armenian government declared their independence from the Soviet Union. One month later, Armenians went to the polls again, this time to elect a president. Ter Petrossian won with over eighty per cent of the vote.[74]

Starting along the road of building a truly independent state, Armenia confronted many continuing problems. The war in Nagorno Karabagh escalated, without any resolution in sight, and after the dissolution of the Soviet Union, it became an issue for the international community, as a dispute between two sovereign states. By mid 1992 this had turned into an all out war between the two republics that threatened to spill over into neighbouring countries and in which national pride, revenge and popular anger were all equally mixed. This tiny enclave straddles a deep political divide that separates not only the historically Christian world from the Muslim world, but also the Turks of Anatolia with other Turkic peoples. It divides Turkey's secular Islam from Iran's Islamic fundamentalism, and NATO from CIS forces. This divide forms an axis of instability, running from the Balkans, through Turkey and Transcaucasia to Central Asia. Furthermore, the security interests of three regional powers collide in Nagorno Karabagh; Turkey, Russia and Iran.[75]

The conflict in Nagorno Karabagh has produced catastrophic results, the cost for the 180,000 inhabitants of this small enclave, both Armenians and Azeris has been heavy: the war has taken the lives of more than 30,000 people, with many more grievously injured and tens of thousands homeless. The war has driven virtually all of Nagorno Karabagh's 40,000 Azeri Turks to the relative safety of Azerbaijan and an estimated 20,000 Armenians have settled in Armenia. Armenian forces emerged victorious, occupying a large chunk of Azerbaijani territory adjoining Karabagh, which has resulted in the enclave being under the control of an unrecognised ethnic Armenian government since 1994. As Azerbaijan's strongest ally in the region, Turkey's reaction to this development was to impose a blockade on Armenia, essentially shutting off Yerevan's roads and rail links to the West. Turkey maintains that normalization of relations with Yerevan can only proceed if Armenian forces withdraw from the occupied Azeri territory.[76]

There appears to be no solution to this conflict in sight, unless one side is willing to give in. Armenia has once again found itself in a potentially threatened position, lodged between Turkic neighbours. Arguably, it was the party's control that prevented long standing ethnic rivalry from breaking out into open conflict. The inter-ethnic violence that broke out in February 1988 over Nagorno Karabagh was the most notorious example of what could happen once control weakened. Confronting the problem, one of Ter Petrossian's first appointments was taken from the American Diaspora. A Los Angeles businessman, Raffi Hovannisian, was invited to take up the post of minister of foreign affairs, thereby firmly establishing Armenia as a new player in the western world and sending a message of hope to the Diaspora. Hovannisian's appointment, however, was short lived, as only a year later Hovannisian resigned at the request of the President. [77]

There have been other Armenians from the Diaspora who have been able to retain their offices in the Armenian government, and this begs the question of why Hovannisian did not survive whilst others did? There was clearly a homeland-Diaspora factor in Hovannisian's dismissal; however, it is more accurate to understand his resignation as a result of the clash of two ideologies: that is between the traditional and pragmatic approaches to foreign policy making. Furthermore the impact of Hovannisian's dismissal was felt by the Diaspora, regardless of ideology. At the very least, Hovannisian's dismissal led to the need for the Diaspora to re-assess its relationship with the homeland. At the same time, the Dashnaks accused the government of wanting to influence or even control the Diaspora. Maroukhian, an ARF leader, argued 'if Diaspora-homeland relations are to work, a great deal depends on the political policies adopted . . . they must be able to view our Diaspora reality without descending into it and taking sides'.[78] Toloyan has argued that the Armenian government most likely did not want the Diaspora to remain a 'wild card' and preferred to control or influence the Diaspora through existing organisations or by circumventing them. The appointment of non-affiliated Diaspora members to government suited such a policy. Clearly, faced with the task of governing a fledgling new Republic, the Armenian government did not prioritise the issue of Diaspora-homeland relations and citizenship. Thus for many Armenians within the Diaspora the relationship with the homeland was one of constantly recurring promise and disappointment.[79]

From August to December 1991, two competing governments existed in Moscow. The one led by Gorbachev, slowly disintegrated, as independence movements in the republics sapped the strength from the centre. The other, led by Yeltsin, became stronger and populist, erasing the ideals of the all-union government. The end came on 1 December 1991, when the Ukraine overwhelmingly approved independence. A week later at a closed meeting in Krushchev's old hunting lodge, Yeltsin met with the elected presidents of Belorus and Ukraine where they agreed to terminate the Soviet Union and form a Commonwealth of Independent States (CIS). The formation of the CIS marked the death of the Soviet Union in its 74 year.[80]

The demise of the Soviet Union and the consequent rise of nationalist groupings in the Armenian republic brought about significant ideological and institutional changes in the Diaspora communities. Specifically, the discrediting and
collapse of Soviet political institutions in Armenia undermined the ideological
legitimacy of the pro-Soviet political parties in the Diaspora. Confronted with
these realities, the political stance of some of these parties became anachronistic.
In contrast, the traditional nationalist ideology of the Armenian Revolutionary
Federation, assumed maximum legitimacy, as the independent republic gained
general acceptance in the homeland and throughout dispersion. Initially, this
period was marked by a general quest for inter-party cooperation, necessitated by
the deteriorating economic and political conditions in the homeland. This short
interregnum of relative ideological quiescence, however, ended after the proclamation of independence. The transformation of the Karabagh Committee into the
Armenian Pan-National Movement (APM) and its rise to political dominance in
the homeland set the stage for renewed inter-party competition in the Diaspora.
Encouraged by the nascent democratic surroundings, the three parties of the
Diaspora established their presence in the republic in order to participate in the
evolving political process. Having engaged in seventy years of bitter polemic,
these parties had the opportunity to engage in electoral contests and assume the
responsibilities of governing, a task which neither the APM nor the Diaspora parties had much experience. Consequently, the political struggles of the homeland
were exported to the Diaspora, where the APM sought to build its own constitu-
ency. These inter-party conflicts could be considered a normal part of democratic
political life. The problem was that conditions in the homeland were not normal:
democratic norms and practices were not firmly rooted in the republic nor the
Diaspora. Nevertheless, despite the emergency conditions brought on by the
Karabagh crisis and the Azerbaijani blockade, there were no serious attempts to
suspend the divisive inter-party struggles through the formation of a national
unity government that would unite the parties and factions within Armenia and
the Diaspora at a time of national peril.[81]

The collapse of the Soviet Union fundamentally changed international politics. Suddenly, one of the super powers was gone, replaced by a weak cluster of
states. The majority of former republics, including Armenia, joined the CIS,
which attempted to maintain some military and economic links between the various republics. The result was that some republics began to look further than this
loose arrangement for allies. Armenia tried to play both Turkish and Iranian
cards, whilst Azerbaijan attempted to bring Turkey directly into Transcaucasian
politics. Indeed, the post Soviet world was not a world of equals. All the republics that emerged from the Soviet Union were relatively weak economically and
militarily. Nevertheless, Armenia made a gentle and successful transition to
democracy under its nationalist president, Levon Ter Petrosian.[82] The relative
success of the new Armenian regime and the overall spirit of optimism is
encouraging for Armenia. It has also fostered a re-assessment of Diaspora
attitudes and institutions, urging Diaspora communities to actively contribute
towards a new democratic Armenian nation state.

The momentous events in the Soviet Union, from 1985 onwards, had a powerful effect on the Armenian Diaspora, with regard to its structure, ideological

prescription and priorities. Initially the earthquake triggered these changes and Armenians throughout the world initiated successive campaigns to dispatch funds, medicine, and basic essentials. The impact of the demise of Soviet power, the proclamation of Armenia's independence, the Karabagh crisis and the ensuing Azeri-Armenian confrontation, galvanized the Diaspora communities outside the Soviet Union. It soon became evident that the Diaspora communities would be called upon to play a crucial role in sustaining the homeland. The newly independent republic and the survival of Karabagh fundamentally required a mobilized Diaspora that could provide not only economic assistance, but also political and even military aid. Indeed, for the geographically disparate Armenian communities, these were awesome burdens, but Armenian political groups successfully lobbied their host governments to extend economic assistance to the republic.[83] More importantly, the post Communist Republic of Armenia has officially defined the Armenian nation to include the world-wide Diaspora, a policy in accordance with the feelings of many Diaspora Armenians.[84] The creation of such an effective symbiotic relationship is a challenge that requires enlightened leadership in both the Diaspora and the homeland itself.

To commemorate the 86th Anniversary of the Armenian Genocide, students and staff from California State University gathered around a model of the Armenian Martyrs Monument at Fresno's Free Speech Area on Tuesday 24 April 2001. Guest speaker, Deran Koligian stated:

> We need to raise our proud voices to give ourselves every reassurance that we will be around hundreds, even thousands, of years from now. . . . We have done so much and come so far that to give up in our efforts now . . . would be to dishonour those who preceded us. The evidence is irrefutable and includes many eyewitness accounts and statements from the US Ambassador to Turkey at the time. Unfortunately today's Turkish government is still persisting in their denial that the Armenian Genocide ever took place.[85]

He went on to say "through a well financed world-wide propaganda effort, the modern Turkish government attempts to revise history". He commended France for its lead among Western nations to officially recognize the Genocide, and criticised the United States government, who are heavily influenced by the State Department's military ties with Turkey, for its reluctance to use the proper description of Genocide. The Armenian Students Organisation and Armenian Studies Programme have continually commemorated the Genocide on campus on April 24th for more than twenty five years.[86]

In a resolution adopted on 28 February 2002, the European Parliament spelt out to Turkey the cost of continuing to deny the Armenian Genocide. It declared that Turkey must recognise the Genocide of 1915 if it means to fulfil its ambition of joining the European Union. The resolution which also called for Turkey to lift its continuing economic blockade of Armenia, therefore linking the present and the past, is the latest in a growing number of statements of recognition from national and international bodies. The strength of support was demonstrated by a 391-96 vote against an amendment to delete reference to the Genocide. Nicolas Tavitian, director of the EU office of the Forum of Armenian Associations in Europe, which coordinated the effort, stated "If Parliament has its way, Turkey cannot join the EU unless it ends its campaign of denial of the Armenian Genocide and makes its peace with history. We hope the Turkish government will hear this principled message and create the basis for reconciliation as called for by the European Parliament". He further stated "Armenia has always been a strong advocate of regional cooperation as an instrument for creating a more favourable environment for addressing more contentious political problems." In other words, Armenia and the Genocide are facts not only of history but of geography with which Turkey must come to terms as relations in the region evolve. Coming eighty seven years after the Genocide, the resolution emphasised for Turkey, that far from fading with the passage of time, the Genocide is assuming greater international prominence. Furthermore, the success also underlined the effectiveness of lobbying by Diaspora communities throughout Europe, in combination with representatives of the Republic of Armenia.[87]

The emergence of an independent Armenian republic has clearly elevated the question of the Armenian Genocide and its international recognition. It was, however, the campaigning effort of nearly forty years by Armenian Diaspora groups in various host countries for Genocide recognition that established the environment in which State policy could advance. Within the various Diasporas the Armenian Genocide has been the central reference point of their collective memory. A formalization of this history was critical, not only for its own reasons, but because of the Turkish government's denial which has become increasingly strident, the more Armenians became vocal on the issue. More importantly, the effort by Diaspora communities to win recognition by their respective host countries has been joined since 1998 by a much more public stance from the Armenian government. Robert Kocharian won election to the presidency with an explicit promise to make Genocide recognition a central objective of foreign policy. This position has achieved notable success in that France, Italy, Sweden and Lebanon have issued Statements of Recognition in the past two years alone. This was in sharp contrast to the administration of Levon Ter Pertrosian's, which emphasised the need to establish relations with Turkey, without preconditions over the Genocide or the war in Karabagh.[88]

Armenian activists, however, within the Diaspora suffer many problems. The total Armenian population in the entire world is approximately seven million, in most instances, not enough to force a favourable conclusion or pressure those who could. Furthermore, the Armenians in the Diaspora are subject to the pervasive and almost inevitable forces of assimilation. Nikola Shahgaldian, a senior analyst with the Rand Corporation, recently commented in a seminar entitled "Ethnicity and Political Development in the Armenian Diaspora" the degree to which such assimilative patterns are operating when he noted that "today roughly less than forty per cent of Armenians in the Diaspora are proficient in the correct use of their language".[89] More importantly, the attempts to rejuvenate the Diaspora through terrorism succeeded to a point, but essentially it began to alienate the non-Armenian communities, who after all must be won over if the Armenian agenda is ever to be achieved. Thus, notwithstanding widespread public support and sympathy, practically all non-Armenians, as well as many Armenians themselves, probably judge the Armenian cause as being desperately anachronistic. It is probable that Armenian activism will persist however it is unlikely to achieve any fundamental goals other than symbolic resolutions of sympathy.[90]

The turbulent events in the homeland since 1987 and the Diaspora's response to those events reinforced certain long term trends in the Diaspora. Firstly, the traditional organisations were thrown into disarray as their raison d'etre was challenged by the emergence of an independent homeland. Secondly the institutional malaise, particularly of the traditional organisations was coupled with the Armenian government's policy of favouring non-traditional organisations. At the same time, although relief efforts for the homeland were to some extent centrally coordinated, attempts at a unified political and humanitarian response to the events in the homeland were generally unsuccessful and short-lived. Thus, the homeland provided both a rallying point for some Diaspora Armenians, whilst at the same time exacerbating long-standing cleavages between the ARF and other parties. In the new Diaspora-homeland configuration, however, the partisan cleavages diminished in significance and were superseded by cleavages between the traditional organisations and the more professional task-orientated non-partisan organisations. Within the Armenian Diaspora communities this was reflected in the liberation of previously marginalized Armenians who experienced a renewed homeland orientation and were able to by-pass the traditional cleavages in establishing relationships with the Armenian homeland.[91]

CHAPTER FIVE

METHODOLOGY

I came to study the Manchester Armenians, having selected the Armenians as the ethnic community amongst whom I wished to conduct research. I made several trips to Manchester and London, contacting the acting Bishop of the Armenian Apostolic Church and gradually expanding my contacts from this initial starting point. I was helped by several members of the Armenian Institute[1] based in Kensington and in particular by a half Armenian lady in her eighties, whose grandfather had been minister of the Armenian Church in Manchester in 1904. Her father was active all his life within the Manchester Armenian community and for forty two years was Honorary Secretary for the Manchester branch of the AGBU. She provided me with valuable information regarding the early Armenian emigrants and introduced me to useful contacts. Like her father, she has been involved with the Armenian community throughout her life and helped with the formation of the Young Armenians Association and is an active member of the Armenian Ladies Association. Respondents were also obtained from a variety of sources, including the Armenian Apostolic Church and associated organisations in Manchester, published lists of Armenian individuals and Armenian businesses as well as snowball referrals. Great care was taken in the selection of respondents to ensure that the selection represented the various sub-groups and categories within the Armenian community. Because visible activists, professionals, the clergy and self-employed business people are among the established elite of the Armenian community, the more recent immigrants, young people, and those of more humble means were interviewed to gain a more rounded picture. In addition the sample includes Armenians from Iran, Iraq, Greece, Lebanon, and Egypt and their accounts inform us of Diaspora communities in their countries of origin. Thus, the respondents for this research include Armenians from a variety of backgrounds.

This research is an ethnographic study of members of the Armenian Diaspora community in Manchester, in which the principal form of data is audio-recorded talk, elicited through focus groups and individual life histories. Ethnography is a wide-ranging term with different traditions within different academic disciplines;

however, common features often identified are that it involves empirical work in order to study people's lives. Essentially, all ethnographic studies examine people and aspects of their lives, and social worlds, which result in the production of a research text. Moreover, this text aims to be qualitative and non-reductive, incorporating change and process without resorting to simplistic aetiological or causation models. Arguably, the ethnographic researcher is able to obtain an insider's view of a specific community and thus understand other people's world-view, rather than taking the outsider's perspective of the conventional scientist.[2] Ethnographic research produces situated knowledge rather than rigidly defined universals and captures the fine details of social life.

Qualitative versus Quantitative

Qualitative methods have played a considerable role in political science, from the study of groups and individuals inside the formal political arena, to the political attitudes and behaviour of groups and individuals outside it. The origins of the different qualitative techniques lie in anthropology and sociology. Participation observation was first used in anthropology to study other cultures and intensive interviewing techniques have been widely used in sociology. Qualitative methods, however, have long been used across a number of sub-disciplines within political science and have proved to be the most appropriate techniques in the study of such issues as individual beliefs and subjective interpretations of human actions, whether they are relatively powerful or powerless in the political arena. Such phenomenon, as well as the theories that political scientists' use in seeking to explain and understand them invariably cannot be quantified. Qualitative methods, therefore, have consequently best been employed in empirical research addressing such issues.[3]

The use of qualitative methods is tied to a specific epistemological position. Issues of method raise the long-standing debate between two contrasting epistemological positions, 'positivism' and 'realism', about similarities and differences of methodology between the natural and social sciences.[4] Broadly speaking the former advocates the application of the methods of the natural sciences to the study of social reality. The latter maintains the view that there are fundamental differences between the study of people and the objects of enquiry within the natural sciences, and therefore social scientists are required to understand subjective meanings of social action and reality. Although the issue of qualitative versus quantitative is well argued, it is worth developing the important differences between these two traditions. Quantitative methods are closely associated with a positivist epistemological position. Positivists claim that facts can be gathered independently of values and that careful observers can be impartial and thus achieve objectivity.[5] Critics of positivism have questioned the possibility that knowledge can be free of researchers' values. Claims to objective, impartial or unbiased knowledge of social issues are always expressed in culturally specific and emotionally or politically loaded terms. It should therefore be recognised that the researcher always brings their assumptions and biases to any research situation. A casual glance at the mass media can produce numerous current examples of scientists being challenged by lay people and also disagreeing with each other.

By way of example, over the safety of mobile phones, infant vaccinations, genetically modified foods, breast implants or the causes of global warming. There are numerous examples of social researchers disagreeing over the notions of family, rights, tradition, religion and community, the causes of crime, racism, the crisis of 'masculinity' and the effect of working on mothers on their children. More importantly, as for everyone, what scientists believe or say they do and what they really do have a very loose fit.[6]

Relativists refute the idea that objective, universal and timeless knowledge is possible. All that can be known is already interpreted within a particular language of knowing, relative to time, place and culture. There is no external reality and only a socially constructed reality in which people attach subjective meanings to their own actions and interpret their own situation and the situation of others. This ontological position implies that there is no rational objective science that can establish universal truths. No science can exist independently of beliefs and values and the concepts we create to understand the world.[7]

The problem with this relativist position is that it leads to a self refuting paradox; namely if relativism is true, then its truth is only relative. In seeking to avoid this relativist trap, few social scientists have argued there is no objective reality and no criteria on which to evaluate competing theories. Realists, for example, have argued that there is an objective reality independent of beliefs and values and that it is possible to evaluate competing theories and establish truth, although proof cannot be established conclusively because there are only different degrees of positive confirmation.[8] Thus explanation involves describing and understanding people as conscious and social human beings and their motives, experiences and subjective interpretations are a fundamental component of causal process. This epistemological position is associated with the qualitative research tradition.[9]

A further difference between the two methods is the way in which each tradition applies its analytic categories. Quantitative research is deductive and qualitative research is inductive. The aim of quantitative research is to isolate and define categories as precisely as possible prior to the research, and then to determine with great precision, the relationship between them. The aim of qualitative research, however, is to isolate and define categories during the process of research. In other words, all quantitative research requires a hypothesis before research can begin. The qualitative researcher expects the nature of analytic categories to change during the research process, and thus does not require a hypothesis to begin research.[10]

More importantly, the qualitative researcher specifically looks for patterns of inter-relationship between many categories, rather than a sharply defined relationship between a limited set of categories. This could be represented as the trade-off between the precision of quantitative methods and the complexity-capturing skill of qualitative methods. "The quantitative researcher uses a lens that brings a narrow strip of the field of vision into very precise focus. The qualitative researcher uses a lens that permits a much less precise vision of a much broader strip".[11]

A further difference of these methods is related to the data reporting ability of the respondent. Some questions elicit quick and easy responses, in other words, the respondent can quickly identify what is required and report it without ambiguity. Other questions are far more demanding and it is much more difficult to determine what is required, in other words they struggle to identify and articulate a response. Thus, when the research questions allow interviewees to respond unambiguously, closed questions and quantitative methods are used. When the research questions are likely to cause difficulties and imprecision, more flexible qualitative techniques are more appropriate. A final difference between these two methods is the number and kind of respondents used for research purposes. Quantitative research necessitates a sample study of size and type to generalise the larger population. In qualitative research the issue is not to produce readily testable generalizations, it is that of access. The qualitative interview does not discover how many and what kinds of people share a certain characteristic, it only endeavours to gain access to such cultural categories. How many and what kinds of people share this cultural category is unimportant, it is the cultural category, the very subject matter, that is paramount to the qualitative researcher. Qualitative research does not survey the terrain, it mines it: it is much more intensive than extensive in its objectives.[12]

The differences between the two methods have certain implications. Firstly, the two research approaches emphasise two very different intellectual habits and frameworks. This should always be considered when one tradition seeks to master the other. By way of example, even though qualitative methods have been made more transparent and routine, quantitative researchers will not be able to master qualitative methods merely by learning a few techniques, and vice versa. The qualitative tradition requires a certain mind set, and assumptions of how we view the world, thus requiring new methods of conceptualising research problems and data. Secondly, quantitative and qualitative methods are never substitutes for one another, because they observe different realities and this distinction should be honoured. We cannot draw quantitative conclusions from qualitative studies and quantitative studies are unable to explain how people experience the world in which they live.[13] Essentially, researchers on both sides of the debate are correct and each approach has its drawbacks. Quantitative research often forces responses and individuals into categories they may not fit in order to make meaning. On the other hand, qualitative research focuses too closely on individual results and often fails to make connections to larger situations or possible causation. We should respect what each of these methods has to offer and in doing so, we can learn to use them and exploit their respective analytic advantages.

Methodological Reflections

As in any social science discipline, ethnic research raises methodological concerns regarding researchers and their interactions with the people under investigation. In qualitative studies of this type, the researcher is recognised as being the ethnographer or life history interviewer. The subjective experiences of human beings constitute the paramount data to be extracted, and as such qualitative researchers spend much of their time worrying about the impact their experiences and values have on the research process. Moreover, this is particularly problematic in ethnic research. In other words does qualitative interviewing generate richer and more valid findings when it is conducted by 'insiders', researchers who belong to the same social or cultural group as the people they are studying, or by 'outsiders' and if so, what strategies can be implemented to minimise inevitable biases, stemming from being reared in a different dominant or minority ethnic group?

The relationship between researcher and researched has become a matter of intense controversy in different contexts. This has included women, people with disabilities, gays and lesbians and minority groups. With this in mind, it is often suggested that members of an ethnic minority distrust people from a different ethnic group, and this is extended to the researcher, preventing access or distorting the quality of the research. Thus research into this experience should be conducted from within the community. The issue surrounding the advantages and limitations of the 'outsider' and 'insider' perspectives has produced volumes of dialogue between social scientists of various disciplines and has long been an object of debate by researchers in the qualitative tradition. On the one hand, critics of cross-ethnic interviewing would argue that people from ethnic minorities are not simply inhibited in their communications to an outsider, with the information being passed through a cultural filter, but that there are dimensions to ethnic minorities' experiences which are invisible to the outsider. In studying a group to which one belongs, one can use one's knowledge of that group to gain deeper insights into their opinions and experiences. Furthermore, the researcher and researched are on a relatively equal footing, reducing the likelihood of power relationships, thereby the interview becomes a mutually reinforcing process or, at least, the researcher and researched establish common understandings based on the preconceptions of the dominant linguistic group. By way of example, having an unusual name[14], dressing similarly, dietary habits or religious rituals. The outsider is thus unlikely to either possess the language, nor the cultural equipment to understand that experience. It would not only be impossible to understand the perspective of the interviewee, but there would also be a strong likelihood of imposing one's own cultural norms on the interview process. In other words, group membership provides a special insight into matters otherwise obscure to others, based on one's knowledge of the language and one's intuitive sensitivity and understanding of the culture and its people.[15]

Outsider research, however, has been shown to have clear advantages in that by not belonging to a group under study, the researcher is perceived as neutral and may be given certain information not given to an insider. Researchers working in their own communities face power relationships and barriers to understanding that may be less apparent. Depending on the information being discussed or the questions asked, insiders may be construed as having different political perspectives or indeed antithetical political views. They may be considered too judgemental of individual actions or attitudes expressed by the interviewee that may not conform to the perceived norms of the ethnic group, which could lead to self-censorship in responses. By way of example, in interviews with members of certain ethnic minority groups, a hybrid insider/outsider status has shown to work effectively. The researcher has partial shared understanding of historical myths, customs and language with the researched but is unthreatening and comes across as genuinely interested and eager to learn about the culture of origin. Furthermore, interviewees may also compare themselves unfavourably to an interviewer perceived as an insider if both are of the same age, gender, have the same educational level, social class and background, but the interviewee does not perceive themselves as succeeding professionally or occupationally as the interviewer. This sense of inferiority can be disempowering for the interviewee.[16] Insider researcher may thus be an intrusive research method, in other words, the greater the intimacy, the greater the danger of self censorship, suspicion and possible hostility.

Furthermore, the significance of insider/outsider does not have to be the same from the beginning of an interview to the conclusion. Where interviews take place in respondent's homes, familiar territory generates confidence. The researcher is invited to their home as a guest and the balance of power is more likely to tilt in the respondent's favour. Moreover, arguments for the exclusion of outsider researchers with ethnic communities on the basis that the relationship of power between researcher and researched, tends to be unidirectional, clearly ignores the fact that the researcher is totally dependent on the respondent's cooperation in the research process and the negotiation which occurs during the course of any exchange. Clearly power relationships between researcher and researched depends very much on the specific content, the research method, and in the case of interviewing, the actual interview situation. Thus, the balance of power in an interview situation of non-ethnic matching does not have to tilt in the favour of the outsider researcher. In certain circumstances and for certain research questions, the ethnic matching of researcher and researched may be appropriate, but this should not be viewed as a general strategy. Indeed more can be understood from considering it as an interactive factor in the dynamic content of the interview, rather than singling it out as the dominating dimension. Skin colour or ethnic background are not the only social markers and are not always relevant to respondents, depending on the topics to be discussed. Other dimensions such as gender, class, age, education and professional status may all emerge with different significance during the course of an interview.

Indeed these questions arise both for insider and outsider researchers because of the increasing recognition of the partiality of the researcher's knowledge. This partiality exists because of the researcher's 'positionality' in relation to the research questions and to the subjects of research. Positionality refers to the shaping of perspective by identifiers such as class, occupation, gender, race, sexual orientation or indeed several of these interacting with each other, as well as location. These can all affect the researcher's perspective and also that of the person being interviewed. Thus, any form of research involves issues of power, however, these are particularly relevant to ethnographic research, as it often involves people who are positioned as 'others' within large-scale relationships of domination and subordination. By way of example, the coloniser studying the colonised, a white person studying people of colour, or an established citizen studying a Diaspora or immigrant community.[17] Thus all knowledge is socially constructed and objectivity is not attainable because people's perceptions and interpretations are shaped by the understandings they bring to any situation. As such researchers need to be reflexive in assessing how the circumstances of the interview dynamic might be affecting the discourse that is constructed between the researcher and the research subject.

Reflexivity in the research process is widely agreed. What reflexivity means and how it can be achieved is much more difficult. Reflexivity generally means attempting to make explicit the power relations and the exercise of power in the research process. By way of example, identification of the exercise of power, power relationships and their effects in the research process as well as ethical judgements that frame the research and mark the limits of shared values and political interests and accountability for the knowledge that is produced—why researchers tell some stories rather than others and how their knowledge is authorised.[18]

Researchers should, therefore, be aware of the ways in which their own biography is a fundamental part of the research process. It is both the experiences of the researched and researchers which are important. This position assumes researcher reflexivity, specifically how the researchers experiences has or has not influenced the research process. This awareness of oneself should address issues such as the choice of research topic, theories, methods, research questions, data collection, results and interpretation. This understanding is at variance with the argument that only minority scholars can produce credible knowledge about minority ethnic groups. Instead, it suggests that scholars researching ethnicity should examine self consciously the influence of institutional racism as well as stereotypical preconceptions by the dominant culture, and the way it shapes the development of their research, rather than assume a colour blind stance.[19] This is an extremely different posture from that advocated by unbiased or objective research, in which one denies the influence of one's status, be it ethnic origin, gender, class or other social status, in the shaping of knowledge. This requires that we examine the social construction of our own identity not just that of those we study.

The debate surrounding insider outsider issues, however, has greatly evolved in recent years and has demonstrated that the personal relations of the researcher and researched dynamic are not reducible to the insider outsider dimension. If the notion of insider is taken up uncritically it brings with it a danger of essentialism, meaning the assumption that all those who are in a particular social category or ethnic group share a common perspective. By way of example, even with generalised identities like disabled, blacks or working class, it is not always very obvious who is inside and who is outside the group. As we add more descriptors to define the identity of any given community, for example, black, middle class, female, graduate, we are more likely to create people who stand as insiders or outsiders. Most importantly the insider researcher will always be something of an outsider in his or her community by virtue of becoming a researcher.[20] As such attempts have been made to move from a dualistic perspective to a more nuanced approach in which intermediate categories are interposed between insider and outsider in order to cover situations where the researcher's position is more fluid and ambiguous, such as the outsider within.

Nevertheless, the goals of insider research remain crucial in terms of the validity of the research. It is still important to question the extent to which we can actively achieve real empathy when we do not share the crucial characteristics of those we interview. With all the best intentions, differences that impede under-standing will continue to exist and interviewees may have reasons to suppress aspects of their experience that they believe the researcher could not comprehend or is not entitled to know. In this sense, it is possible to agree with Robert Merton that 'we no longer ask whether it is the insider or outsider who has monopolistic or privileged access to social truth; instead, we begin to consider their distinctive and interactive roles in the process of truth seeking'.[21] Both perspectives have the possibility of distortions and preconceptions of social reality; however, it is the role of the researcher to assess the distinctive advantages and limitations of each perspective in relationship to the specific research. More importantly, discovering the participant's own definition of the terms insider and outsider is essential as this could affect the kinds of information gathered and the interactive process within the interview sessions themselves.

Focus Groups

The main reason for choosing focus group interviews for the initial stage of research is that they are compatible with key assumptions within the qualitative paradigm. Within the qualitative tradition, the nature of reality is understood as phenomenological and that multiple perceptions do exist. When we refer to peo-ple's feelings and beliefs, we are concerned with what takes place, in terms of thinking and acting upon those beliefs. These subjective states refer to our 'inner' world of experiences, rather than the outside world, thus we focus on the mean-ings that people give to their environment, not the environment itself. Further-more, a fundamental belief underlying focus groups is that individuals are asked to take part in a discussion where their diverse opinions are desired. The interac-tions between the respondents are recognised as having the ability to add depth and scope to the knowledge gained. Finally, the nature of knowledge, within the qualitative tradition, is influenced by perspective. Knowledge is explained by describing a particular set of issues in relationship to a particular context. The aim is not to generalise to larger populations, rather to describe findings within a par-ticular situation. Thus, the underlying principle behind focus groups is not to elicit principles that can be extended to a wider population but an interactive dis-cussion that gives a greater understanding of perceptions, beliefs, attitudes and experiences from multiple points of view and to record the context from which those understandings were derived.[22]

Focus groups developed as an important part of market research, but are now widely used across social science disciplines as a means of assessing attitudes. In the social sciences this interviewing technique appears to be gaining in popularity and has tended to be viewed as an adjunct to other methods, complementing indi-vidual interviews, and has commonly been used to refine research questions. In this context, they are a particularly useful forum for discussing both the past and issues such as ethnicity. There are a variety of definitions of focus groups but these definitions usually contain the following principles:

- The group is an informal assembly of target persons whose points of view are requested to address a selected topic.
- The group is small, six to twelve members, and is relatively homogenous.
- A moderator with prepared questions and probes sets the stage and induces participants' responses.
- The goal is to elicit perceptions, feelings, attitudes, and ideas of participants about a selected topic.
- Focus groups do not generate quantitative information that can be projected to a larger population.[23]

It is important to remember that the whole purpose of the focus group is not on consensus building, it is on obtaining a range of opinions from people about issues thus, the attention of the focus group interview is on the subjective experiences of the participants. Focus groups differ from other small group interviews in that small group interviews are conducted to ascertain people's point of view. In contrast, focus groups are better organised, more formal and produce information that results from analysis of the transcriptions from the interviews. A further distinction is that small group interviews are often used for consensus building or problem solving. It is not an explicit goal in focus groups to reach a consensus, rather, the goal is to ascertain individual perspectives and encourage people to express different points of view.[24]

The main emphasis of a focus group is the interaction between the participants, and not that between participants and the interviewer. Interaction is crucial because interaction between participants highlights their view of the world, the language they use about an issue and their values and beliefs about specific situations. Interaction also enables participants to ask questions of each other, as well as to re-evaluate and reconsider their own understanding of their life experiences. A moderator rather than an interviewer, whose role is to centre the debate and ask some probing questions by adopting a posture of 'sophisticated naiveté', thus guides focus groups.[25] This disposition encourages the group to talk in depth with confidence, but also to be prepared to elaborate on issues for the outsider. By way of example, when specific subjects were raised such as the Armenian homeland, it was important for the members of the group to elaborate on what they meant by the Armenian homeland as the danger is to assume your own understanding of such a concept. Furthermore, do not be surprised if the respondent's have very different perspectives of the relevant concepts that arise during focus groups.

The moderator's role also involves balancing the two main constraints on a focus group: namely individuals who dominate the discussion; and a sense of group pressure which can build up from a majority perspective, which discourages a minority of participants from expressing their opinions.[26] It should be noted, however, that during the focus group sessions, individuals who attempted to dominate or talk over members of the group were usually dealt with by other members of the group. It was not necessary, therefore, during the focus group sessions to intervene on a regular basis. In other words, the focus groups were in a sense regulated by the participants themselves.

There are several assumptions underlying the focus group interview. Firstly, that people are valuable sources of information about themselves. Secondly, that people are capable of self-reporting and are able to articulate their opinions and feelings accurately. Thirdly, that the best procedure for eliciting information regarding opinions and feelings is through structured group conversation. Finally, and most importantly, there are effects of group dynamics that enhance the likelihood that people will speak openly about a specific subject. For example; snowballing, when the statements of one respondent initiate a chain reaction of additional comments; stimulation, when the group discussion generates excitement about a topic; and spontaneity, because participants are not required to answer every question put to the group, their responses are more genuine. Underlying these assumptions is the belief that information obtained from a focus group interview is genuine information about what each person feels rather than a group mind set in which people conform to what others believe.[27]

A precise understanding of the research aims facilitates the use and application of the focus group interview; however, when considering the applicability of focus groups, the researcher must also assess the potential abuses of this research tool. Thus, to approach a focus group without a precise notion of what information is required from the participants is unlikely to be of value. One of the common abuses of focus groups is inadequate planning for the focus group sessions. It is necessary for the success of a focus group that extensive planning is undertaken. Because focus groups are informal, do not assume there is no need to plan the questions and probes.[28] Therefore, the success of the project is directly related to how clearly the research problem is identified. It is essential that the topics to be discussed are clearly identified and limits are set. It is preferable to limit the scope of the focus group rather than attempt to accomplish too much: what information is required, what is not required? What specific question or aspect of the research study is the focus group designed to address? As this research focuses on ethnic identity and how this is reproduced and maintained within Diaspora communities, the aim of the focus groups is to:

- Develop a general understanding of target groups' perceptions of their ethnic identity; and
- Identify the language and key concepts that target groups use to discuss their ethnic identity.

It is anticipated that the focus group sessions will produce:

- Key ideas that relate to their ethnic identity ('Armenianness' (Haygaganoutyoun), and how strongly the participants feel about these key ideas.
- A better understanding of key Armenian associations.
- Specific language and themes relating to their ethnic identity that the participants use and that the significance of such language can be described.
- Further design and refine research questions.

Focus group interviews typically last between one and three hours. When considering a focus group site, it is important to remember the main goal is to promote the comfort of the participants, therefore, when you select a setting for conducting the focus group, it is more than just the physical environment, it should provide a comfortable space that facilitates a relaxed atmosphere in which people feel free to express their opinions, and conveys the extent to which you value their participation. The Manchester focus groups were held in the Holy Trinity Church community halls. The atmosphere was relaxed and comfortable as this is the place where Armenians typically gather together and discuss topical issues. In a sense, the focus group meetings were no different to the discussions that usually take place when groups of Armenians get together. Furthermore, Armenians that did not regularly attend church or indeed did not attend the church at all were willing to come along and participate in these group discussions.

A common misconception relating to focus groups is that they are imprecise in the way in which they are organised and conducted. Certainly, the discussion may often give the impression of being informal; however, it is actually the result of a precisely planned session with clear objectives and carefully structured questions. Although the intention of the focus group is to produce an informal atmosphere that will facilitate participation, it should be noted that the focus group may be an unnatural setting for some people. In order to overcome this, the moderator should ensure that people feel at ease and comfortable about the proceedings. In this sense, I was fortunate in that I was able to meet with most of the participants prior to the focus group sessions which resulted in a more informal and relaxed atmosphere. Participants will be unable to articulate openly if the general environment feels threatening or if questions are ambiguous or inappropriate. Most importantly, if the moderator is incompetent in encouraging discussion or disrespectful of the integrity of responses, there is a real danger that natural and flowing discussion will be thwarted. This is significant when conducting focus groups where there is an inconsistency between the culture and the language of the moderator and participants. Due care should therefore be taken to ensure misunderstanding or indeed alienation does not occur.

The precise number of focus groups required to address the research questions is difficult to predict. The number of focus groups conducted is based on the purpose of the study, the information the individual researcher requires, the nature of the focus group and the success of the first focus group. It is, however, unwise to conduct only a single focus group and at least two focus groups with different participants allows the researcher to confirm the initial group's responses. Two things should be considered when selecting the number of focus groups. Firstly, there should be an adequate number of groups so findings produce themes or key ideas. Secondly, a sufficient number of focus groups to reflect the range of participants who need to be interviewed. By way of example, four focus groups were held with the Manchester Armenian community (the first comprised eight people and the remainder six people). Upon completion of the fourth focus group, I was satisfied that the aims of the focus groups were fulfilled. Thus it is recommended that focus group interviews continue to be conducted until the moderator can confidently predict how some of the participants are going to respond.

Organising focus group interviews requires more planning than other types of interviewing as getting people to group gatherings can be difficult. It was, therefore, initially anticipated that these focus group interviews could be carried out at the Second Armenia Diaspora Conference in Yerevan during the last week in May 2002[29], where over 3,000 members of the Armenian Diaspora from different countries attended the conference. Because the research goals for conducting focus groups often differ from those of quantitative research, the procedures relating to sampling are often not directly applicable. Qualitative research methods, such as focus groups, are designed to select members, based on predetermined characteristics, in this case being a Diaspora Armenian. Thus, when there is a large cohort of individuals who meet these predetermined characteristics, it is possible to randomly select participants from that group. Due to the intensive schedule of events at the conference, however, this proved to be impossible.

It is not always easy to identify the most appropriate participants for a focus group. If a group is too heterogeneous, whether in terms of gender or class, or professional and lay perspectives, the differences between participants can make a considerable impact on their contributions. Alternatively, if a group is homogenous with regard to specific characteristics, diverse opinions and experiences may not be revealed. Participants in focus groups need to feel comfortable with each other, therefore, meeting with others whom they think of as possessing similar characteristics or levels of understanding about a specific topic will be more attractive than meeting with those who are perceived to be different. The first focus group of eight people, therefore, was selected from my own Armenian contacts to discuss issues relating to their ethnic identity and community relationships. The participants (male and female) were therefore largely equal in social status, knowledge and experience, so that confidence was generally high and nobody felt threatened or unable to voice their opinions. This is an extremely useful way to recruit participants: a contact person or persons who represents the desired criteria, and is aware of others who meet those criteria.

Compared to traditional sampling in quantitative large-scale studies, this procedure may seem extraordinarily straightforward. The involvement of participants, however, may not be as easy as expected. By way of example, many members of the general public, let alone minority ethnic groups, are suspicious of research or researchers for that matter. This suspicion can be generated from cultural differences, prior experiences, or indeed the unfamiliar and perhaps threatening domain from which research originates. Thus, a potential abuse of focus groups is the temptation to resort to convenient samples, which are less than desirable and could result in abandonment of the project.[30] Nevertheless, my own experience of focus groups was positive and productive. Once you have generated interest in the process of focus groups, the fundamental prerequisite for success is a willingness to participate in the process. The participants were informed of the general purpose of the focus groups, that it is a research discussion. They were not, however, informed of the specific research questions as they may have become too sensitised to the issue before the focus group interview. Most of the Armenians I approached were willing to participate in focus groups. Indeed asking their opinions, being listened to genuinely and knowing that their experiences are interesting to someone outside their cultural community appears to be a valuable and fulfilling experience for many people.

One misunderstanding regarding focus groups that can lead to abuse is that the information elicited from the groups is easy to analyse and the findings are readily apparent. It may involve an extensive amount of time to summarise, analyse and identify common themes. There may indeed be some key findings that are apparent; however, more subtle findings will involve much more time and extensive scrutiny of the data. Interpretation of data is not always straightforward. Similarly, it is possible for participants to discuss issues you may feel irrelevant, as was the case in one particular focus group where an interesting but heated discussion regarding football took place, however, such expression may indeed be extremely important to identity and care should be taken not to overlook such representations. Furthermore, the strength of an individual's concerns, or intensity of feeling, may not be apparent in the written transcripts. Clearly inaccurate transcripts will be recorded if due attention is not paid to the participant's nonverbal responses i.e., intonations, facial expressions, body language as well as frequency of participation. All these non-verbal responses should be recorded in some way and need to be taken into account when interpreting results.[31]

Life Story Interviews

The focus group sessions were followed by life history interviews to refine and further explain the findings. One of the reasons for choosing life history interviewing as a method of research is its qualitative nature. Life histories are an acknowledgement of a simple, but important point; that for many social processes, the past is a crucial factor in understanding the present. In order to understand the present perspective of an individual, we need to know as much as possible about their personal history, and to locate that personal history within the history of contexts. This enables us to understand, rather than recycle personal accounts of their life. Furthermore, life histories are an acknowledgement of the importance of the interaction between individual's lives and social and institutional structures. Clearly individual's actions are reflected in their life histories, but equally, individuals' experiences reflect structural realities, which affect their experiences and actions.

Today, more and more researchers in various disciplines are using the life history approach as a method of inquiry. Biographic narrative interviews, enables the interviewee to provide an uninterrupted narrative of their own life. They are asked to tell their story, in their own way, beginning wherever they like and for as long as they like. This allows a person to narrate the story of their life in all its dimensions: personal, spiritual, social and economic. This initial narrative, which may last ten minutes or three hours, is their told story. Treated as text, this is the focus of analysis, which is supplemented by further questioning which begins only when the initial narration is brought to an end by the interviewee.[32] Thus, life history interviewing offers researchers access to people's ideas and memories in their own words, rather than in the words of the researcher. This is an important factor, as the social world in general is understood as an interactive process i.e., constructed by individuals who actively contribute meaning to it, both through their interpretations and through actions based on those interpretations. Therefore, construction and interpretation of social phenomenon such as ethnicity can best be understood by an appreciation of one's research subjects' own understanding of their circumstances.

Life history interviewing differs from conventional ethnography as it does not involve long periods of researcher participation in the life of the interviewees. It also differs from the highly structured interviews used in survey research, based on rigidly defined questionnaires and closed questions, by including interaction between researcher and interviewee. As opposed to quantitative questionnaire type, during which the researcher determines the interview questions and language, employing qualitative techniques leaves the content and language more open to negotiation. Thus, a more interactive approach can give interviewees greater discussion over the pace and content of the interview and direct the flow of conversation. Most importantly, the respondents are able to ask questions themselves, allowing the respondents the space to discuss openly their own values and account for their own actions. These methods are undoubtedly the most effectively employed where the aim of the research is to examine people's subjective experiences and the meanings they attach to their own experiences. It permits people to talk freely and to offer their interpretation of events as it is their perspective that is paramount.[33]

In contrast to a pre-defined questionnaire, the researcher's interview guide is used as a checklist of specific topics to be raised after the initial narrative. The central difference of this form of interviewing from both the structured and semi-structured interview is its open-ended character. The order in which issues are raised is not of importance. Open-ended questions are used to allow the interviewees to talk at length and freely on any given subject that may be of particular importance to them, allowing them to lead discussion. This method provides the possibility to challenge the preconceptions of the researcher, as well as allowing the interviewee to answer questions within their own frame of reference. In other words, by drawing upon ideas and meanings with which they are familiar provides a greater understanding of the subject's point of view. It could be argued that this is a licence for the interviewee to talk about an issue in any way they choose. For example, one of my interviewees was extremely hostile towards recent immigrants in Britain and talked for a lengthy period on issues that could easily have been construed as racist. This apparent disadvantage, however, can be turned into an advantage because there is a concern for the perspective of the person being interviewed, and such issues apparently diverging from the specific topic, can actually divulge something about their anxieties.[34]

The establishment of rapport in life history interviewing is of fundamental importance, given that the method itself is designed to elicit understanding of the interviewee's perspective. It is important to remember, therefore, that language is more than an act of speaking it is also an act of representation. If we hope to move beyond official representation, and discover how things actually are, then it is necessary to seek the trust of the individuals being interviewed. Spradley[35] views the establishment of rapport as a four-stage process. Firstly, there is the initial apprehension between the interviewer and interviewee. Indeed, this is understandable if the parties are strangers, and it should not be considered as a personal weakness on either part. In order to overcome this, both parties must begin to talk to each other, which is assisted by the use of descriptive questions. By way of example, you could ask what terms they use for particular places such as Armenian associations, or how they perform certain tasks in relation to cultural practices, which enables the researcher to ask questions around that topic using the language of the interviewee. The use of such descriptive questions assists the second stage of achieving rapport: exploration. This is where both parties begin to discover what each other is like and how the interview will proceed and for what reasons. This is further assisted by the use of descriptive questions by both parties, which leads to the third stage: cooperation, where each party begins to know what is expected of each other. The fourth stage is participation:[36]

> A new dimension is added to the relationship, one in which the informant recognises and accepts the role of teaching the ethnographer. When this happens there is a heightened sense of cooperation and full participation in the research. Informants begin to take a more assertive role. They bring new information to the attention of the ethnographer and help in discovering patterns in their culture.[37]

An average life story interview may need two or three sessions and can take anything from one to eight hours. Because of the length of time involved in such interviews, these are normally conducted on a small sample of research participants. These are normally private, one to one encounters between interviewer and respondent. Sessions should be held at a time convenient to the respondent and in a suitable location, which offers privacy, comfort and familiarity. There is often no better place than the respondent's home.[38] Indeed all six of my life history interviews were carried out in the respondents' homes. Breaking up the interview into separate sessions, a break for lunch perhaps, gives people time to remember and explore the past, and makes recollection more of a reflexive process. Furthermore, this takes the pressure of a single session, when the respondent might feel obliged to cram everything in. When discussion flows naturally, issues discussed during one session can be reflected upon by the respondent, and then brought to the next session. The interviewer can also benefit from the pause between sessions. Most importantly, because of the length of the interview, it is possible to understand the rationale of the respondent and the correlative thinking that enables them to form a particular judgement. Finally, this method draws attention to related issues, locating the respondent's attitudes and behaviour in the context of their individual biography and broader social position, therefore enabling the researcher to draw out meaning, process and context.[39]

Having identified the population for study and the location in which to conduct the fieldwork, however, it was necessary to locate the Armenians in Manchester. Initial contact was made through the Armenian Apostolic Church in Manchester by attending the church service on the first Sunday of every month and luncheon sessions over several months, thus gradually expanding contacts from this starting point. There are also many activities sponsored by Armenian voluntary associations and I attended as many of these gatherings as possible.[40] Indeed, this is the route used by many Armenians themselves to enter the community, particularly those Armenians who have few or no contacts previously established within the London or Armenian communities.

There is also an Armenian Directory of all Armenians and Armenian businesses in England which enabled me to select participants from the Manchester area randomly. From the initial contacts and the Armenian Directory, a list of proposed interviewees was drawn up, who were contacted by letter, outlining the research objectives and assuring confidentiality. Six were carried out. The first principle of qualitative methods such as life history interviews is that 'less is more', where meanings rather than frequencies are important. It is essential to work with greater care with a small sample, than more perfunctory with a large sample of interviewees. This group of respondents is not intended to represent some part of the larger world, however, it offers the opportunity to view the complex character, organisation and logic of Armenian ethnic identity.

The life history seeks to achieve a deeper insight into a person's biography. The respondents, however, in a qualitative interview of this nature are subject to several risks. By way of example, life histories can be extremely time consuming, privacy endangering and emotionally demanding in ways that quantitative interviews rarely are. It is difficult for such problems to be anticipated at the outset of an interview, therefore researchers must ensure that the respondent is not overtly or subtly pressurised by the interview process. The standard ethic protocol in Appendix B is one example of how respondents' rights can be protected.[41]

Nevertheless, life history interviews can often have a profound effect on the research subject who may have never discussed their memories. They are unlikely to have recalled and reflected on their whole life over several hours. For most people, however, recalling their life story is a positive, if emotional experience from which they can gain much satisfaction and a renewed sense of perspective. Moreover, this method gives the respondent the opportunity to engage in an unusual form of conversation. They find themselves in the presence of the perfect conversational partner, who is willing to listen eagerly to anything the respondent has to say. This leads to other assets such as the opportunity to make oneself the centre of attention, to state a case that is otherwise unknown, to engage in an intellectually challenging process of self understanding and even to experience a kind of catharsis. All of these advantages suggest that for most respondents the benefits of life history interviews outweigh the risks.[42]

Qualitative Data Analysis

The transcripts from the focus group discussions and life story interviews will comprise the data for analysis and interpretation. There is, however, a great deal of literature regarding how and why to use qualitative research methodologies but there is considerably less information on what to do with the data after the research has been conducted. Analysis begins by describing the samples of both the focus groups and individual life history interviewees and transcription should be initiated as soon after the focus groups or interviews are conducted. The tape recording of the focus groups and interviews is essential because the participants' words are important, and this also gives the benefit of easier concentration on the face-to-face interaction, and non-verbal gestures. There are, however, a variety of problems with collecting and representing talk as data. While some qualitative researchers insist that transcripts should include everything that is said, Lilian Rubin[43], for example, defends the practice of organising edited transcripts in terms of previously developed categories of interest rather than verbatim records of interviews, although she does listen to the entire tape as she proceeds with analysis.

Following each interview I listened and transcribed everything that was said and then organised the text into specific categories of interest. The resultant familiarity with the data has led to some sub-themes developing in each main area of focus. Such themes evolved throughout the whole research as a continuation of the researcher's understanding and experience of academic debate in this research area which has resulted in the process of selecting key words, concepts and key interview excerpts. By way of example body language, the words of the participants, the emotional level associated with responses and convergence from several participants on a particular issue (not necessarily all). It should be noted, however, that categorization is not always clear-cut and many issues appear complex and inter-related.

Conclusion

The problem of taking difference into account in social research is not easily dealt with by methodological rules. We cannot escape the complex interrelations of power that constitute ourselves and situate us in relation of difference. Taking account of difference in the research process is a sensitive, contested, personal and often painful process. There are often long and complicated stories behind our differences. How researchers contribute to the negotiation of research relationships and how they perceive power, difference and otherness affects the representations that they produce as knowledge and their own accountability for this knowledge. With this in mind, we should not assume that outsiders are unable to generate credible research with different ethnic groups. While individuals from within a community have access to a particular kind of understanding of their experience, this does not attach special authority, though it may attach special interest to their own representations of that experience. Moreover, while we might acknowledge the limitations of the understanding which someone from outside a community can develop, this does not mean that they cannot develop and present an understanding or that such understanding is worthless. Individuals can indeed benefit from the understandings which others offer of their experience. It is almost certainly a different understanding from that of insiders and will depend, among other things, on the extent to which they have immersed themselves in the world of the other and portrayed its complexity through the outside perspective of the structures which surround and help to define the experience of the community.

This requires an acknowledgement of the complex, multiple, and contradictory identities and realities that shape our collective experience. If the challenge of qualitative analysis is to understand the multiple intersections between life histories and social structure, then the various ways in which we view ourselves and our relationship to others should be part of that analysis. It follows logically from the discussions above that any account of a research project is an interpretation rather than an objective description. As we learn to see the world through the experience of others, a process that is itself antithetical to the views of privileged groups, we can begin to construct more complete and less distorted views of ethnic identity.[44] This research does not claim to be representative or make sweeping generalizations about other Armenian Diaspora communities. By seeking to illustrate some of the complexities of ethnic Armenian identity, this research emphasises process more than content amongst a small sample of ethnic Armenians at a particular moment in time, thus providing a snapshot of their lives.

Finally, it has become increasingly fashionable for individual researchers to 'personalize' their accounts of field work however; there have been few systematic attempts to reflect upon the experiences and emotions that are reported in an epistemological sense.[45] Research methods texts remain relatively silent on the ways in which field work affects us, and how we affect our field work subjects. Nevertheless, it is perhaps more common to find a personal dimension in the recollection of field work and the analysis of data, although the increasing awareness of the personal nature of field work is not something the methodological literature gives substantial attention. Thus, it is important to remember that in writing, remembering and representing our field work experiences, we are involved in the process of identity construction. Through examining the intimate relationships between significant others, we are able to understand the processes of field work as practical, intellectual and emotional accomplishments.

CHAPTER SIX

THE MANCHESTER ARMENIANS

This chapter deals with my case study on the Armenian Diaspora in Manchester and examines the social and political processes that maintain and shape their individual identity. In particular this study analyses the way in which Diaspora peoples balance lives rooted in a particular territory while also sharing very different social spaces. Diaspora as a conceptual tool and empirical reality, understood as a transnational social network relating to both the country of origin and the country of settlement can give a more profound understanding of the social reality in which migrants live. In addition, fluid bases of identity associated with the recent scholarship on hybridity emphasises the ability of individuals to cut and mix. Today many members of a Diaspora community are bilingual or even trilingual, with multiple points of origin. They are often able to determine what is missing in their country of settlement. Knowledge and awareness has increased to the point of cosmopolitanism but at the same time cultural values which sustain solidarity have not been threatened. Diasporas can be thought of as positioned between the host land, homeland and images of the Diaspora themselves.

This research illustrates that the cohesion and maintenance of the Armenian community does not derive from homogeneity or a collective ideal, it is maintained and reinforced by the acceptance of a symbolic framework which is multi-layered and expressed in a variety of ways. Because of the fluid nature of symbolic ethnicity it is able to incorporate the diversity of expression that exists within a single ethnic group. The resultant familiarity with the data has led to some themes developing. Such themes evolved throughout the whole research as a continuation of the researcher's understanding of academic debate in Diaspora studies, however, categorisation is not always clear cut and many issues appear complex and inter-related. This case study illustrates there are an innumerable combination of possibilities in defining what it is to be Armenian.

Armenians represent one of the older immigrant communities in Britain; however, it was not until the nineteenth century that a sizeable community emerged in Manchester. The first Armenian settlers in Manchester were textile traders, small manufacturers or retailers who came originally from Turkish or

Western Armenia in the Ottoman Empire. Their main purpose in Manchester was to arrange trade connections with Constantinople, Smyrna and Trebizond. While the Greeks in the early nineteenth century controlled most of the foreign trade of the Ottoman Empire, the Armenians had a strong hold on the internal trade. As the demand for English textiles gradually increased, the more enterprising Armenians came to Manchester to procure textiles, either for their own firms or on commission for others. They exported silk, cotton, and other fibres as well as various metals to the Ottoman Empire. By 1848 there were three Armenian merchant houses in the city. The early Armenian community in Manchester was close knit and mobile, visiting Constantinople or Smyrna at least once a year, combining family and business commitments. Some had agencies, or commercial interests in Paris, Marseille, Cyprus and Egypt, where Armenian settlements were already well established. By the 1850's these Manchester merchants were rich, as a Lancashire historian observed: 'the Sultan's dominions were taking more Manchester piece goods than all the European countries put together.'[1] The success of these early immigrants and the events of the Crimean War and the Russo-Turkish War of 1877 encouraged others to follow.

By the end of the nineteenth century there were over fifty Armenian businesses in Manchester alone and a thriving community. Over the years more Armenians came from a wide range of places such as Isfahan, Tabriz, Tehran, Baghdad, and others came from the Caucasus, Tiflis, Athens and Alexandria. During the repressive rule of Sultan Abdul Hamid II over the Ottoman Christian minorities in the late nineteenth century and the massacres of the early twentieth century, more Armenians arrived from Sassun, Van, Moush, Karin and Zeytun. These early Armenians created the nucleus of the present Armenian community. In 1862 there were only sixteen established firms in the city, yet this small community hired a chapel at 151 Rumford Street in Chorlton-on-Medlock. By 1870 they had built their own church in Upper Brook Street, at a cost of nearly £3,000, subscribed by the communities of Manchester, Liverpool and London. It was the first Armenian Church to be built in this country. Various philanthropic organisations, such as the Armenian General Benevolent Union (AGBU) and the Armenian Association of Manchester were established by these early immigrants and they were the pioneers of the Diaspora in Britain.[2]

The Manchester community today is a small community with around 500 families listed in the Armenian Directory and only 200 families are registered on the church mailing list. Manchester may have been a magnet for Armenian merchants from the 1840's to 1914, but surprisingly few of their firms survived for more than a generation. The collapse of the cotton trade after the First World War, climate, health, foreign competition, and the subsequent events in Ottoman Turkey resulted in many Armenians leaving for the United States, particularly California where there is a large and thriving Diaspora community. Many of the younger generation went away to study and did not return. They valued Manchester's educational opportunities, sending their children to good local grammar schools, or public schools as boarders, followed by university and a professional career.[3] Others married and left the area, spreading out from the original heartland of South Manchester into Cheshire, Bradford and Leeds and joining the larger London community. As many drifted away, however, more newcomers from

Cyprus, Iran, Iraq, Lebanon and Syria have added vigour to the older settlement. Unlike many other nationalities whose populations originated in a common location, Armenian families are characterized by geographically dispersed origins. Consequently Armenians have relatives in many countries and most of their ties to family members can be traced to a time prior to their families' settlement in England.

Motives for Armenian Migration

The primary trigger of large scale Armenian emigration from the historic homeland virtually always involved some form of religious persecution, political oppression, forced relocation or escape from physical annihilation. Chapters Two and Three provide such an historical analysis of the mass dispersal of the Armenian people thus providing a broad framework for Armenian dispersion and patterns of migration. Later migration to the United Kingdom, however, from a variety of countries of origin was for the purpose of education or on the initiative of families and individuals. An important factor in migration motives is the extent of social mobility in the host country or more precisely 'the possibility of a distinctive creative, enriching life in tolerant host countries'.[4] Robin Cohen emphasises this characteristic as a significant factor in the success of Diasporas. Nowhere is this more evident than in the Western Diaspora communities since modern pluralist democracies such as the United States, Canada, France and the United Kingdom offer a fair degree of tolerance and security for ethnic minorities. Two of my respondents offer a typical explanation, describing how their short term plans to get an education turned into permanency in England:

I came here in 1978 because I wanted to study engineering. I attended Leeds University, however, when the revolution in Iran broke out, my parents could no longer send me any money. I did manage to get a job to fund my studies so I stayed. Then I met my wife and we eventually settled in Manchester.

I came here first to do research—I was doing atomic chemistry and I had been granted a scholarship from Baghdad. I returned to Baghdad then came back to do further research for my PhD and that is when I met my husband who was also studying here. I did not finish my PhD as by that time I was having a baby and I had to give it up but we settled here.

A family based reason for immigration was for unification with relatives already living overseas, thus people may travel abroad because they are attached to a family or other social network that has migrated. In a chain migration process, several respondents were influenced by contacts in England. Since the propensity to migrate can be transmitted along family networks, having relatives abroad is often correlated with one's own emigration. This approach focuses on networks and emphasises the links that migrating people can access in locations of settlement. Such was the case for one of my respondents, having spent his childhood in Iran, he currently resides in Manchester with his wife and children. His parents still reside in Iran. He explains how he depended on family contacts in order to plan his move to England and assist in his settlement:

My uncle was living in Manchester and he had a good job as a university lecturer. My parents also had some friends living in Stockport. They assisted in all the paper work and I lived with my uncle until I found suitable work and accommodation. They introduced me to many other Armenians who made me feel welcome in their homes and explained about the ways of the English, simple things like transport and going out. My sister wanted to come here with her husband and children but the government would not let her in, so she went to Germany. This was very difficult for her at the time, but now it is easy enough to keep in touch and for us to visit.

Similarly, a Baghdad couple, who visited Manchester over a ten year period to see relatives, were finally able to settle here six years ago with their two sons:

My brother and cousin both had businesses in Manchester, after visiting them for so long and meeting many Armenians that were settled here, we yearned to set up home here and wanted our sons to be educated here. We were very lucky, they helped us considerably, not so much financially but with the system you know and both our boys are now at university in Manchester. I am a freelance artist and my wife helps with the cooking for the church luncheons. I miss my mother and father but they wanted the best for us so they understand.

Indeed according to the interviews conducted, information and emotional support is far more frequently exchanged than financial remittances between family members. A characteristic of a transnational community is transnational relations with relatives or individuals in other Diaspora communities. One of the factors leading to the emergence of transnational networks is the ease and speed of communication and travel, by comparison with earlier dispersions where immigration often led to isolation from family and friends. According to my sources, many Armenians have taken other Armenian families and friends in from a variety of places whilst they have looked for accommodation and employment. The moral support and connections provided by informal networks are able to open many avenues for new immigrants. When funds are extended, they tend to be unidirectional, mostly to parents in their countries of birth. Today, many authors[5] emphasize the role of information, informal networks for finding work and adapting to a new environment in sustaining Diaspora communities. Such networks include personal relationships, family and household patterns, friendship and community ties, and mutual help in economic and social matters. These links provide vital resources for individuals and groups—informal networks based on familial connections, or on a common place of origin, that bind Diaspora communities in a complex web of social roles and interpersonal relationships. Thus contemporary immigrants can easily sustain their kinship networks globally.

Kotkin views Diaspora cultures as expansionary groups being manipulated to exploit new opportunities in what he refers to as 'the making of global tribes'. Kotkin argues that strong Diasporas are the key to determine success in the global economy, and are likely to possess three characteristics, namely: a strong identity; an advantageous occupational profile; and a passion for knowledge. A strong ethnic identity fosters distance from the larger society that can be used for creative purposes. Furthermore, their unwavering loyalty to the Diaspora community inspires confidence born from their strong sense of identity. Certainly the persecutions suffered in the homeland, the denial of the opportunity to develop their own country, and their minority status in dispersion has combined to drive the Armenians to succeed whenever conditions were favourable. Therefore, the persistent quest for economic well being and educational achievement in Diaspora settings was a form of compensation for the Armenians' inability to develop their homeland as well as a device to achieve a sense of security in foreign environments.[6] Thus, Diasporas are outsiders as well as participants, comparing and learning from their experiences in the host country and other societies. Those members of society who belong to a Diaspora characteristically have an advantageous occupational profile, are more strongly represented in the professions and are less vulnerable to a volatile labour market. Finally, a passion for knowledge is characterised by a desire for education, specifically degrees, vocational or professional qualifications, which are the passports of the successful members of a Diaspora.[7] The Armenians in the case study often referred to their enjoyment of material and social advantages that are difficult to obtain in their countries of origin, including a higher standard of living, a greater degree of personal autonomy, friendly social relations in public settings, numerous cultural amenities, a wide range of occupational opportunities, easier access to higher education, freedom from military service and a welcome release from the political uncertainties of the Middle East. For instance:

> We bought this house in 1938. Both our daughters went to boarding school and then university. We have done really well. I cannot understand all these refugees these days moaning and wanting greater facilities, they should be proud to be here, look what Britain has to offer—what do they say when in Rome. The English have been good to us. This is a Christian country and it should remain so. We wouldn't be allowed such freedom in other countries. Take it from someone who knows.

> When I came to this country I was only seventeen years old, I came to study at university and as such I did not have to do my military service in Iran. My brother is still in Iran and they are struggling, his family that is, it is difficult for them. I feel proud to be here and would never consider going back to Iran. I have a good job and a good standard of living.

A central feature of migration networks is that they span national borders and often allow elements of communal interaction, transnational social spaces, to develop between discrete nation states. Such networks ranging from personal contacts among family members and friends to migration channels (broad patterns of social linkage developed within religious or social groups, academic networks and cultural communities).[8] While Armenian emigrants travel across geographic spaces and national borders, many remain within familiar networks and these provide newcomers with resources and a sense of familiarity in otherwise unknown settings. As such the culture shock associated with moving is moderated. Migrants may be in a different environment but in coming here they are able to maintain a way of life socially and linguistically, and even in terms of diet and recreation that is not very much different from the one they left behind. Accordingly their experience of migration may be quite distinct from that conjured up in established literature that assumes geographical movement equates with loss of ties and social interaction. Reflecting the power of Armenian networks, one respondent describes her feelings of comfort:

> My Armenian friends are only a phone call away, or I can hop in the car or on the train to London. In London they have many Armenian cultural events which I try and attend. It is such a comfort to listen to the children recite Armenian poetry or watch them dance. We always get together and put on some good Armenian food. Apart from the climate, it is just the same, we move in the same circles.

A representative from the Armenian Institute explained how they are able to help newcomers, emphasising how all Armenians are aware of the community organisations:

> It is not that obvious to outsiders but we are a very close knit community. Just by virtue of being Armenian you will very quickly learn of the various formal or informal organisations that are accessible to many. Like all immigrants, Armenians naturally face many challenges upon arrival: immigration papers, employment, housing, insurance, legal advice etc., When they arrive in England most people are a little lost, as we all are in the beginning. I am able to supply all the information they need about schooling, banks, housing and doctors. We try to help each other and this enables them to settle more easily. It is not easy when you are faced with lots of paperwork in any situation. Furthermore, we hold numerous cultural events throughout the country in an effort to bring us all together.

To designate a community as transnational it should possess certain qualities and characteristics including the community's recognisable presence in different parts of the world. A normal pattern of concentration might involve many countries with the largest community concentrated in one specific country, like the Armenians and Jews in the United States and the rest in smaller clusters. The American Armenian community is estimated at 1.5 million of which nearly half live in California. Armenians commonly have access to informal networks in many countries that can provide a broad range of resources ranging from job opportunities, housing and social life. The fact that Armenians are involved in chain migration and rely on transnational networks is consistent with the literature on voluntary migration.[9] By way of example:

> We have family and friends in America, you know there is a place called Little Armenia there. We have visited several times and we know all about how to apply for a Green Card and which avenues we need to take. They have many more Armenian organisations there and full time Armenian schools. We receive a lot of information via email regarding job opportunities. Our children are at primary school at the moment, however, but when they are a little older that is where we would like to settle.

> There are lots of Armenians in California. Some of our family live there. I have only been once but I regularly receive newsletters and newspapers as well as

emails from the Armenian organisations in America. A lot of Armenian academics live in America—mind you they come here to talk to us. They are much more active over there also, lobbying the government on political issues. Mind you there are many more of us there. There are literally hundreds of Armenian organisations. The community is open to all Armenians and they make you feel very welcome. I would like to go live there eventually.

Despite the virtually free movement of capital in the age of globalisation, no countries welcome mass migration. Members of a Diaspora have benefited where states sanction selective migration such as the enticement of business migrants and the relative laxity in respect of family migration particularly in the United States. Notwithstanding the official control of migration, there has been the rapid development of a 'migration industry' comprising lawyers, travel agents, recruiters who sustain links with origin and destination and who are driven by financial considerations. Points of departure and arrival, however, are also linked by friendship and ethnic networks organised by the migrants themselves. Restrictions on immigration have also revitalised old Diaspora practices, that of sojourning. Many of today's migrants are people of considerable wealth and portable skills who are helped by the global communications and transport revolutions, by the need for states to attract foreign investment, by the legal protection accorded to minorities in receiving countries and by the custom of sojourning itself. A diasporic consciousness with roots in several locations is highly familiar with networking and sojourning as opposed to permanent settlement in one nation state.[10]

Migration networks therefore are not unidirectional. Just as they facilitate exit, they allow migrants to stay in touch with their country of origin and expedite return if they so desire, thus maintaining links with their country of origin. Such factors as flexible notions of ethnic identity, access to and participation in social networks, family history in several nations, and the ability of people to sustain cultural competence and legal status in more than one single society allows Armenians to maintain meaningful relationships in multiple settings at one time. For example:

I travel back to Iran twice a year to visit family and friends. My father is involved with the Armenian Church so he knows most of the Armenian community in Tehran and indeed Isfahan, where I was born. When he comes here to visit he assists in the church service. I have recently been offered a job also which I am considering. It would be relatively easy for me to go back and work in Iran for a while if I so wished. I still hold an Iranian passport.

I worked in America and Argentina for a while before returning to Manchester. I am originally from Iraq and travel back to visit relatives but I have children now so we are settled for the time being.

The experience of Armenian migrants emphasises their ability to combine resources and networks from multiple locations in order to maximise their freedom and independence from the confines of any one nation state. Transnational networks clearly provide Armenians with a variety of resources, however, given the diverse characteristics of Armenian dispersal, and the varied locations in which they settle, it is important to note that these networks provide different resources to their members, reveal disparate criteria for participation, and may be more or less exclusive in permitting people to join. With this in mind migrant networks are capable of restricting membership and withholding benefits as well as providing resources. By way of example, Robert Mirak[11] comments on the alienation of the more recent Armenian immigrants from the Republic of Armenian (Hayastantsis) in California who are charged with living off the welfare system, an anathema to the self-reliant older generation, and therefore excluded in many instances from communal assistance. Furthermore, whenever there is a crime within the Armenian community it is blamed on the Hayastantsis. Thus they may provide new opportunities to some, while limiting the options of others.

In the few historical accounts of Armenian immigration to the United States, scholars have capitalized on the cultural characteristics of Armenians with regard to the demands of immigrants by dominant American society.[12] The Armenians' skill as entrepreneurs and those valued by American society made it possible for them to succeed. In addition many have highlighted the Armenian love of and value for education as a reason for their upward mobility in the United States. Henry notes in summarising her findings on occupational mobility that for Armenians education has been the major avenue for occupational mobility. It was evident for some Armenians in the sample that their reputation was extremely important to them. For example 'everyone knows how hard working we are' or 'we strive to be successful, you must always work hard and get a good education'. With this in mind it could be argued that the stereotypical views about the Hayastantsis are as much to do with class as it does with ethnic identity. The recent immigrants from Soviet or the Republic of Armenia to America did not bring any money with them thus entering a lower social class. Therefore the stereotypes that divide their community are influenced by American society that castigates those that contaminate their country. These comparisons are used by insiders and outsiders in order to measure a group's perceived attributes as good immigrants who do not contaminate American society.[13] Thus, ethnic groups involve the positing of boundaries in relation to who can and cannot belong, according to certain criterion which are heterogeneous, ranging from the credentials of birth, language or conforming to cultural or other symbolic practices. In other words, the way in which membership of an ethnic group is demarcated is socially motivated and depends upon the preferences of its members. The fact that the recent Hayastantsis do not possess entrepreneurial skills or a strong work ethnic, the established members of the Diaspora may exclude them. In other words how the boundary is contructed is not only diverse but is also contextual and relational to other groups.[14]

Like other social structures, access to migrant networks and the resources they may provide is a conditional process. They vary according to the characteristics of the migrants in question, the nature of the receiving society, conditions in the country of origin and other factors. Information may be passed on by one channel but motivation to move may come from another. Networks may shape motives for settlement in a particular country and patterns of adjustment, however, they are not accessible to all and different networks may offer their members dissimilar resources. Nevertheless, by understanding migration as a network based progress, we can consider both macro and micro factors and integrate them into the rich fabric that links and shapes migration. The network approach emphasises that migration is embedded in a series of political, ethnic, familial and communal relationships, including some that cross borders. Migrating populations often remain connected to more than one national context.[15] The network model is particularly useful therefore for understanding the experience of the Armenian Diaspora because they regularly have access to transportable skills, border-crossing social ties and can often obtain resources in multiple locations.

The Community

The internal differentiation of Armenians and the apparent absence of readily identifiable corporate interests is not easily applicable to Cohen's ethnic group viewed as 'interest group'.[16] Cohen argues that ethnicity should be regarded as a type of political resource for competing groups. Moreover, among non-Armenians there is little or no awareness of Armenians either as a category or a distinct ethnic community. One of my respondents stated 'all the way through school everyone thought I was Jewish, they just assumed my sister and I was Jewish—I used to say we are Armenian but they were not interested'. The identification of Armenians with Jews is not a new phenomenon. Christopher Walker writes of the myth of the 'Armenian Jew' which has emanated from the historical stereotype of the Armenians as clannish and good business men.[17] Similarly one woman claimed her eldest daughter when applying to university to study geography, the tutor said to her 'are you Indian, because she was olive skinned and because Indian names are difficult to pronounce, you see even if they are university lecturers they do not know who we Armenians are'. Indeed few people know where Armenia is, what language they use and what religion they are. They do not compete with non-Armenians as a group either occupationally, residentially or educationally in terms of the discernment of others. In other words Manchester Armenians often work beside one set of people, live beside another and spend their free time with another set of Armenians. On the whole interaction between Armenians takes place outside their other activities rather than in terms of them. Thus within these other activities Armenian identity may be of little or no importance.

With regard to their employment and their residence, their Armenian identity is secondary and sometimes irrelevant. Since information on place of employment is not available for Armenians in the British National Census Records, there are no comprehensive statistical records on the distribution of occupation and workplace for Armenians. From my observations and discussions with Armenians it is possible to state with reasonable certainty that there is no concentration of Armenians in any specific workplace or industrial sector, with the exception of small family run businesses. As such the dispersal of Armenians throughout a variety of places of employment may be associated with the types of occupations Armenians are commonly employed in. They do appear to be concentrated in the skilled white collar or professional sector and educational levels appear to be high and several of my respondents had received University education in this country. Clearly this sample is not intended to be representative; however, it has been very common for Armenians arriving in Britain with the original purpose of furthering their education to settle here subsequently. That is to say that for some Armenian immigrants, England was pre-selected for its educational facilities and unsurprisingly many of those now settled in Manchester and London have attained high educational levels.

Manchester Armenians are residentially dispersed throughout most areas in Manchester and they do not form a visible concentration of shops and restaurants catering to an ethnic population. Although there is no data available for the Manchester community, if one considers the maximum figure quoted for the size of the Armenian population in Greater London of 18,000 and that this is scattered over a city with a population of nine million, even a relatively greater presence of Armenians in several boroughs (there are more Armenians in Acton, Ealing, Chiswick, Wembley and Muswell Hill i.e., the affluent residential suburbs of West and Northwest London) does not, by any means demonstrate a concentration sufficient to leave a visible ethnic stamp on any one residential area. Therefore, Armenians are not giving priority to residential location in the establishment and maintenance of relationships with their ethnic cohorts. As Talai[18] suggested in his 1989 study of the London Armenians, there may be external factors such as income and accessibility to a wide range of accommodation which facilitate the residential dispersal of Armenians, however, there are grounds for believing that this pattern is not entirely coincidental. The more dispersed Armenians are the more invisible socially they are and the more invisible they are the greater their freedom of movement within the non-Armenian host society.

The social anonymity of Armenians in Manchester is due not only to their small numbers but also because Armenians seek to maintain a low profile. Armenians are not easily distinguishable in terms of their appearance and both men and women dress along contemporary European lines, and are often mistaken for different nationalities. They are usually highly competent linguistically and indeed some may speak two or three languages fluently. All my respondents spoke English with relative ease and many had prior knowledge of the language before settling in this country. Both St Sarkis in London and Holy Trinity in Manchester are in secluded areas and provide no external indication of the Armenian character of the churches, with the exception of a small plaque. Combined with the fact that the majority of Armenians belong to the Armenian Apostolic Church or some other Christian denomination, they have no diacritical ethnic markers which make it easier for them to be inconspicuous in Manchester and elsewhere in England.

The only area in which Armenian identity is publicly noticeable is the fact that almost all Armenians have retained an Armenian surname distinguishable by ending 'ian' or 'yan'. I am only aware of one person whose name did not correspond to this rule and he had no idea why this was the case. One respondent informed me that she was advised to change her name because it would enable her to gain employment as a teacher. Also a head teacher had suggested that she write something on her application form that suggested she was white. Neither do Armenian parents appear to be in any hurry to endow their British born children with Anglicised Christian names. All of my respondents had Armenian Christian names, including the youngest members of the group.[19] Two of my respondents who were Armenian women and had married non-Armenian men did take their husband's surname so they were functioning with a name which gave no indication of their origin. The same applies to children of mixed marriages where the husband is non-Armenian, however, one of my respondents adopted her mother's maiden name. An ethnically identifiable surname signifies to all Armenians that this person may be 'one of them', however, Armenian names in themselves need not necessarily identify Armenians to outsiders but they do identify the person as not of British origin, as an immigrant. It is possible, therefore, that Armenians may be categorised on the basis of their country of origin.

People with mixed ethnic backgrounds present interesting cases as they have at least two ethnic groups from which to claim and negotiate an ethnic identity. Root[20] identifies four basic reasons why a multi ethnic person would choose to identify with a particular group regardless of how others may view them. Firstly, one enhances their sense of security by understanding a distinct part of their ethnic heritage. Secondly, parental influences stimulated by the encouragement of grandparents promote identity, thereby granting permission to make a choice. Thirdly, racism and prejudice associated with certain groups lead to sharing experiences with family, thereby assisting the individual to develop psychological skills and defence mechanisms. The shared experiences help to build self-confidence and create the sense that one can cope with the negative elements often associated with the group. Fourthly, gender alignment between parents and children may exert influence on ethnic and racial group formation.[21]

Interestingly, Talai suggests that Armenians may sometimes use their Armenian identity to disassociate themselves from any potentially negative cultural traits which may be associated by non-Armenians with their country of origin. He uses the example of a Lebanese-Armenian woman who was involved in a conversation with an Englishman who criticised the vulgarity of Lebanese women. The Lebanese Armenian pointed out that the reason she was different was that although she was from Lebanon she was Armenian. Similarly a Lebanese Armenian boasted about how, when on holiday, people had not been able to work out her nationality and they assumed she was either Arabic or Jewish. Within the same conversation she also referred to the alleged vulgarity of Lebanese women unlike German and French women, presumably excluding herself as an Armenian from this appraisal.[22]

Within an Armenian context, country of origin becomes emphasised to make a distinction between groups of Armenians. Armenians may characterise themselves as Lebanese, Egyptian, Iraqi, Iranian, Middle Eastern or Armenian depending on the circumstances and depending on whom they are talking to. The important advantage the Armenians have in Manchester is their relative social anonymity, thus most non-Armenians have no stereotypical ideas about what being Armenian means, how they dress, how they speak, what are their customs. Therefore an Armenian can portray their ethnicity to a non-Armenian and stress particular aspects of it, such as Greek or Iranian origin and distinctiveness without fear of challenge. By way of example, two respondents emphasised that they could not eat food prepared by Iraqi Armenians stating that it was just not the correct way to prepare this particular Armenian dish. Likewise an Armenian Lebanese woman when trying to emphasise the unique nation status of her ethnicity to a young English woman, stressed that although originating from Lebanon, she was not Arab. To make the point she stated that 'Lebanon is not my home and very few Armenians picked up any Arabic customs'. The relationship of Armenians to Lebanon was not challenged by their non-Armenian listener because she had never heard of Armenians before.[23] Arguably had this been said during an Armenian gathering there would no doubt have been a heated argument, for many Armenians agree that they have been influenced by the cultures of the different countries in which they originated. As one 93 year old Armenian man stated to me:

> Culture is something or nothing, when somebody says what is your culture, how can you possibly answer that, everyone is different. We are all a mixture we Armenians, we embrace some things and discard others. We can, however, say we are Armenian because we are the same religion, we may or may not speak the language proficiently but we are one people. We have our writings, our history, our books—whether we use it or not it is there for us should we wish to.

The identification of another person as a fellow member of an ethnic group implies sharing the criteria for judgement—'two people playing the same game'. The critical feature of an ethnic group for Barth is the characteristic of self-ascription and ascription by others, in terms of general identity, determined by origin and background. Essentially, belonging to an ethnic group implies possessing certain characteristics judged by others and oneself relevant to that identity, none of which can be categorised within a descriptive list of objective cultural differences. Clearly the mutability and variability of an ethnic group's cultural characteristics demonstrates that it is misleading to view ethnic groups as individuated by their cultures. It is necessary to look at the scope of the group, which may in reality be determined by other factors, so that a common culture may serve as a focus for group identification rather than being what generates the boundaries of the group. This relationship permits the possibility of development of their social relationship to include practically all areas of activity. Conversely, a 'dichotomization' of others as not belonging, strangers, limiting understanding and restriction of interaction to areas of assumed common understanding and mutual interest.[24]

Bhabha emphasis the constantly changing boundaries of Diaspora communities and the narratives which constitute their collective cultural discourses by those cultural hybrids that have lived because of migration or exile in more than one culture. As a construct it refers to the state of hybridity where we are asked to examine the overlapping edges and mixing of cultures.[25] The Armenian Diaspora bears the traces of specific cultures, languages and histories which have shaped them but they are the product of several interlocking histories and cultures. As Chambers stresses 'ethnicity is always open and incomplete involving the continuous reinvention and reconstruction in which there is no fixed identity'.[26]

When discussing the manner in which they established friendships upon first arrival or settlement in Manchester, only two stated that they had made friends in their residential neighbourhood and one of these had established relationships through his management of a local post office. By friendships I explained to my respondents that I meant friendship to mean a relationship that goes beyond casual and brief 'passing the time of day' encounters of the street. One respondent stated 'our neighbours are lovely people, we always say 'hello' or 'good morning' but we have lived here ten years and they have never been in our house and we haven't been in theirs'. He further stated 'I like English people, all the people I work with are English, no sorry one is Irish but we do not socialise together'. Similarly, one lady told me:

> I work in a primary school and one of my children attends the school . . . my little girl has lots of English friends and goes for tea, however, I do not socialise with English people, my husband is Armenian and when we have free time, we visit our Armenian friends as a family, it is just more comfortable for us.

Thus Armenians do not congregate through residential location, occupation, nor educational establishments. There are no full time Armenian schools in London or Manchester. The only Armenian educational establishment in Manchester is the Armenian Supplemental School which meets for four hours weekly on a Sunday at the Armenian Church. This is in sharp contrast to the American Armenian community. In the late sixties and seventies a more prosperous community, expanded by newcomers from the Middle East and encouraged by the national revival of ethnic studies, established full day professionally staffed and well financed schools with Armenian and non-Armenian curricula. There are twenty one full time schools and these operate in addition to the seventy current Saturday language schools. The growth of parochial schools is also evident in the Canadian Armenian community where the Canadian government, prompted by the French speaking minority in Quebec, has encouraged multiculturalism and given financial support to ethnic minorities.[27] Armenians who have received some part of their education in Britain, however, have attended a non-Armenian school where the Armenian language, history, religion or cultural traditions form no part whatsoever of the curriculum. The implications of this for education and fluency in the Armenian language are a deep concern amongst some Armenians and will be discussed later in this chapter. Therefore where and when Armenians get together and interact with one another occurs within their leisure time in the exchange of visits between private homes, and through participation in Armenian Church and association sponsored events. If Armenians wish to come together they must make a conscious effort to do so due to their dispersed nature. This can be exceptionally difficult however, due to family or work commitments or indeed mobility restrictions.

Most regular contact between Armenians occurs within their leisure time in the exchange of visits between homes and participation in community based gatherings. Leisure time can mean different things to different people. Not all Armenians in the sample study were employed outside the home, some are retired and some women were engaged in the full time management of the home. By way of example, one of my respondents, an architect by trade who had worked with non-Armenians, had been actively involved in the Manchester community throughout his working life but since his retirement and the onset of chronic arthritis he was unable to attend any of the community based gatherings, let alone the church, unless his daughter was able to drive him. Another respondent, a woman with two young children could no longer attend the church but still had regular contact with other Armenians but these usually took place at home or their homes. Keeping up with church or community based gatherings can often prove difficult. Furthermore, they often do not live in close proximity to their Armenian friends and have to travel long distances in order to be with other Armenians. Thus the Armenian community is far from all embracing and to be involved in it as an active member requires a conscious effort at communicating and making time to be with Armenians. It takes time and commitment to be an active member of the Armenian community; however, this has raised rather than weakened the awareness of Armenians about their ethnic identity and community.

The Armenian Apostolic Church

Much of the community activity in Manchester revolves around the Holy Trinity Armenian Apostolic Church and its associated organisations. The church has adopted many English ways, the increased use of English in the services and the promotion of Men's and Women's associations. The Armenian Ladies Association of Manchester was founded in 1908 under the chairwomanship of Mrs Akabi Jamgochian. The association's aims were to help the community socially and educationally; to raise funds for needy Armenians elsewhere; and to support the Holy Trinity Church by caring for the priest's vestments, the fabric of the church and the flowers etc., The Armenian Association of Manchester, also known as the Young Men's Club was established in 1911. Its Articles of Association claim that 'every Armenian can become a member by paying the fixed subscription'. Its purpose was threefold: to have a centre where Armenians can gather to further their moral, physical and cultural development; give moral and financial help to national benevolent purposes; and have no connection with political parties. The moral, physical and cultural development was to take the form of lectures and debates, musical and theatrical presentations and social evenings and outings.[28]

The church, for Armenians away from the homeland, is more than a place of worship; it is a symbol of their national identity and unity as being a focal point for the community. Indeed the Armenian Church throughout its long history has been committed to its struggle to maintain the spiritual, cultural and political identity of the dispersed Armenian communities throughout the world. No other institution has had a greater impact on shaping the national identity of Armenians than the Armenian Apostolic Church. The Armenians have the distinction of being the first nation to adopt Christianity in 301 AD, despite sustained pressure to convert to Zoroastrianism and indeed Islam from the eighth century onwards. In these circumstances of adversity, the Armenians viewed themselves as the 'flock of New Israel', 'uz-hod nor Israeli' committed to the Christian faith, which eventually became the ideological foundation of a peculiar religio-cultural nationhood centred in the Armenian Apostolic Church. Therefore, as discussed earlier the establishment of Christianity is a crucial landmark in Armenian history, not merely for its importance in the fourth century, but because to contemporary Armenians, church and faith appear to have been the fundamental instruments, shaping and preserving the Armenians as a people. The creation and dissemination of the belief that 'we are a chosen people' has been crucial for ensuring long term ethnic survival. Moreover, Armenians throughout the ages have regarded themselves not simply as a 'people' 'zhoghovurd' but as a 'nation' 'azg' even after the loss of independent statehood. This sense of ancient nationhood has also persisted in diverse Diaspora settings throughout the centuries.[29]

Practically all of the Armenians in the sample described being Armenian as their most immediate and powerful base of identity. They viewed themselves and other Armenians as members of the same ethnic group despite linguistic, class and geographical differences. All Armenians young and old mentioned their pride in being the first nation to adopt Christianity thus implying that there is an essence to their identity. In the past this belief was fostered to establish difference and indeed superiority as Christians among Muslim powers. As Smith suggests 'religion has provided the most intense energy for many pre-modern ethnies, especially those who have evolved a myth of ethnic election'.[30] Arguably religions can provide additional cohesion to bind a diasporic consciousness but they do not comprise Diasporas in and of themselves. Most Armenians profess to be members of the Armenian Apostolic Church, many Irish, Poles and Italians are Catholic, and Judaism may unite members of the Israeli Diaspora. Indeed such an overlap between religious faith and ethnicity is likely to complement social cohesion. Secular members of these communities, however, are part of their respective Diasporas. Furthermore the myth and idealization of a homeland and return movement is absent in the case of religions. As Cohen states 'one might suggest that their programmes are extraterritorial rather than territorial'.[31]

Nevertheless, the church stands as a focal point for Armenians and the Manchester church holds services on the first Sunday of every month which is attended by many from the city and surrounding areas. Powerful conservative forces appear to keep the church alive. The fear of assimilation has strengthened the church and its social and educational activities as a national focus. An effort is being made to promote an English educated clergy and the church is served by a priest who is studying theology at Mirfield College which is affiliated to Leeds University. The liturgy is long and has changed little over the centuries, however, a new service book has been introduced in Manchester in the last four years which has come from California. Alongside the Armenian script is a transliteration in English letters and then the English translation. The Armenian Church, although very firm in its theological position is open and tolerant towards other denominations and faiths. Its motto is 'Unity in essentials, Liberty in doubtful matters and Charity in all things'. Perhaps because of their history, their constant contact with people of many cultures and religions, their extensive trade routes and their patterns of migration, there is a genuine recognition that different religions, national languages and cultures are all complementary. One Armenian cleric who had lived in war-torn Lebanon described the Armenians' attitude to warring neighbours as one of 'positive neutrality', an uncomfortable position to be in, one might imagine, but one with which the Armenians are all too familiar.

During the 1960's the church cellars were cleared, cleaned and converted into a social centre by the resident priest's three children and their student friends. Members of the Armenian community donated money and provided a kitchen, toilets, central heating and furniture for the centre which can accommodate over 100 people. Indeed over the years Armenians have become skilled and dedicated fund raisers. During the late nineteenth century, members of the Armenian community were aware of the terrible events that were taking place in the Ottoman Empire and the suffering that many of their families and friends were facing. They began not only to raise funds but to raise awareness among the authorities and local people in order to assist their campaigns. Hundreds of thousands of pounds were sent to relieve those suffering from the effects of famine, to build orphanages for the survivors of the genocide and more recently to support the victims of the earthquake which hit the town of Spitak in 1988.

When Diasporas are involved in issues that extend beyond the borders of their host country, the significant actors apart from the Diaspora communities are the host government and to a lesser degree, transnational institutions. The scope and intensity of Diaspora activities including those that affect international relations are determined by the material, cultural and organisational resources available to them. Opportunities in some countries are not equally available to all migrant groups. Some minorities experience severe constraints while others are free to pursue their interests. More importantly Diaspora activity depends on their inclination and motivation—a call to unity to maintain their solidarity and exert group influence.[32] The point to be made is that activities by Diaspora communities including those that relate to international affairs vary as much with the opportunities available to them as with their skills and resources.

By way of example, the Hayestan Fund was set up within days of the earthquake—Hay being the Armenian name they give to themselves and the church in Manchester became a depot for the sacks full of clothing donated by sympathisers. This small community raised £25,000 for three pre-fabricated houses, which were flown to Armenia in a Russian cargo plane and were erected by a team of Lancashire firemen. The community raised a further £7,000 for an ex-Ministry of Defence mobile bakery and the firemen again volunteered to set it up. In addition the struggle for Nagorno Karabagh and the blockade of Armenia added to the tiny republic's problems. Noteworthy among the many charities at the time was Aid Armenia Northwest which provided medical supplies, beds and lockers. In 1999 Dr Nahabedian, a surgeon from Lebanon, living in Cheshire, and local volunteers shipped medical goods valued at £100,000 for use in a Karabagh old people's home and a Yerevan hospital.[33]

The Armenian Church also serves as a Sunday school and classes have been set up during the last ten years in an attempt to keep the Armenian language alive. The social centre is also used for Armenian dance, folk music, celebrations, meetings and lunches. Folk and liturgical music and dance remains extremely popular both in informal and professional groups. On the notice board that greets people in the entrance to the hall is the following poem, a powerful reminder of what it means to be Armenian:

> A nation smothered with the blood of its own sons and daughters
> One and a half million,
> One and a half million innocent lives
> Buried with dreams still in their eyes
> Rivers of blood, pyramids of corpses

Disgrace to humanity, bewilderment of sanity
A nation was to be swallowed
By the darkest appetite of history
A race was to be vanished
And another denying its attempt to kill
Like smoke in the night
A nation was to die!
But it was reborn, resurrected
The seeds of the fading flower grew taller
And the one and a half million, doubled, tripled
Standing tall, remembering . . .

Only a small proportion of the Manchester residents regularly attend the Church Divine Liturgy which is held on the first Sunday of every month. There is usually between thirty and eighty people attending the church, and community based activities every month, however, the community organisations remain important focal points. With a population residentially and occupationally dispersed, the Armenian community activities remain the most visible and permanent markers of the Armenian presence in Manchester. Furthermore, they appear to be traditional landmarks of Armenian communities worldwide. Most of the communities from which the Armenians originate all appear to have had a church and in most cases a school and a community centre. Being unpaid volunteers, most of the organisers of the Manchester Armenian activities do so in their spare time and a large number of people have been successfully attracted towards a commitment to unremunerated service and thus developing and sustaining their community. The only fundamental issue which has the consensus of all the Armenian associations, however, is that Armenian ethnicity should be preserved and that organised voluntary action must be taken in order to preserve it. What form this organisation should take, what actions it should undertake, who is best equipped or most committed for the undertaking of these tasks are issues by no means agreed upon. In a population dispersed and heterogeneous as the Manchester Armenians, where a community is defined and maintained in terms of public collective gatherings, no matter how infrequently, this enhances the very existence of the community, rather than hastens its dissolution.

The Armenian Church, in its capacity as a permanent marker of the Armenian community, and its affiliated organisations is also able to serve as a gateway into the community. Indeed the Armenian community based organisations play an important role in introducing new members of the community to established members, and in maintaining contacts between Armenians locally as well as globally. A newly arrived Armenian who has few previously established contacts with Armenians in Manchester, and no knowledge of the activities of the Armenian associations can be fairly confident that if an active community does exist, it will have an operating Armenian church. The social activities at the Armenian Church can provide initial personal contacts with other Armenians as well as information about the activities of other Armenian associations. As new members to the community develop their contacts, both personal and associational, they are able to be far more selective about the manner of their participation in the Manchester Armenian community and their dependence on the institutions is inevitably weakened over time.

The Armenian organisations not only provide a framework for new relationships but can also provide the means for previously established relationships to be reactivated. This is particularly evident when Armenians who would not normally attend regular church services attend memorial services, such as April 24th Martyrs Day, or Christmas or Easter services. The drawing power of the churches on these occasions can provide Armenians with the opportunity to meet new acquaintances or friends with whom they have lost contact. For some Armenians this provides the impetus for attending church, as one respondent claimed 'I always attend the special church services because I met someone I used to go to school with in Iran and we have kept in contact ever since. You never know who will be visiting from abroad'. Similarly, one respondent whose parents were visiting England from Iran visited the church whilst they were staying with him: 'it is important for them as they attend church regularly back home, so I took them to church here'. Only a proportion of the Manchester Armenians may attend the church on a regular basis but many more attend the special services or when they have relatives or friends visiting on a nominal basis.

Due to its historic role the Church continues to view itself as fulfilling many of the functions of a state. This is particularly true of the Diocesan Church, which is linked to the homeland through its affiliation with the Catholicosate of Echmiadzin. Certainly for many Armenians the Church has represented the 'visible soul of the absent fatherland' and this is a role that Armenian intellectuals have nurtured over the years, emphasising the coherence of the Armenians due to the efforts of their Church.[34] Nevertheless this idealistic perception does not seem to be borne out by the facts. Moreover the Church is increasingly being relegated to the realm of the symbolic. By way of example, all of the respondents interviewed stressed the importance of Armenia being the first state to adopt Christianity:

> The Armenian Church is the first state Church in the world and we were the first Christians—in every Armenian community there is a church. It is our identity.

> We were the first people in the world to adopt Christianity. The Armenian Church is extremely important it has kept us together.

> In every community we have a church, for us it is not just a religion it is the core of the community. Our church is unique and our hymns are not like other churches. A lot of people have not heard of Armenians but we were the first people to adopt Christianity, our church is very important.

> Everywhere, where ever there are Armenians there will be an Armenian Church, it follows us, we were the first and that is important. Had we not embraced the Christian religion history may be different, however, we did—our church symbolises this . . . we were the first and we are proud of that.

Nevertheless, despite these statements and similar statements that were raised by many people in the focus groups, only two people attended the church on a regular basis, and one of those admitted to not being religious—'I am not a religious man but it is important to keep in touch with other Armenians plus the food is excellent at the church'. Most of the respondents did however attend the church at Christmas and Easter. Furthermore many of the women I spoke to after the church service had not attended the service themselves. They either came to the church halls to prepare the luncheon or to partake of the luncheon or listen to the lectures that were held in the hall. Thus Armenians will visit the Church without actually attending the service inside. In particular the gatherings that take place in and around the churches attract Armenians who might otherwise never visit the institution. Three respondents did not attend the church in Manchester and attended their local parish churches, although they were married in the Armenian Church and their children were baptised there. Only one person admitted to being devoutly religious 'it is only through embracing our unique church can we truly be Armenian because the church encompasses our life force'. According to a former deacon of the London church of St Sarkis in Kensington, 'Armenians were more devout in the Middle East because their host societies were also more devout, but the secular nature of Western societies has unavoidably influenced a trend towards secularization among Armenians residing within them'.[35]

A few respondents expressed regret at the decreasing number attending church, particularly the young, and compared their experiences in their country of origin where there was a much higher attendance however in general it was accepted as a natural and inevitable consequence. For instance:

In Iran we are very separate to the Muslims and we go to church much more often, plus the services are different. . . . I used to really enjoy going to church with my family, my father was connected to the church—what do you call it? Here we can attend any church as it is a Christian nation . . . the Armenian Church means that we are Armenian and we speak Armenian but church is a church, Christ's church there is no difference.

My childhood in Baghdad was very happy and when I was a child I learnt that I was connected to the church. The Priest used to come to the house a lot, over here it is much more difficult. We used to have lots of celebrations and we would all eat together at home with the priest, with lots of singing. It was very nice. It is a shame that we Armenians are now scattered all over the world and things are not done as they used to be, although some people try to keep it going. The world changes, the young are not so much interested in church affairs now, and people have to change too.

Back home the church was much more connected to the community and the priest used to visit us regularly, they do here but you have to make an appointment. It is not the same. The young over here are not interested in going to church . . . it is boring for them, maybe they will change when they get older. . . I would like my boys to attend the church but I cannot force them, they come with us sometimes on special occasions.

The Armenian Apostolic Church, however, as its name suggests is a national church and the priests in London and Manchester do play a significant role in the community outside the church. They can be approached for assistance by Armenians who are neither members of the Armenian Church nor any church or openly atheist. Many Armenians still marry in the church even where the spouse is non-Armenian. Therefore the Armenian Apostolic Church, as an institution distinctive to Armenians, is an important symbol of Armenian ethnicity and its continuity. In this sense the importance of Christianity whether that religion is part of your day to day life has become essentialised. Some Armenians found satisfaction and religious meaning in attending the Armenian Church however, others felt it was simply a way of retaining an Armenian identity, socialising children and gaining access to a community. As Armen Gavakian has suggested in his study of American-Armenians, symbolic religiosity for first and second generation Armenians involves mainly the implicit affirmation of their secular life through the rites of baptism, marriage and death, and participation in major religious holidays and festivals. For those of the third generation who are further along the assimilation scale, the Apostolic Church is on the whole offering very little. In other words more and more Armenians are choosing to attend only the secular activities of the Church and to maintain only a loose association with it, whilst in some cases obtaining their spiritual nourishment elsewhere. Ironically, it seems that the Church by its very nature is particularly suited to play a role in the future of symbolic ethnicity, because of its strong emphasis on national symbols and sacred traditions.[36] As long as there is a building in Manchester designated as the Armenian Apostolic Church and a visiting priest, the Church as an institution will remain, always available in reserve for weddings, baptisms, deaths or on important religious and social occasions such as Christmas and Easter.

One reason why essential cultural definitions are problematic is that even though Armenians do differ from other groups in one way or another, Armenian scholarly discourse falsely assumes that there is an essence of Armenian culture. By way of example, Armenians are not the only ethnic group who place importance on their religion. Thus the church may claim to be the essence of a particular culture but they are common cultural markers for many different groups. Armenians and other ethnic groups, however, continue to define themselves in essential ways and this is perpetuated in a society which asks 'where are you from?' Armenians therefore distinguish themselves from other ethnic groups by stating their religious history—the first official Christian nation. In the context of Britain they are asserting that they are good citizens assuming that Christianity is equated with the West. Religion is therefore used to declare their cultural difference from their countries of origin in the Middle East. For example, 'We come from Iran but we are not Iranian, we are Armenians, Christians'.

The use of Christianity to establish Armenians as the 'ideal immigrant' has been perpetuated by the West's contribution to Orientalism. Edward Said defines Orientalism as 'the study of the Orient by Western scholars who place their culture in direct opposition to the East[37]'—the power of Western scholars to define other cultures in opposition to their own superior culture. Those who were Orientals were backwards and uncivilised as opposed to advanced, civilised and culturally superior Westerners, which is equated with Western Christendom. For instance 'Christian peoples are actually more civilised, much more educated and polite . . . the English have been good to me and we have had a happy life but that is because they are a Christian people'. Thus the Armenians' use of Christianity reinforces their good or ideal immigrant status as it confirms they are most like

Occidentals than Orientals. More importantly it separates the Armenians from 'the dreaded Turks', Muslims who they consider uncivilised and cruel. This is consistent with Barth's analysis that ethnic identity is a means to create boundaries that enable groups to distance themselves from one another.

Armenian Organisations

There has been a significant decrease in the number of traditional ethnic organisations operating on a local and national basis, particularly those affiliated to the Armenian political parties since the emergence of the Independent Republic of Armenia. There has, however, been a significant increase in the form of non-traditional transnational organisations, particularly those task-orientated organisations which provide Diaspora Armenians with the opportunity to engage in development work in Armenia.[38] As discussed previously the Diaspora-homeland relationship is central to Diaspora identity since by definition the Diaspora exists in relation to the territory from which it has emigrated. More importantly it could be argued that modernity has a double impact on ethnic expression in that it acts as a homogenising force in society while at the same time alienating individuals and in doing so reinforcing the search for diversity. Stuart Hall is perhaps the most intuitive observer of this condition:

> The face to face communities that are knowable, that are locatable, one can give them a place. One knows what the voices are. One knows what the faces are. The recreation, the reconstruction of imaginary, knowable places in the face of the global postmodern which has, as it were, destroyed the identities of specific places, absorbed them into this postmodern flux of diversity. So one understands the moment when people reach for those groundings[39].

The search for groundings can be understood as a backlash from the ever widening global opportunities available to confront the challenging of a sense of belonging, a meaningful ethnic identity. For hybrid identity to flourish this involves the restructuring of existing structures and discourses or the creation of new ones. In the case of the American Armenian community, both have occurred, creating a whole assortment of cross cleavages that transcend partisan loyalties.[40] This has a trickle down effect to other Diaspora communities as the American community could be described as the mother community.

The Manchester branch of the Armenian General Benevolent Union (AGBU) is an international organisation known for the schools it has established in Armenian communities throughout the Middle East and in the United States. It was established in Cairo in 1906 by Boghos Nubar Pasha (1851-1930), the son of a former Prime Minister of Egypt, together with some influential friends and has served as an important charitable function as a sort of 'Armenian Red Cross'. Initially the AGBU's purpose was to provide education for Armenians in Ottoman Turkey, in its broadest most practical form. A year later, a co-founder of the charity came to Manchester in search of funds and organisers and a committee was formed. It is also renowned for its literary publications and for its financial assistance to Armenian students who are suffering hardship. Although internationally the AGBU is associated with the Armenian Democratic Liberal Party or Ramgavars, its activities are restricted to cultural and educational matters on a transnational level. As far as I am aware there are no Dashnak organisations operating in Manchester today although there are many Dashnak affiliated organisations operating on a transnational level. Indeed, there are literally hundreds of Armenian organisations operating on a transnational level.[41] Furthermore, today outside of Lebanon the Diaspora political parties could be considered as social clubs, as it is only in Lebanon where they run candidates for office. Moreover, while the history of the political parties, the Dashnaks, Ramgavars and Hunchaks act as a backdrop to contemporary references and claims in Manchester, it is as components of the symbolic repertoire of the Armenian community. For instance:

> In Lebanon and elsewhere in fact, the Dashnaks are the true Armenians, they are very patriotic and they know everything about Armenians, they fly the Armenian flag. Of course, there are other political parties, the Ramgavars are the rich ones you see but we do not belong to any. How it is in England now, the liberals went to be the Social Democrats that is what the Ramgavars are like. The Dashnaks all they ever wanted was for Armenians to be free like in 1918-22. The Dashnaks always they said, we want a free Armenia . . . we do not want the Russians . . . we want a free Armenia, if you see the tricolour flag, that was the Dashnaks. My father was a Dashnak, they always worked the hardest . . . in America it is the same.

> They killed the Archbishop you know the Dashnaks in America . . . they were against the Soviets but they shouldn't have done that. I should say that we do not have the English coldness, we are passionate and strong, you say something to Armenians and they go off the deep end, they are impulsive. Most of the organisations for the young, the scouts Homenetmen[42] are all affiliated to the Dashnaks—you were either one of them or you were against them . . . it is silly now.

> I know that all the people I knew and my family knew did not accept those that were Dashnaks. They were a revolutionary arm, beyond the pale. My father used to say to us, do not talk to them they are Dashnaks, they will get you into trouble.

Among the younger generations of British Armenians, however, there is little knowledge, let alone understanding of the traditional ideological and partisan cleavages that divided their parents and grandparents. Even among those who are aware of those cleavages, there is an overall lack of interest in perpetuating them. By way of example, several of the younger Armenians who participated in the focus groups knew of the Armenian political parties, particularly the Dashnaks and their political activism. They were aware of the history but didn't feel they were relevant now Armenia was an independent republic although they did say that their parents often talked about the divisions between people who had antithetical political views in their countries of origin. Bakalian[43] noted in her study of American Armenians, that there was a significant drop in the influence of Dashnak and anti-Dashnak ideologies and identifiers among the third generation, implying that on the whole these ideologies are able to influence American

Armenian life only to the second generation. For the children of American born parents, the imported political agendas of earlier generations are seen not only as irrelevant but also as harmful. This is despite attempts by many elites to argue that these cleavages are useful in that they heighten the political mobility of the community. With the increasing marginalization of the political parties, especially the Armenian Revolutionary Federation and the emergence of new organisations, of which most are transnational, in the Diaspora it is interesting to compare the success of the different organisations in recruiting Armenians. Among my sources and respondents, however, there was a general agreement about the lack of involvement of English born Armenians in community life, particularly the traditional structures and a general concern over the long term capacity of present organisational forms to embrace and mobilise future generations. There is genuine concern amongst many Armenians regarding the absence of English born Armenians in community life. A church representative stated:

> We need to be able to create something that they want to become involved in and by this I mean we need to understand the younger generation, what it is to be Armenian in England today, we need to connect with their mind set, if that is possible so the church will have to evolve and have different kinds of activities that may attract the youth.

Similarly, an Armenian academic expressed deep concern over the long term capacity of the present organisational forms to mobilise future generations:

> The way things are at the moment, the Diaspora will not be permanent, we are not able to communicate beyond the third generation anything of intellectual value. . . . Our organisations are run by immigrants, and still have immigrant mentalities. We need the third generation, they are still part of our family and it is their forefathers who have built what we have today.

When discussing the lack of youth involvement during the focus groups, the majority of older Armenians blamed the inadequacies of the traditional ethnic organisational structures, particularly the church, in dealing with the problems. The most common response was to reaffirm traditional modes of Armenian identity and much of the debate fell short of offering real solutions to the problems. This lack of involvement is symptomatic in the American Diaspora and an article by Saghrian[44] started off by observing that for many American Armenian youths 'the Armenian Question',[45] political parties, schools, Armenian culture, political activism and similar approaches not only do not exist, but are considered dangerous, since they can threaten their comfortable 'Americanness'. The problem, he argued, was due to a crisis of identity that is characteristic of Western society in general, and which challenges the basic values that have sustained the Armenian nation over the centuries. Furthermore, this problem was intricately related to the malaise in Armenian life in general and called for a more sober assessment of the state of the Diaspora. He does not suggest, however a reassessment of the expectations placed on American Armenian youth, and reaffirmed many of the traditional modes of Armenianness: a sense of belonging to the Armenian culture and homeland; active involvement in Armenian organisations and community life; and learning and speaking the Armenian language.

There is at the same time, however, recognition that events in the Armenian homeland have stimulated interest in Armenia, its culture and heritage. Indeed many of the English Armenian youth were now rallying to the cause of the homeland and homeland issues provided an outlet for feeling Armenian without the stuffiness of traditional institutions. One respondent argued that professionalism is the key to getting the youth involved:

> The way to get the youth involved is for them to become successful, if you work hard and get a good education you can help your communities. Many of the young become actively involved in projects in Armenia, nobody knew these people but after the earthquake they were drawn back into the community. When they get involved in exchange programmes they have a renewed sense of pride in being Armenian. That is the key to get the young involved, they want to do things, make a difference, not just go to church and eat with other Armenians.

The turbulent events in the homeland since 1987 and the Diaspora's response to those events reinforced certain trends in the development of the western Diaspora communities. The traditional organisations were thrown into disarray as their raison d'etre was challenged by the emergence of an independent Republic of Armenia. The institutional malaise, particularly of the traditional organisations was highlighted and the internal crisis, coupled with the Armenian government's policy of favouring non-traditional Armenian organisations, particularly in America, strengthened the alternative organisations. The American Armenian community has been impacted by the massive influx of immigrants from the Soviet Union and the Middle East, and the fusion of American born and immigrant groups was a revitalising experience for both the older and more recent members of the community. Adalian argues that the line separating the two groups has become blurred and has also reinvigorated the Americanised portion of the Armenian community.[46] Thus the homeland provided a rallying point for the English Armenian communities and this development was reflected in the liberation of previously marginalized forces, particularly the young, which experienced a renewed homeland orientation and were able to by-pass the traditional organisations in establishing relationships with the homeland.

One explanation for the emergence of interest in ethnicity beyond the first generation is Marcus Hansen's 'Third Generation Return' which was actually based on the emergence of interest in Swedish history. Hansen argues that 'what the son wishes to forget the grandson wishes to remember'.[47] In other words, the second generation Armenians (that is the children of immigrants) were typically keen to forget their ethnic heritage and simply wanted to make a life for themselves and their children. Many members of the third generation, that is the grandchildren of immigrants, however, seem to take a renewed interest in their ethnic heritage, particularly their history. This suggests that the third generation return may itself only be another variety of symbolic ethnicity. Third generations can obviously attend to the past with far less emotional risk than first and second generation people, who may be still trying to escape it.[48]

Clearly new non-traditional forms of ethnic expression were needed to accommodate the views of a whole generation of Armenians and there is a shift to a greater interest in practical, professional and task-orientated involvement towards the homeland. The eighties and beyond witnessed the emergence of a whole new array of Armenian organisations and movements that offered an alternative to the existing traditional structure and discourses. The Armenian Assembly of Europe representing Armenian organisations acting in European countries focuses its attention on issues relating to international relations, as well as human rights, economic and cultural cooperation. Aid projects for Armenia, lobbying for Karabagh and joining a political action committee such as CRAG (Centre for the Recognition of the Armenian Genocide) are just a few examples of this kind of involvement. There are many youth programmes supported by the Armenian government and various Diaspora organisations designed to keep the young tied to the land, culture, language, religion and people of the Armenian state.

The most popular of these organisations is the Armenian Volunteer Corps which was set up approximately three years ago to provide Diaspora Armenians with the opportunity to engage in long term service and development work in Armenia. Whilst visiting Armenia in May 2002 I spoke to many young Armenians from a variety of host countries who were involved in a variety of projects including building affordable housing, teaching English to orphans, developing small business and improving public health in Karabagh, as well as working on legislation to protect Armenia's cultural heritage. The AVC is sponsored by the Fund for Armenian Relief and will cover volunteers' rent, health insurance and provide an adequate living stipend in Armenia. Those wishing to volunteer their services are required to raise money from their local Armenian community to defray the cost of their travel, thereby becoming a representative of their Diaspora community and a potential link for further support. One of my respondent's children had recently come back from a year's voluntary work in Armenia and was hoping to return and work at one of the many non-governmental organisations NGO's that operates in Armenia. He was involved in several projects there and found the experience extremely valuable, he became fluent in the Armenian language and learnt a lot about the cultural heritage, he said 'he feels more Armenian now and wants to contribute more'.

Involvement in the work of the Land & Culture Organisation (LCO)—a youth programme run by the American Armenian community and supported by the Armenian government, carries great symbolic significance for those involved, since it is an act of preserving the architectural and other visible aspects of the national heritage. Volunteers for this programme, however, have to support themselves whilst in Armenia. By working on the land, the participants develop a stronger sense of their ethnicity and a sentimental attachment to the homeland. At the same time, working on the land is an activity with practical benefit for those living in Armenia, thus appealing to the functional component of British-Armenian ethnicity. When reflecting upon the experiences of visiting the Armenian homeland and indeed their countries of origin many respondents felt it allowed young Armenians to develop a more complete Armenian identity, master the Armenian language and indeed reduce the chances of marrying a non-Armenian. For example:

My son went with the LCO to Armenia. His Armenian language is perfect now and he feels more in tune with his Armenian identity. He worked at the Armenian Development Corporation for three months and is considering taking up a job with them. Mind you we often visit Tehran where my parents live and he has met many young Armenians.

I would like both my children to visit Armenia when they are old enough. It is important that they learn about our customs and meet young Armenians. I know you might think this is bigoted, but I would prefer my children to marry another Armenian.

The opportunity to visit the homeland is wonderful. Ours is such a small community and it gives them the chance to socialise with other young Armenians. It is better when Armenians marry together because you are of the same mind. We can never say to each other—you do not know you foreigner, if your mentality is different, it will never work. There is a Greek saying which translates 'always wear a pair of shoes made in your home town'.

Despite the usefulness of Hansen's thesis, the generational thesis cannot be applied uniformly to all members of the third generation. Its application must be subject to a number of other factors including the place of origin of the immigrant ancestor, community involvement, as well as the influx of new immigrants which makes it difficult at times to distinguish developments owing to generational mobility from those relating to social and economic mobility. Nevertheless, the idea of third generational return provides a useful tool in understanding the phenomenon of renewed ethnic interest. One such example is Michael J Arlen Jr whose father had worked hard to disassociate himself from anything Armenian, and changed his name from Dickran Kouyoumdjian and married a Greek woman. He lived in England for some time before moving to the United States. In his memoirs Arlen Jr recollects a sense of distance between himself and his father (referred to as his 'other side'), which his father refused to discuss even when his son showed signs of curiosity. Arlen became conscious of being escorted throughout his life by a kind of shadow of being Armenian. Arlen eventually took a trip to Soviet Armenia during which he became aware of his own transformation from apathy towards Armenian affairs to an almost prejudiced passion for all things Armenian. Arlen's highly symbolic act of visiting the homeland resulted in his professional and passionate involvement in the American Armenian community and a book written not in Armenian but English, for an American audience, not Armenian.[49]

The Armenian Homeland

For seventy years the dominant discourse portrayed the Diaspora as a temporary condition and the guiding rhetoric was the aspiration of returning to the homeland. The Dashnaks maintained that the Diaspora could not be an end in itself rather it was lived as temporary and transitory: the eventual return to the homeland was deemed essential and inevitable. This notion emerged when the aspirations of a generation of ARF affiliated leaders exiled from Soviet Armenia in the 1920's combined with the hopes of the deracinated survivors of genocide. The Diaspora was to think of itself as exilic, existing provisionally until its eventual return and while it waited, it had to engage in an organised struggle to sustain Armenian identity. [50] The myth of return functions as a source of purpose and destiny for the Diaspora in that it is providing an ideological justification for the perpetuation of the Diaspora and its structures.

Indeed since historical times, Armenians have perceived the Diaspora as a temporary phenomenon, a transient existence that would culminate in the inevitable return to the homeland. The return to the homeland is seen almost as an eschatological concept being viewed as the precondition of collective redemption. Many Armenian clerics use the Christological illustration of death and resurrection when describing the Armenian experience of the genocide and the spiritual imagery of re-birth is often used to describe the re-establishment of the Armenian homeland. This psycho-spiritual predisposition has been a pervasive and persistent feature of the Armenian dispersion, although with the passage of time many Armenians have had to establish roots and a sense of permanence. [51]

Therefore, at least in rhetoric, the Diaspora was presented as a means to an end, the end being the homeland, its restoration and security. At the same time, however, there was an increasing willingness to acknowledge that given the opportunity most Diaspora Armenians would not return to the homeland, at least not to live. The rhetoric about going back is often just that, rhetoric—'we are and most of us will remain Diaspora'. Of the many Diaspora Armenians who have visited Armenia since 1988, only a fraction were likely to settle there permanently. There are marked differences in culture, mentality, and socio-economic conditions between the homeland and the Diaspora. As an American AGBU representative pointed out:

> There is a difference. First of all there is a terrible difference in mentality so that it is like Armenians who come from Armenia or Armenians who come from Beirut . . . there is a great difference in people just as mine is different from being American. So, I mean, I do not think any of those people who have lived here for most of their lives will go to live in Armenia . . . they talk about it but there is no going back[52].

In 1991, the Los Angeles Times featured a very interesting article which examined the phenomenon of return in the light of Armenia's newly found independence. The article explained that 'after decades of exile, Armenians around the world now face the possibility of return to an independent homeland . . . the opportunity presents both a victory of perseverance and a vexing personal dilemma.' The article stated that for many Diaspora Armenians the 'myth of return' was 'the core of their lives'. One interviewee was quoted as saying 'it has all happened so suddenly . . . now the dream is becoming a reality, what do you do?'[53] Certainly from my focus groups and respondents there was a general consensus that the idea of return was idealistic, in theory it is what the Diaspora has embodied but in reality few people want to go and live in Armenia on a permanent basis. Nevertheless many of my respondents felt it was important to visit the homeland. For instance:

It is impossible to understand your identity without visiting your homeland, you need to know where you come from, feel your feet on your own soil. . . . I am too old now, it will kill me if I go there.

It is very important to know your culture so we are arranging a trip next year. Our friends went to Yerevan last year and they were quite upset at what they saw, they are so backward and they could not understand what they were saying . . . their Armenian language is different to ours you know. . . . They said to me the toilets are disgusting wherever you go and you must take your own toilet rolls . . . however I want to go and see for myself.

We should never forget who we are as if an English person is born abroad they retain their culture and self belonging of being British, they visit England. I believe every culture should do that . . . we are a great nation. I have been to Armenia and I fell in love with the place, however, my relatives are in America and that is where we are heading.

It is important to remember that when Diaspora Armenians talk of return to their homeland they are in fact engaging in a process of double imagination as the majority of Armenians in the Diaspora do not originate from the Republic of Armenia. Most Diaspora Armenians originated from Western Armenia in the Ottoman Empire and in reality their true homeland is the lost lands of Anatolia in Turkish Armenia. This being so, the majority of Diaspora Armenians have no practical means of return since resettling in the Anatolian provinces of modern day Turkey is not an option, though some have visited Mount Ararat. It is only the recent migrants, following the break-up of the Soviet Union, that originate from Eastern Armenia, the Republic of Armenia. Nevertheless many Diaspora Armenians travel to the Republic of Armenia as a kind of pilgrimage, a symbolic leisure time gesture towards their homeland.

The fact that Diaspora Armenians relate to the Republic of Armenia is the construct of double imagination as the Armenia imagined by most of the Diaspora is the Armenia of their Western Armenian ancestors and nothing like the Eastern Armenian homeland. Indeed this double imagination is highlighted through greater interaction between the Diaspora and the homeland and the realization of the differences between these people. This gap is more evident in the Western Diaspora. Armenians living in Western countries are the least likely to migrate to Armenia, since modern pluralist democracies such as the United States, Canada, France and the United Kingdom offer tolerance and reasonable security to ethnic minorities. Moreover there are obvious economic advantages in remaining in these countries and very little to entice the Diaspora back to the homeland on a permanent basis. All this could, of course, change if the homeland was to achieve greater economic and political stability or extend its boundaries to include historic Armenian territories in Turkey. Armenians may also be more likely to return if the economic conditions in the host country deteriorated or there was persecution. Thus instead of fleeing from one host country to another, they might seek permanent settlement in the homeland. An article in the Armenian Review, written in 1987 pointed out that:

American Armenians will stay put because they like peace, prosperity and freedom and because they are losing their identity . . . the ones who might realistically be expected to return to Armenia are those in the Middle East. Only in hostile Islamic societies can Armenians maintain their identity and pass on to their children the dream of moving to the homeland.[54]

Certainly most of my sources and respondents believed that at the present time the Diaspora is a permanent condition but that it can be mobilised in response to events in the homeland. Furthermore, on the one hand they believed that the Diaspora and the homeland shared some common origin, despite ideological and language differences and differences in mind set. As one respondent stated 'we are all Armenians we may have been dispersed and our language changed over time but we are one people'. On the other hand increased homeland-Diaspora interaction confirmed the political division of labour between the Diaspora and the Republic of Armenia, leading to a more definite role for the Diaspora. Interestingly, Toloyan states that 'in Armenia, they want service and money from the Diaspora, not thoughts or opinions; from America they want coke, music and jeans, no serious ideas please'. They want the products of one system, Diaspora organisation, solidarity, work, sacrifice—and again the material benefits of the West but no merits or ideas of that system like contracts, free elections, free communications etc., Why learn something about the systems of thought, organisation and behaviour that may have promoted the prosperity and generosity of Armenians in the Diaspora! Thus for many people in Armenia, their encounters with Armenians from the Diaspora are power struggles. They have a strong desire to assert what they have and what they know but what they have and what they know is very limited, by international standards. A great intellectual void is expressed in their assertions of self sufficiency and the biggest danger according to Beledian facing Armenia is that feeling of superiority.[55]

Nevertheless, the Diaspora was naturally better suited to encourage foreign investment in Armenia and to lobby for the recognition of the Armenian Genocide, since the homeland needs to walk a diplomatic tightrope in its relations with neighbouring Turkey. Thus the division of labour between the homeland and Diaspora and the varying cultural settings that the Armenian communities find themselves in give the Diaspora a unique sense of what it is to be Armenian. Although beyond the scope of this study, this begs the question of how does the Diaspora view itself with regard to the homeland and how much autonomy does and should the Diaspora have? As simply part of a larger Armenian nation and therefore a means to an end, that end being the homeland. Indeed citizenship in the new Armenian republic was granted, not only to all living within its territorial boundaries, but also to those Armenians in the Diaspora who wished to exercise that right. As one of two nations existing within a larger transnational Armenian nation. Or as a nation itself—self-sufficient in identity and purpose. Arguably an answer could be given that incorporates all three perspectives, however, the impact of the question lies in its ability to stir sentiments one way or another[56].

The Armenian Genocide

Diaspora need not be divorced from historical specificity. Clearly the concept of Diaspora questions fixed identities yet it embodies the need to attend to the historical conditions that produce diasporic subjectivities. The overriding sense of purpose for the Armenian Diasporas has been perpetuating its identity and this is inextricably linked to the Genocide. Maintaining identity was indeed the best response to the attempt to annihilate the Armenians but the Diaspora was unable to fashion a single uncontested identity—it is complex and contradictory. How will the Armenian youth relate to the historical memories and cultural heritage of their parents and grandparents? Janus, the figure from Roman mythology whose gaze is simultaneously directed both forward and backwards suggests a certain temporarility—the figure at once looks to the future and the past which characterises the situation of many Diasporas.[57] Armenians within the Diaspora are caught between individual and organisation forces which are utilised towards the reinforcement of communitarian connections and the cosmopolitanism of modernity. Ethnicity as process allows us to view this contravention as a duality between correspondence and difference.

The struggle to come to terms with the Armenian genocide continues to this day. One of the main difficulties is that the Armenian genocide has been overshadowed by the events of thirty years later. Everyone knows about the Jewish Holocaust and the Jewish community has done much to ensure that those events are at the forefront of our consciousness and that these terrible events are remembered and taught to our children. Few people, however, know of the Armenian genocide. As one respondent claimed 'the un-mourned, unburied bodies of the victims are carried around in the psyches of the survivors and their grandchildren like ghosts'. At Britain's first Holocaust Memorial Day in 2001, the Armenians were not initially invited, until intense pressure was brought to bear and the government made some concessions.

The quest for political recognition of past injustices has been intensified by the ominous developments of the past quarter of a century. The deterioration of Armenian communities in the Middle East, particularly Lebanon and Iran, brought thousands of immigrants, especially to the United States. These immigrants with fierce political and cultural commitments to their heritage swiftly assumed control of many of the Armenian American organisations. At the same time, in the intellectual arena, Armenian academics led by Professor Richard Hovanissian redoubled efforts to inform Armenian and non-Armenian audiences about the historical reality of 1915 and to repel the attempts perpetrated by pro-Turkish scholars to whitewash the genocide. The Armenian National Institute was established in Washington in 1997 to gain international reaffirmation of the genocide and combat denial. The intense concentration on the genocide, however, replete with documentaries, workshops, tape-recordings of the survivors, and above all the drive to recognise 24 April by the American Congress as a day of remembrance has to some a negative side effect. As with the Jewish absorption with the Holocaust, the Armenian fixation on 1915 tends to create a 'garrison mentality' or cultural parochialism in which a self-critical attitude towards Armenian issues is often avoided.[58] For example:

We have been refugees and we have been massacred. If you ask us why this happened to us, you look left, right, they are all Muslim countries that is why. If we go back back back, Persia, Turkey . . . half of it really belongs to us. It is not because we are Armenians that we have suffered—it is because we are Christians.

Mohammed came and then the Muslims. Christian peoples are actually much more civilized, much more educated, and more polite. You can always tell a Christian whereas Muslims tell us that we are nothing, all the time because we are surrounded by non-Christian peoples. We did such a lot for them (the Turks), we were good businessmen and we helped them but then they say go away we do not want you. Russia is Christian so we looked to Russia for protection. My father always used to say you cannot see the truth unless you are telling it . . . this is the truth what I am saying, I am a nonagenarian now I have seen everything, this is the truth.

The genocide has only been officially recognised by France and Greece although every government in this world knows what the Turks did to us. Turkey does not recognise it . . . it is difficult you see because justice must begin. If the Turks say no, then where are all these Armenians? I would say the English people have been good to me and supportive and we have had a happy life here but you are a Christian people.

Historians have suggested that cultural parochialism has therefore developed a kind of one-dimensional ethnocentrism within the Armenian Diaspora communities. Armenians have been guided at all times and places by a single ideological motivation, that of self-determination or freedom, or after the adoption of Christianity, the preservation of their particular faith. Mythological heroes and villains have been defined in their relation to these fundamental goals. According to Suny, the notion of a single narrative for all of Armenian history or a unifying theme is more a literary conceit than an accurate description of Armenia's complex and fragmented history.[59] Indeed some Armenians in their self-criticism have diagnosed this parochialist syndrome and termed it 'ailamerzhutiun', which implies a reluctance to accept outside influences that may prove detrimental. This, as Dekmejian argues, has produced specific behavioural patterns among the new generation of the Diaspora. For example, in the choice of educational specializations and career goals, Armenian students appear to favour the applied professions, rather than abstract theoretical subjects, the arts and advanced fields of research in the social and behavioural sciences. While the traditional Armenian emphasis on education is maintained, the quest for knowledge for its own sake has given way to pragmatic education, thus weakening the potential for creativity and hindering the emergence of a 'world-class' Armenian intelligentsia.[60]

As I have argued earlier, however, Armenians may experience this with greater intensity, but the difference is perhaps quantitative rather than qualitative. Ethnocentrism, fatalism, parochialism and conservatism are terms that could be used to describe any ethnic group. In other words, the critics of Armenian political and cultural norms and institutions are themselves falling into a trap of ethnocentrism, by seeing the Armenian experience as unique in a negative sense. More importantly an essentialist view of Armenians and other ethnic groups, that as a people they have always and everywhere possessed a core of discernible, ethnically determined qualities, has been for political nationalists the basis of their political ideology. The continuous existence of the Armenians as a historic people, their origins in ancient Armenia provides them with the right of self-determination, nationhood and a historically sanctified claim to the territories that constitute Armenia. Because this view of Armenian history plays such an important political role for Armenians, as indeed it does for nationalities, any attempt to dispute it, or revise this single narrative of history, must be done with a great deal of care and sensitivity.[61] Certainly ethnic identities may seem invented, irrational and arbitrary to the outside observer, but they are generally regarded as immutable and sacred to those holding them, who will actively resist challenges to them.

The psychological impact of the genocide cannot be over emphasised. Although the terms exile, dispossession and vulnerability were not new in the Armenian discourse, they took on a new dimension amongst the post-genocide Diaspora. This sense of vulnerability is described by many Armenian authors. By way of example, Hovannisian writes that Armenians were "condemned to a life of exile and dispersion, subjected to inevitable acculturation and assimilation on five continents".[62] The Armenians' sense of abandonment has been exacerbated by the denial of the Armenian Genocide by successive Turkish governments and compounded by Realpolitik. There are many countries; Britain included who refuse publicly, at least, to acknowledge that the Armenian genocide ever took place. At the same time, however, the political and symbolic expressions of genocide remembrance have flourished through ethnic education, commemoration, monuments and the preaching of the church. As such the discourse of vulnerability and victimization has been fostered, reinforcing the sense of abandonment, while little has been offered in helping Armenians deal with the psychological impact of the genocide.

Language

Ethnic traditionalists argue that the loss of language means loss of identity—it is the carrier of culture. Among the sample most of my respondents could speak two or three languages fluently, including Armenian. For some of the British born Armenians the Armenian language is relegated to the symbolic because of its low utilitarian value. Furthermore, they argue they remain Armenian without language fluency. Thus a common language may be a typical component of an ethnic group but is neither necessary nor sufficient to distinguish ethnicity.

The diversity of background is reflected in differences occurring between Manchester Armenians. They speak two major forms of the Armenian language; Western and Eastern Armenian. When discussing the lack of fluency in Armenian and actual instruction in the language, then both Eastern and Western speakers tend to distinguish one from the other. Only Armenians of Iranian origin and newer immigrants from the Republic of Armenia[63] employ the Eastern inflection, however, reference to Eastern Armenian speakers is often synonymous with Armenians originating from Iran. Difficulties in communication amongst

Armenians were stressed but in the majority of cases emphasis was by Western Armenian speakers regarding their lack of understanding Iranian Armenians. For instance 'it is very difficult for us to understand Iranian Armenians because they mix Farsi in with the language'. Or 'in the homeland where the Eastern language is also used, they do not use such foreign words so we have no difficulty in understanding them when we travel there'. Debates over which dialect is correct or more true to the Armenian historic tradition is a constant concern for many Armenians throughout the Diaspora and the issue of which inflection is the authentic one is not so easily resolved:

> I was in the Armenian House (in London) about five to six years ago and there was a terrible argument going on. When I came in, they stopped and said, Oh he can tell us which one is right. Do you know, they were arguing about which dialect is the more correct one, the Eastern or the Western. I said look there isn't a right or wrong dialect. So long as you have a language and you can communicate that is all that matters. If you ask me which one is more correct phonetically, then I have to say the Iranian because they pronounce all the letters in the alphabet, the Western Armenians do not. But what does that matter? The important thing is that you are all Armenians and you belong to one nation.[64]

Despite these internal difficulties, however, Armenian emigrant parents often fear that their children will lose their Armenian identity if they do not learn the language proficiently. As discussed above, there are no full time Armenian schools in Britain, only the Supplementary schools which are affiliated to the Armenian Apostolic Church. As these usually only operate for four hours weekly, the pressure of teaching their children the Armenian language rests on the parents. Among the sample where both parents were Armenian the children were usually reasonably fluent in Armenian. Within mixed marriages, however, particularly if the mother was English, Armenian language fluency was low. As such many Armenian fathers felt that migration had prevented them from sharing a common language, culture and life-shaping experience with their children. As two respondents described:

> My children cannot speak any Armenian at all, I used to try and teach them but my wife is English, they went to English schools, their friends at school are English and that is their life, they have a different mentality to me. . . . It is very difficult when family visit from abroad because they are unable to converse. There are no full time Armenian schools here, so what are we supposed to do. They go to church sometimes but they do not understand the service.

> Most of our friends are Armenian and their children do speak Armenian, however, ours only speak a little because their mother is English. As with all mixed marriages, children take their mother's tongue. The irony of the situation is that my wife actually speaks more Armenian than they do, they have been to the Armenian language school and have the books, but they are not interested . . . it is not important to them. The main problem I have is when I try to discipline my children, they dismiss me as if I am old fashioned and say you do not understand, your culture is different.

Similar problems were cited by Jewish émigré parents in America. A Los Angeles based Israeli psychologist describes the source of the generation gap in the United States:

> Israelis send their kids to public school and they have this little American running around at home. So where do we meet in the family? On what value system do we meet? There is no value system that Israelis can give to their children as Americans because they don't know it. The children bring home the American culture; their parents don't know it. That is why the breakdown occurs.[65]

Language and speaking the Armenian language does carry significant importance for the immigrants. A number of my respondents felt it was not possible to stay Armenian without speaking the Armenian language. For instance 'language states who you are and who you are not'. Loss of language means loss of identity for some. In this sense language is not merely the transmitter of culture but contains within it the very essence of that culture. Thus in the absence of territory, it is language that functions as the space for imagining the nation. This argument is particularly salient for the Armenian Diaspora since in the absence of a state, it is the language and the Church that provides a tangible identifier upon which national consciousness can be built. In cases where a people do not possess a territory such as the Kurds, Basques and other stateless minorities, the preservation of language as a symbolic link to the ethnic past, rather than as a means of communication may play a significant role.

With this perspective it is not possible to be a true Armenian without speaking the language. Therefore, a different language may be a significant marker of an ethnic group. Consequently the preservation of language may be central to the preservation of that culture. Language is a means of generating imagined communities and of providing a means of defining a group's boundary. It connects this generation with those who went before it. Nevertheless, a common language may be a typical component of an ethnic community but it is neither necessary nor sufficient to distinguish ethnicity. It is possible to be a member of a distinct ethnic group and have limited knowledge of that group's native language. British born Armenians have argued that they are living proof that it is possible to remain Armenian without maintaining language fluency. One young girl stated:

> I do not speak Armenian fluently, just a few phrases here and there. . . . I know how to greet my grandparents and that pleases them. Ideally I would love to be able to speak and read the language but I have other priorities, however, I am still Armenian that can never be taken away from me. I am going to Armenia next year and hopefully I will learn the language then.

One of my respondents was ten years old when he arrived in Manchester. He explained:

> I think in English now. I came here when I was a boy and I was thinking in Armenian until I went to Manchester Grammar School and I thought in English. My children do not speak Armenian. It is my fault, of course, I should have taught them but you know I was into other things . . . but there are

Armenians who teach their children. I spoke English all the time at home. Its funny you know when the Armenian priests speak English I cannot make out what they are saying, their English is dreadful. I am Armenian and proud to be Armenian but I think in English. By the same token my children do not speak the language but they are Armenian through and through.

In this sense, language retention would be ideal but it is not possible in a pluralistic society. Furthermore, recent research on American Armenians has shown a clear generational decline in the use of the Armenian language.[66] There are many difficulties involved in encouraging bilingualism, particularly among the younger generation for whom attending an Armenian day school is not an option. Some American Armenian youths have attended the language schools and summer camps, however, the Armenian language does not appear to have anywhere near the practical everyday utilitarian value of English. Thus language retention may involve learning just a few key words or phrases that would give some connection with family members or it could mean the learning of greetings, words denoting foods, songs, hymns or poems.

With regard to language, it should be emphasised that whilst the communicative and the symbolic may co-exist, they are separable. Within majority populations the language of daily use is usually the language which reflects the dominant culture through the media and education. Among minority groups, however, the value of language as symbol can remain in the absence of the communicative purpose. Language can also function as a means of secret communication within the ethnic group. The symbolic use of key rings, wall hangings, even tattoos where its intrinsic appeal is often just as important. Even in its symbolic form, this kind of language and alphabet functions as a boundary marker. The Armenian language, however, is an ambiguous symbol partly because there are key dialects such as Western and Eastern, as well as variations from individual to individual. By way of example, only Armenians of Iranian origin use the Eastern inflection whilst Western Armenian speakers originate from a number of places. Furthermore, the difference between communicative and symbolic language mirrors a more general one between public and private ethnic markers. On the one hand, it could be argued that the public characteristics will be early casualties in assimilative or pluralistic contexts. On the other, private and symbolic characteristics continue to survive because they promote the continuation of group boundaries without impeding social mobility and access.[67]

CHAPTER SEVEN

SUMMARY

Armenian history is packed with migration and inter-cultural contact. Throughout their long history, even before global ethnoscapes[1] Armenians had contact and interaction with other peoples. In its strategic geographical location, the historic Armenian homeland was at the crossroads of the East and West, and was host and victim to many empires of different cultural groups. These contacts facilitated the expansion and creation of the Armenian Diaspora and their resultant communities. Dispersion, therefore, whether voluntary or involuntary has been a way of life for the Armenians especially after the fall of the Bagratid dynasty which ruled the medieval kingdom of Ani (885-1045). The rise of Cilicia was the most eloquent expression of such dispersion. These immigrants grew numerous and powerful establishing an independent principality under Prince Ruben I. The Armenian kingdom of Cilicia (1080-1375) became an Armenian Diaspora and the epicentre of Armenian political, cultural, economic and religious activity shifted away from the traditional homeland. The legacy of Cilicia is significant in that it provided a strong link with Europe through trade and inter-marriage with the French monarch and through contact with the Crusaders who passed through. The Armenians controlled the overland trade routes between the Orient and Europe up until the nineteenth century.

In the wake of the collapse Cilicia, there emerged a belt of Armenian communities, old and new, extending from South East Asia to Europe. By the turn of the nineteenth century, however, some of these communities had disappeared and others had grown acquiring greater significance. Indeed the Armenians developed large Diaspora elements long before force compelled complete dispersion under Sultan Abdul Hamid in 1895-6 and the Armenian Genocide of 1915. If the designations Eastern (Russian) or Western (Turkish) are relatively new in Armenian history, the distinction they signified encompassed the age old convergence of Eastern and Western elements in Armenian culture. It is also important to remember that the early influence of Persian culture on Armenians was mixed with elements of Hellenism contributing to the distinct blend and character of Armenians. As a result Armenians have always inhabited the crossroads and have embraced hyphenated identities. Armenian identity was never clear cut and Armenian migration to Britain is merely an extension of their historical experience.

Early networks developed through conquest and trade, however, have now been superseded by the emergence of selective migration opportunities in the global capitals. An important factor in recent migration is the extent of social mobility in the host country. For instance, Manchester in the mid nineteenth century used to be a thriving textile metropolis and magnet for Armenian merchants. The first Armenian Church in Britain was built in Manchester in 1870. By the beginning of the twentieth century many Armenians joined the larger community in London or left for the United States. Global cities such as London are centres of global transport and global communication. The net result of these features of global cities is that they become progressively more integrated into other global cities.

Many members of a Diaspora are people of considerable wealth and transferable skills who are assisted by the global communications and transport revolutions, by the need for states to attract foreign investment, by the legal protection accorded to minorities in receiving countries and by the custom of short term contracts overseas. Armenians may have worked in a variety of places before settling down in Manchester, although not necessarily on a permanent basis. Similarly many expect to uproot themselves in the future to join other Diaspora communities, particular the mother community in the United States. A diasporic consciousness with roots in several locations is highly familiar with transnational networking and sojourning as opposed to permanent settlement in one nation state.[2]

It is apparent how the new notions of space and the new connections between global cities are advantageous to Diasporas. One of the factors leading to the emergence of transnational networks is the ease and speed of communication and travel, by comparison with earlier dispersions. Clearly, members of a Diaspora are more mobile than people who are rooted in national spaces. They have multiple connections in a variety of countries of origin, the homeland and other Diaspora communities. Unlike many other ethnic groups whose populations originated in a common location, Armenian families are characterised by geographically dispersed origins. Since the propensity to migrate can be transmitted along family networks, having relatives abroad is often correlated with one's own migration. The moral support provided by such networks is able to open many avenues for new migrants. They change their places of work and residence more frequently. In the age of globalisation their language skills, familiarity with other cultures and global contacts makes many members of a Diaspora highly competitive in the labour market.

Compared with members of their country of settlement, those who belong to Diasporas characteristically have an advantageous occupational profile. They are more often strongly represented in the professions and self employment and as such are less vulnerable to a volatile labour market. A passion for knowledge is usually reflected in a desire for education—degrees, vocational or professional qualifications are the hallmark of the successful members of a Diaspora. Armenians are concentrated in the skilled professional sector and educational levels appear to be high. They valued Manchester's educational opportunities, sending their children to good local grammar schools or public schools as boarders, followed by university and a professional career. It has also been very common for Armenians arriving in Britain with the original purpose of University education to settle here subsequently.

The connections that Diasporas have between various countries are advantageous for Diasporas and they are major players in the global arena. Globalisation has improved the practical, economic and effective roles of Diasporas. As they become more integrated into their surroundings, their power and importance are enhanced by working and living successfully in the global cities. The experience of Armenian migrants emphasises their ability to combine resources and networks from multiple locations in order to maximise their freedom and independence from the confines of any one nation state. There are contradictions to globalisation, however, such as ethnicity, nationalism, religious fundamentalism and other forms of social exclusivism. These all appear to be on the increase, thus at the cultural level a perverse feature of globalisation is the multiplication of identities. In a globalizing context, groups and individuals do not become culturally identical but rather it produces the growth of new kinds of cultural difference in the interface between the global and the local.[3]

The cultural identities as an outcome of diasporic experience can be explained and understood from different angles and definitions given by many theorists. Cultural identities are emerging that are in transition drawing on different traditions and synthesizing old and new traditions, without assimilation or total loss of historical traditions. Hall describes this development as 'the evolution of cultures of hybridity' and associates the development of these cultures with Diasporas.[4] Perhaps we should think of identity as a production which is never complete, always in process and always constituted within, not outside representation. Diaspora identities are those that are constantly reproducing themselves through difference. As such each Diaspora community has modified its way of life, blending elements from its own heritage with elements of the mainstream. The use of English in the Armenian Apostolic Church is a clear example. Even so, within their travels and hyphenated identities there are more complex markers of identity. This means keeping any values and customs from other groups. By the use of transnational strategies, which exposes them to many cultures, Diasporas are in an advantageous position to pick and choose characteristics.

Diasporas are often better suited to determine what their group shares with other groups and when they perceive their cultural practices may be a threat to the majority groups in their countries of settlement. For instance, due to the persecutions suffered in the homeland and the denial to develop their own country, combined with their minority status in dispersion[5] this has encouraged the Armenians to excel whenever conditions were favourable. The persistent quest for economic stability and educational achievements has acted as a mechanism to achieve a sense of security.[6] Indeed Robin Cohen recognises this as a significant characteristic of Diasporas. Nevertheless this quest for economic elitism may bring visibility which in turn could bring negative reactions from the majority populations. With this in mind, and as this case study illustrates, the Armenians do not congregate through residence, occupation nor educational establishments. The more dispersed Armenians are the more invisible socially and the more invisible they are the greater their freedom of movement. Thus while economic ties are quickly established with the larger environment, they remain socially anonymous as this is seen as a threat to their survival.

The Armenians' skills as entrepreneurs are highly valued in Western societies and the stereotypes that divided the American community are influenced by a society that castigates those migrants who rely on benefits. Furthermore, Armenians use their Armenian identity to disassociate themselves from any potentially negative traits which may be associated by non Armenians with their many countries of origin. The dichotomization between insiders and outsiders in the study of ethnic groups suggests the critical focus of investigation becomes the ethnic boundary that defines the group. It is at the same time important to remember that these boundaries are not only defined from within the group but from outside, by the conditions of the host society and by global currents. Fluidity implies interaction with other groups and interaction is the core for the maintenance of the group. It is through interaction that identities are constructed and reconstructed.

This being so, what defines an Armenian. If the traits of a group are produced and then re-produced over time and space—what keeps an ethnic group intact? What are the values that make up Diaspora identity? The definition of Armenian identity has always varied widely within each community and from one community to another. The Diaspora is made up of fragmented societies that speak in multiple voices, have different attitudes and different expectations from the Diaspora and the homeland. The Armenians share common historical memories of the genocide, a spirit of solidarity, may speak the same language, and many other bonds that result in a partly shared, diverse culture but the illusion that they are one language, one culture, and one church must be discarded.

The notion of symbolic ethnicity allows for a more voluntary and flexible expression of ethnicity which allows the individual to develop a form of ethnic expression that is appropriate to their circumstances. Because of the fluid nature of symbolic ethnicity, it is able to incorporate the diversity of expressions of identity that exist within a single ethnic group. If one is to consider the range of options available to the average Anglo Armenian, as well as any other ethnic group, in the areas of marriage, career, political affiliation, geographical location and taking into account generational differences that exist within any ethnic community, as well as diversity in place of origin, and the influx of new immigrants, it becomes evident that there are an innumerable combination of possibilities of defining 'Armenianness'. In this sense ethnic identity in modern pluralistic societies is highly relativistic and individualistic.

An ethnic symbol must exhibit an unusual degree of flexibility if that symbol is to survive if a sense of ethnicity is to be preserved within that group. In its essence, however, symbolic ethnicity has its origins in the immigrant ancestors. Ararat remains a powerful symbol for Armenians across the world; a symbol of the homeland for a community in exile. Its name has been given to various books, journals, businesses and restaurants. Armenians name their houses after it and the national football team is called Ararat. The Armenian Apostolic Church as an institution distinctive to Armenians is an important symbol of Armenianness because of its strong emphasis on national symbols and sacred traditions, whether given religious or secular meaning. The Armenian language in whichever variety is related to the symbolic because of its low utilitarian value. Greater value is placed on the symbolic manifestation of the language involving books, key rings, iconography, jewellery and tattoos, to name a few. In every Armenian home and organisation Armenian calendars, books, placemats, pictures of Mount Ararat were evident to name a few. Symbolic ethnicity allows ethnicity to be self perpetuating and re-imagined without being destroyed or lost to the community. Such re-imagination occurs at a faster pace and the outcome is a more fragmented and decentralised set of identities. Consequently there are different degrees of ethnic mobilisation within an ethnic group. Among some people there exists a degree of ethnic awareness which is not a daily routine but is only activated in times of crisis, national holidays, days of remembrance or interaction with other Armenians.

Certainly patterns such as loss of language, reduced community participation are all characteristics of assimilation, however, assimilation and ethnic reassertion can and do occur simultaneously. In discussing this paradox Bakalian points out that the majority continue to maintain high levels of Armenian identity, fierce pride in their ancestral heritage and a strong sense of 'we-ness' or 'peoplehood'[7]. Anny Bakalian who has applied the notion of symbolic ethnicity to her empirical study of Armenians in New York and New Jersey gives a description of symbolic ethnicity as a 'selective', 'visible', 'convenient', and socio-economically 'low cost' form of ethnic identity. Its priority is on preserving culture as an artefact rather than living it out in every day life. Symbols are adopted that most easily blend with those of the host country. At the same time other symbols are emphasised that fill the gap created by contemporary life, particularly those symbols relating to family and a sense of belonging. Thus what one Armenian may view as a compromise of long held sacred cultural norms, others may view as ethnic rejuvenation.

Symbolic ethnicity provides the rallying point despite the community's fluid boundaries and there is a strong continuity despite the shift in how the symbol may be perceived. Therefore, the change in ethnic expression between generations in the Armenian Diaspora represents a change in form but not in substance. The ethnic identity of the later generations still maintains core values and symbols which are interpreted in such a way that it makes sense to that generation. Nevertheless over time there is likely to be less of an ethnic repertoire to draw upon and the symbolic ethnicity of each successive generation will be less comparable to the ethnicity of the immigrant culture. Symbolic ethnicity is likely to persist and increasingly characterise the identity of future generations of Anglo Armenians and over time the traditional institutions and discourses will continue to decline.

With this in mind it could be argued that the constant influx of immigration will facilitate the preservation of ethnic identity in its symbolic form. Since a regular flow of immigrants, however, cannot be guaranteed in the long term, it appears that the answer lies in strengthening both the tangible and symbolic aspects of the Diaspora-homeland relationship. With the increasing marginalisation of the political parties in most Diaspora settings a significant number of the

Armenian youth were now rallying to the cause of the Armenian homeland and homeland issues, thus by passing the traditional Diaspora organisations. The renewed task orientated dimension of Anglo Armenians towards the homeland and genocide recognition will increasingly become the key agent in perpetuating Diaspora identity. For instance, the quest for political recognition of past injustices and the struggle to come to germs with the Armenian genocide continues to this day. CRAG (Centre for the Recognition of the Armenian Genocide) is just one example of this kind of involvement. In the intellectual arena, Armenian academics led by Professor Richard Hovanissian have concentrated efforts to inform Armenian and non-Armenian audiences about the historical reality of 1915 and to repel the attempts perpetrated by pro-Turkish scholars to whitewash the genocide. At the same time, the symbolic expressions of genocide remembrance flourish throughout the Diaspora through commemoration, monuments and the preaching of the church.

Although the guiding rhetoric portrayed the Diaspora as a temporary condition, there is at the same time an increased willingness to acknowledge that given the opportunity most Diaspora Armenians would not return to the homeland on a permanent basis. This is more evident in the Western Diaspora. All of this, of course, could change if the homeland was to achieve greater economic and political stability or extend its boundaries to include the historic Armenian territories in Turkey. There are, however, many youth programmes supported by the Armenian government and various Diaspora organisations designed to keep the young tied to the land, culture, language, religion and people of the Armenian homeland. The renewal of interest in the homeland clearly indicates that the Republic of Armenia remains a significant source of identity for a large number of Armenians. Indeed the Diaspora-homeland relationship is central to Diaspora identity since by definition the Diaspora exists in relation to the territory from which it was originally dispersed.

In summary the opportunities offered by a consumer economy have eroded the obligations of a community and ethnic identity has now evolved into a very self conscious characteristic of an individual's personality. The availability of multiple choices has necessitated that we make decisions throughout the course of our lives. Contemporary Armenians have been attracted to the types of professional organisations that do not have a strong ethnic flavour. Initially events in the homeland drew them into Armenian community life and in doing so they were able to participate through Western forms of professional activism. By working on the land Armenians develop a stronger sense of their ethnicity and a sentimental attachment to the homeland. At the same time, working on the land is an activity with practical benefit for those living in Armenia, thus appealing to the functional component of ethnicity. Ultimately, this kind of activity carries appeal to Armenians of different types of ethnic expression, traditional through to symbolic. Such members of an ethnic community seek to create a more transitory form of ethnic expression, one that does not require time consuming commitment either to a culture that needs to be practised regularly or to organisations that demand full and active participation. In this sense ethnicity is valued for its existential contribution to the life of the individual—for that feeling of belonging to a distinct community that it invokes. The greatest benefit of symbolic ethnic attachment is its capacity to fill the cultural, social and communal gap created by tachment is its capacity to fill the cultural, social and communal gap created by globalisation. As Gans summarizes his understanding of symbolic ethnicity as one 'characterised by a nostalgic allegiance to the culture of the immigrant generation or that of the old country; a love for and a pride in a tradition that can be felt without it being incorporated into everyday behaviour'.[8] Thus, ethnic communities and their boundaries exist not as social structural systems but as worlds of meaning in the minds of their members. Membership comprises not so much of particular behavioural patterns, more of thinking about behaviour in common, attachment to a common body of symbols, a shared vocabulary value.

A social boundary does not simply happen as a reaction of one system to another, it also reflects a variety of symbolic meanings occurring within ethnic communities in which the impact of external factors is understood through the varied subjective experience of its members. I must therefore agree with Clifford that Diaspora is something in between primordial codes of belonging and the wandering installation of alliances envisioned by postmodern theories. 'A 'changing same', something endlessly hybridized and in process but persistently there— memories and practices of collective identity maintained over long stretches of time'.[9] The combination of symbolic practices from the old world and the new opportunities presented in a globalised world give rise to the multiplicity of enriching identities within the Armenian Diaspora. Those ethnic traditionalists who mourn the loss of their language, the declining importance of the church and traditional organisations, or the mixed marriages of their children must not overlook that the mixtures of cultures, tastes, physical appearances that such bonding brings about gives birth to blends of tastes and crossovers of cultures which diversifies not only their identities but also the way we feel towards our position in the world in relation to other cultures.

APPENDIX A

MODERATOR'S GUIDE

1. Introduction welcoming the participants, providing an outline of the topic to be discussed, establish guidelines for the proceedings and set the tone of the focus group.

2. Warm up which provides an opportunity for participants to feel at ease and ask general introductory questions to each other.

3. Clarification of terms. It is important to clarify any terms that may be used during the course of the focus group. The moderator defining the term for the group, or asking questions about the terms, and expanding on the respondent's replies can achieve this. By way of example, "many of you may be familiar with the term ethnicity, in your own words what would you say ethnicity means?"

4. Easy and non-threatening questions. These should be general questions, allowing the group time to understand the process and feel comfortable expressing their opinions.

5. More difficult questions. As the group begins to feel more comfortable with each other, the moderator asks more difficult questions which may require the participants to provide reasons and meanings for their feelings.

6. Wrap-up. Firstly, the moderator attempts to identify major themes and to organise these into a summary. This provides an opportunity to verify how members feel about selected issues. It may be possible to interpret the length of the discussion as an indicator that all members feel the same way. Conversely, however, it may be that only a few members feel strongly and some have different or at least less intense feelings. Secondly, any conversational issues that were not completed during the course of the focus group are recognised, specifically as some questions may not have been discussed as fully as group members would have wished.

7. Closing statements. Firstly, request that all participants of the focus group keep the information stated as anonymous as possible and inform the group that the audio tape will be transcribed and they will be assigned false names for the purpose of transcript and analysis. Secondly, thank all the participants for their participation in the focus group and answer any questions.

APPENDIX B
STANDARD ETHICS PROTOCOL

(To be read by interviewer before the beginning of the interview. One copy of this form should be left with the respondent, and one copy should be signed by the respondent and kept by the interviewer).

Hi, my name is .... I am a researcher on a project, which examines how ethnic identity is reproduced within Armenia Diaspora communities. This project is being sponsored by the Economic and Social Research Council at the department of Politics, University of York, Heslington, York YO10 5DD. Professor Haleh Afshar is my principal supervisor on this project and she may be contacted on 01904 433554 should you have any questions.

Thank you for your willingness to participate in this research project. Your participation is very much appreciated. Just before we start the interview, I would like to reassure you that as a participant in this project you have several very definite rights.

First, your participation in this interview is entirely voluntary.
You are free to refuse to answer any question at any time.
You are free to withdraw from the interview at any time.
This interview will be kept strictly confidential.
Excerpts of this interview may be made part of the final research report, but under no circumstances will your name or identifying characteristics be included in this report.
I would be grateful if you would sign this form to show that I have read you its contents.

.... (Signed)

.... (Printed)

.... (Dated)

Please send me a report on the results of this research project. YES/NO

Address for those requesting research report.

....

....

....
(Interviewer: keep signed copy; leave unsigned copy with respondent)

Notes to the Introduction

1   I use the term 'Diaspora' throughout this research to refer to Armenians collectively, although strictly speaking, within the definition given in Chapter One, the Armenians who fled the Ottoman Empire did not become a Diaspora until there was an independent Republic of Armenia. Repatriation of Armenians, however, was taking place during the Soviet period hence Armenians have always felt they had a territorial homeland to which they could return.

2   Dekmejian, R. H. (1997) p413. For a complete profile of Diaspora communities see Dekmejian, pp421-435

3   Talai, V. (1989) p1

4   Said, E. W. (2000) p396

5   McNeill, W. H. (1986) pp14-22

6   Ballard, R. (Ed) (1994) p1

7   George, J. (2002) p5

8   Gold, Steven. J. (2002) p9

9   George, J. (2002) p3

10   Acculturation: The process whereby an individual or group acquires the cultural characteristics of another through cultural contact. Acculturation is a one way process, in which one culture absorbs another, and is to be distinguished from the two-way process of assimilation, in which homogeneity results from changes in both.

11   Takooshian, H. (1986-7) pp133-134

12   The United States prides itself on its free and unfettered exchange of information however, the decennial Census gives no reliable data on Armenian Americans. Its 'mother tongue' data is based on small samples, it does not report Armenians as a separate nationality and it stopped noting people's religion in 1936. Experienced Armenologists like Arra, S. Avakian "Armenians in America: How many and where?" In Ararat Quarterley, Vol 18 No 1, 1977, pp125-35 must expend great efforts to derive partial data, to guesstimate an answer to the simple query, How many Armenians live in America? Although Canada is historically more attuned to ethnic groups, the world 'Armenian' does not appear in its many official sources: the Green Book, Almanac, Yearbook or the quarterly or annual reports of the Manpower and Immigration Department. The United Nations annual Demographic Yearbook selectively cumulates self-report data from different nations. Census methods vary greatly among nations and rarely include Armenians. Authoritative private sources often contain questionable data on Armenians. By way of example Europa's 1978 Middle East Yearbook contained a paragraph mentioning 900 Armenians in Israel. An identical paragraph appeared six years later in the 1984 Europa Yearbook.

13   Tabibian, J. (1999) pp28-33

14   Tabibian, J. (1999) pp28-33

15   Because the name Armenian Revolutionary Federation would obviously give most non-Armenians in the West a negative impression, the party calls its political arm, the Armenian National Committee (ANC). ANC organisations exist in a number of different countries in the Diaspora.

16   Toloyan, K. (2002) p8

17   See Bourdieu, P. & Wacquant, L. (1992) *An Invitation to Reflexive Sociology;* Castells, M. (2000) *The Network Society*
18   Barr & Toye (2000) cited in *Ethnicities* Vol 3 No 1, March 2003, p31
19   Talai, V. (1989) p12
20   Gold, S. J. (2002) p52
21   Huntingdon, S. (1993) p1
22   Barth, F. (1969) pp10-19
23   Said, E. W. (2000) pp198-215. Edward Said is associated with Orientalism. His analysis argues that the construction of the Orient is intrinsically intertwined with the hierarchical connections the West maintains with the Orient. The Orient is an idea that has a history and a tradition of thought, imagery and vocabulary that have given it reality and presence in and for the West. Thus constructed images of the East have become essentialised as real and uninfluenced by hierarchical relationships and historical contexts.
24   Mirak, R. (1997) p410
25   Appadurai, A. (2002) p192
26   Integration: A social, economic and political process through which distinct identities of various groups are preserved and respected to a certain degree, but are brought into mainstream society. To be distinguished from marginalization, segregation, acculturation and complete assimilation.
27   See Cohen, R. (1997) *Global Diasporas;* Marienstras, R. (1989) *On the Notion of Diaspora;* Saffran, W. (1991) *Diasporas in Modern Societies: Myths of Homeland and Return;* Clifford, J. (1994) *Diasporas*
28   Toloyan, K. (2002) pp26-27. See Panossian, R. *Between Ambivalence and Intrusion: Politics of Identity in Armenia-Diaspora Relations* and Shain, Yossi. *American Jews and the Construction of Israel's Jewish Identity*
29   Rouse, Roger. (2002) *Mexican Migration & The Social Space of Postmodernism;* Appadurai, A. (1996) *Modernity at Large: Cultural Dimensions of Globalisation;* Brah, A. (1996) *Cartographies of Diaspora*
30   Kivisto, P. (2003) pp5-28
31   See Eriksen, T. H. (1993) *Ethnicity & Nationalism;* Gans, H. J. (1979) *Symbolic Ethnicity, the future of ethnic groups and cultures in America;* Jenkins, R. (1997) *Re-thinking Ethnicity, Arguments and Explorations*
32   Anderson, B. (1991) pp37-46
33   Eriksen, T. H. (2001) p279
34   Friedman, J. (1990) p311
35   See Bhabha, H. (1994) *The Location of Culture;* Hall, S. (1996) *Critical Dialogues in Cultural Studies;* Chambers, I. (1993) *Migrancy, Culture & Identity;* James, C. Clifford. (1994) *Diasporas*
36   Bhabha. (1990) *Nation & Narration;* Hall. (1997) *Representation: Cultural Representations & Signifying Practices;* Vertovec & Cohen. (1999) *Migration, Diasporas & Transnationalism*
37   Jenkins, R. (1997) p29
38   See Hovannisian, R. G. (1997) *The Armenian People from Ancient to Modern Times Vol II;* Redgate, A. E. (2000) *The Armenians;* Chahin, M. (Second Edition) (2001) *The Kingdom of Armenia;* McCarthy, J. (2001) *The Ottoman Peoples and the End of Empire;* Walker, C. (1980) *Armenia: the survival of a Nation*
39   Suny, R. G. (1993) p1
40   Gunter, M. M. (1990) p29. Armenians assert that the head of their distinctive church, the Catholicos, has been consecrated in Echmiadzin, a small city near Yerevan since the fourth century.

41 The Holy Apostolic Orthodox Church of Armenian adheres to the Nicaean creed as defined at the Council of Nicaea in 325: '*Christ is a very God, begotten of God, but not a creature of God; Son of God, of one nature with the Father, who came down from heaven, and took flesh and became man, and suffered and ascended into heaven;* Who was, before He was begotten and Who has always been.' In plain language God became Man, in the fullest sense. To the layman, the Nicaean creed seems to uphold the single nature of God, as well as God manifesting himself in three natures, the latter being a Trinitarian statement and its official interpretation. The Nicaean formula was questioned and the following compromise was adopted at the Council of Chalcedon in 451: '*Jesus Christ according to his Godhead is one nature with the Father, according to his humanity is, apart from sin, of one nature with Man.* Thus one and the same Christ is recognised in two natures indissolubly united but yet distinct. Thus the Greek Orthodox Church adopting the Chalcedonian dogma believes in the dual nature of Christ. He is God manifest on earth in the Holy person of Christ, as well as in the secular person of vulnerable man. Chahin (2001) p261

42 Armstrong, J. (1982) pp206-13
43 Hovannisian, R. G. (1997) p438
44 Dudwick, N.(1993) p262
45 Hovannisian, R. G. (1997) p438 & 440
46 Smith, A. D. (1992) pp440-9
47 Walker, C. (1980) p440
48 Suny, R. G. (1993) p9
49 Talai, V. (1989) p120
50 Roger Smith, Professor of Government, College of William and Mary, cited in Graber, G. S. (1996) pxiii
51 Suny, R. G. (1993) pp94-95
52 Suny, R. G. (1993) p115
53 Mirak, R. (1997) p403
54 Gavakian, A. (1997) p112
55 Walker, C. (1980) p441
56 Bhabha. (1990) Hall. (1997) Vertovec & Cohen. (1999)
57 Cohen, R. (1997) p4
58 Cohen, A. P. (1985) p21
59 Gans, H. J. (1979) pp9-17

Notes to Chapter One: Conceptual Considerations of Diaspora

1 The use of the word Diaspora in English was fairly limited until the 1990's when there was a rapid surge of interest with the appearance of a new journal 'Diaspora' edited by Robin Cohen as well as many individual books including 'The Penguin Atlas of Diasporas, dealing with specific issues on the subject.
2 Braziel & Mannur. (2003) p1
3 Rapport & Overing. (2000) p156
4 Toloyan, K. (2002) p1
5 Cohen, R. (1997) p159. There is little documentation on the impact of personnel moving as a result of TNC's than there is on capital or trade flows, yet the numbers are considerable. For instance the case of the Japanese who have moved with their

expanding companies. Kotkin calls the movement a 'Diaspora by design' and argues that because the Japanese had been frustrated in their plans for conventional colonization they enlarged their influence in the world economy. The most important Japanese colony is in the United Kingdom where Japanese factories, banks and corporate offices have investments exceeding $16 billion which employ approximately 90,000. Despite the size the group has remained largely invisible through the development of its own social institutions.

6   For an interesting discussion of archetypal Diasporas, Jews and Armenians see John Armstrong (1982) *Nations before Nationalism*, pp206-13

7   Braziel, J. E. & Mannur, A. (2003) p2

8   Cohen, R. (1997) p181

9   Eller, J. D. (1999) p143

10   Cohen, R. (1997) p28

11   Marienstras, R. (1989) pp119-125

12   Spiurk has a long pedigree, Saint Nerses Shnorhali spoke in the twelfth century of Armenian 'spiurk' scattered in the world. The General Epistle of Saint Nerses Snhorhali was directed 'to all the faithful of the Armenian nation, those in the East who inhabit our homeland Armenia, those who have emigrated to the regions of the West and those in the middle lands who were taken among foreign peoples, and who for our sins are scattered in cities, villages and farms in every corner of the earth.' Translated by Arakel Aljanian, New York Saint Nerses Armenian Seminary (1996) p13 cited in Armenian Forum 1998.

13   Dekmejian, R. H. (1997) p436

14   Marienstras, R. (1989) p120

15   See Sanguin, A. L. (1994) pp495-8

16   Skeldon, R. (1997) p28

17   Dekmejian, R. H. (1997) p437

18   Cohen, R. (1997) p171

19   Saffran, W. (1991) pp83-89

20   Cohen, R. (1997) p184

21   Exodus 19:5-6 cf Deuteronomy 7:6-13 and 10:12-22 cited in Smith, A. D. (1992) p441

22   Smith, A. D. (1992) pp440-9

23   Dekmejian, R. G. (1997) p438

24   Smith, A. D. (1992) pp440-9

25   Rapport, N. & Overring, J. (2000) pp274-275

26   Rapport, N. & Overring, J. (2000) p281

27   Smith, A. D. (1992) pp440-9

28   Schopflin, G. (2000) p7

29   Schopflin ,G. (2000) p236

30   See Hobsbawm, E. & Ranger, T. (1983)

31   Eriksen, T. H. (2001) pp272-273

32   Marienstras, R. (1989) p120

33   Gold, S. J. (2002) p145

34   Milton, J. E. (1986) p334

35   Jenkins, R. (1997) p13

36   The exceptions are those groups that were in effect settler colonies: the British in North America and the Portuguese in Brazil who were able to establish their own hegemony in language and political institutions.

37   Cohen, R. (1997) p186

38	Khachatrian, H. "Armenia: Repatriation may not solve problems of exodus", 12.12.02 *A Eurasianet Commentary*
39	Riggs, F. W. (1999) p31
40	Sheffer, G. (1986) pp1-15
41	Milton , J. E. (1986) pp333-9
42	Cohen, R. (1997) p185
43	Dekmejian, H. R. (1997) p436
44	Cohen, R. (1997) p187
45	Cohen, R. (1997) p187
46	cited in Gavakian, A. (1997) p194
47	Marienstras, R. (1989) pp119-125
48	Saffran, W. (1991) pp83-89
49	A number of books have been written about Armenian origins including personal and collective memories of town such as Adana now in Turkey and villages such as Kessab in Syria (The Kessabtzi Diretory by Rev Vahan Tootikian) In the United States, ancestors from these villages have created their own telephone directories, children's summer camps and annual picnics, all of which helps to continue a sense of belonging to a certain place, already fostered within the extended family.
50	Rigg, F. W. (1999) p6
51	An Armenian millionaire, Las Vegas entrepreneur and major stockholder in Metro Goldwyn Mayer, MGM.
52	Dekmejian, R. H. (1997) p441
53	Dekmejian, R. H. (1997) p438
54	Mirak, R. (1997) p399
55	Rigg, F. W. (1999) p3
56	Gavakian, A. (1997) p26
57	Cohen, R. (1997) p176
58	Rosenberg, J. (2001) *The Follies of Globalisation Theory: Polemical Essays*
59	Wallerstein, I. (1990) p36
60	Giddens, A. (2002) pp93-94
61	Hirst, P. & Thompson G. (1999)
62	Aghanian, D. (1998)
63	Hirst, P. & Thompson, G. (1999) pp7-13
64	Appadurai, A. (2002)
65	Appadurai, A. (2002) pp46-64
66	Scholte, J. A. (2002) p12-13
67	Scholte, J. A. (2002) p13
68	Beck, U. (2002)
69	Scholte, J. A. (2002) p14
70	Eriksen, T. H. (2001) p300
71	Scholte, J. A. (2002) pp18-21
72	cited in Inda & Rosaldo (2002) p4
73	Inda & Rosaldo (2002) pp2-4
74	Eriksen, T. H. (2001) p300
75	Inda & Rosaldo (2002) p28
76	Dekmejian, R. H. (1997) p435
77	Riggs, F. W. (1999) p31
78	Kivisto, P. (2003) pp5-28
79	Rouse, R. (2002) p161
80	Because migration is self-evidently a movement between places, it has commonly been treated as a movement from one set of social relationships to another. Thus

numerous studies have sought to analyse the changes that migrants have undergone by comparing the systems of family organisation, kinship, and friendship in their places of origin with those they have developed in the places to which they have moved.

81   Rouse, R. (2002) p162
82   Rouse, R. (2002) p162
83   Inda & Rosaldo (2002) p20
84   Gillespie, M. (1994) p87
85   There are other Armenian web sites such as Cilicia.com and Hayastoun.com but this is by far the most extensive.
86   Toloyan, K. (2002) p37
87   Appadurai, A. (1996) p42
88   Inda & Rosaldo (2002) p20.
89   Rosenau, J. (1990) pp12-13
90   Inda & Rosaldo (2002) p21
91   Held & McGrew (2000) p11
92   Cohen, R. (1997) pp194-196
93   Gillespie, M. (1994) p5
94   Nonini & Ong (1997) p3-33
95   Kvisto, P. (2003) p28

Notes to Chapter Two: Situating Ethnicity

1   Comaroff, John & Jean. (1992) p39
2   Rapport, N. & Overring, J. (2000) p12
3   Eriksen, T. H. (1993) pp1-4
4   Eriksen, T. H. (1993) p10
5   Anthias, F. & Yuval Davis, N. (1996) p4
6   Moerman, Michael. (1965) pp215-29
7   Within anthropology the term emic refers to 'the native's point of view'. It is contrasted with etic, which refers to the analyst's concepts, description and analyses. The terms are derived from phonemics and phonetics.
8   Barth, F. (1969) pp10-19
9   Hovannisian, R. G. (1997) p439
10   Banks, M. (1996) pp12-13
11   Gilbert. (2000) p25. Situationalism is often equated with instrumentalism, that is to say the view that ethnic groups are formed and maintained to serve particular social ends, principally economic and political ones, so that unless people are in a situation in which ethnicity will serve such ends, it will not be appealed to in group formation. The economy may allocate roles and opportunities differently; some groups may dominate vital sectors of an economy or control governmental offices and security organisations in ways that may be considered unacceptable by those excluded. In these instances, individuals may compete over land, business, assets, jobs, incomes, political offices, access to education, and language and religious rights. Grievances arising from a combination of these factors may be seen by some individuals as vital to group survival and thus provide a basis for solidarity.
12   Cohen, A. (1969) pp198-201
13   Banks, M. (1996) pp33-36
14   Eriksen, T. H. (1993) pp45-46
15   Eriksen, T. H. (1993) p34

16	Epstein, A. L. (1978)
17	Constanides, P. (1977)
18	Werbner, P. (1980)
19	Talai, V.A. (1989) p3
20	Werbner, P. (2002) *Imagined Diaspora among Manchester Pakistanis*
21	Banks, M. (1996) pp36-37
22	Rex, J. (1986)
23	Weber, Max. (1978) pp389-95
24	Weber, Max. (1978) pp389-95
25	Gilbert, P. (2000) p10
26	Gilbert, P. (2000) p10
27	Gilbert, P. (2000) p22
28	Weber, M. (1948) pp171-9
29	Deutsch, K. W. (1966) pp96-105
30	Geertz, C. (1985) pp119-121
31	Hutchinson & Smith (Eds) (1996) p12
32	Cohen, R. (1997) p174
33	Hutchinson & Smith (Eds) (1994) p5
34	Anderson, B. (1983) pp37-46
35	Anderson, B. (1983) pp37-46
36	Smith, A. D. (1996) pp5-17
37	Eriksen, T. H. (2001) p279
38	Eriksen, T. H. (2001) pp281-282
39	Eriksen, T. H. (2001) pp281-282
40	Geertz, C. (1963) pp108-13
41	Nehru cited in Geertz, C. (1963) pp108-13
42	Geertz, C. (1963) pp108-13

43   Banks, M. (1996) pp17-18. The late Yulian Bromley was one of the most well known Soviet anthropologists outside the Soviet Union, and certainly one of the most powerful and influential within it. It must be remembered that Bromley and his colleagues were at the time committed to a Marxist interpretation of history. This view holds that all human societies pass historically through five social formations: primitive communism, slave-ownership, feudalism, capitalism and finally socialism leading to communism.

44	cited in Banks, M. (1996) pp18-19
45	cited in Banks, M. (1996) p19 & 25
46	Tabibian, J. (1983) p21
47	Dekmejian, R. H. (1997) p437
48	Suny, R. G. (1993) p5
49	Friedman, J. (1990) p311
50	Cohen, R. (1997) pp173
51	Rapport, N. & Dawson, A. (1998) p23
52	Eriksen, T. H. (2001) p307
53	Riggs, F. W. (1999) p31
54	Cohen, R. (1997) p175
55	Cohen, R. (1997) p175
56	Cohen, R. (1997) pp175-176

57   For an interesting discussion of Doing History in the Postmodern World see Jenkins, K. (1999) *Re-Thinking History*

| 58 | Bhabha, H. (1994) p38 |
| 59 | Bhabha, H. (1994) p254 |

60 Rapport, N. & Overring, J. (2000) p 364
61 Yuval-Davis, N. (1997) p202
62 Bhabha, H. (1994) pp269-72
63 Cohen, A. (1985)
64 Cohen, A. (1985) p21
65 Hall, S. (2003) pp233-246
66 Lowe, L. (2003) p140
67 Cohen, R. (1997) p131
68 Werbner, P. (2000) p13
69 Hall, S. (1996) p443
70 Hall, S. (1992) pp6-8
71 Chambers, I. (1993) p133
72 Chambers, I. (1993) p27
73 Friedman, J. (2000) pp76-77
74 Clifford, J. (1997) pp267-8
75 Geertz, C. (1985) pp119-121
76 Jenkins, R. (1997) p29
77 Jenkins, R. (1997) p165
78 Comaroff, J. & J. (1992) p51
79 Gilbert, P. (2000) p167
80 Castles & Miller. (1998) p294
81 The Soviet Union, in particular, is an interesting example of the continuing potency of nationalism because the Communists asserted they had solved the problem by progressing beyond nationalism, by separating political power from cultural identity, centralising the former, while devolving the latter. But nationalism had not been permanently erased, only temporarily submerged. Furthermore, the break up of Yugoslavia may not have been caused by ethnic nationalism, but ethnically defined nations have become Yugoslavia's heirs. For a thorough and detailed analysis of Nationalism and the USSR and the Successor States. See Ronald, G. Suny (1998) *The Soviet Experiment*, Oxford University Press.
82 Castles & Miller. (1998) pp295-296
83 Castles & Miller. (1998) pp296-297

Notes to Chapter Three: The Armenian Diaspora Historical Origins

1 Suny, R. G. (1993) p1
2 Redgate, A. E. (2000) p6. It is this smallest territorial Armenian state which is detailed in the Armenian Geography which was written probably before AD636 by the Armenian scholar Anania of Shirak. The most recent explorer of Armenian historical geography, however, has confirmed that this account should not be taken literally as it is not a valid picture of the geopolitical realities of ancient Armenia. For a detailed commentary see Redgate, A. E. (2000) pp6-13
3 Papazian, D. R. (1987) p1
4 Ararat is mentioned in Genesis 8:4 and Jeremiah 51:27. Armenia itself is mentioned in 2 Kings 19:37 and Isaiah 37:38.
5 Talai, V. A. (1989) p116
6 cited in Talai, V. A. (1989) p116
7 Armenians refer to themselves and their country as Hay and Hayastan.

8   Moses of Khoren tells the well known Armenian legend of the unrequited love of Queen Shamiram (The Semiramis of Greek legend) for King Ara the Beautiful. Her pride wounded, Shamiram went to war against Armenia, but in spite of strict orders to her warriors not to harm him, a stray arrow killed Ara. The distraught queen decided to remain in Armenia, the land of her hero. Cited in Chahin, M. (Second Edition) (2001) p45

9   cited in Talai, V. A. (1989) p116

10   Chahin, M. (Second Edition) (2001) p43

11   Walker, C. J. (1980) pp22-3

12   Talai, V. A. (1989) p117

13   Redgate, A. E. (2000) p5

14   Hovanissian, R. G. (1992) p438

15   Smith, A. D. (1992) pp440

16   Suny, R. G. (1993) p8

17   Redgate, A. E. (2000) pp249-251

18   Papazian, D. R. (1987) pp7-8

19   Papazian, D. R. (1987) p8
Whilst visiting Armenia to attend the Second Diaspora Conference in May 2002, I came across an interesting article in 'Mashtots' an independent weekly paper. In this article Professor Ayvazyan, from Yerevan University, claims that Britain could face a 600 year old bill from the Cilicia Kingdom, which has remained unpaid all these years. Ayvazyan has been writing to the Queen of England to demand the return of the treasury of the Kingdom of Cilicia. He claims that King Levon VI of Cilicia managed to escape to Europe, where he sought to mount a final crusade to free the last Christian State in the Middle East. In 1378 he signed an agreement depositing the Cilicia treasury with King Richard II of England for safekeeping until his kingdom regained its independence—King Levon did not live to see his country free again. Furthermore, Ayvazyan claims that the English themselves originally came from the Angltun region of ancient Armenia in the second millennium BC, which is why Levon VI, following the tradition of Armenian rulers, handed the Armenian treasury for safekeeping to those who originally came from Angltun—to the English King. He further suggested that the House of Windsor derived its name from the Armenian word meaning 'gorge of the vineyards'. In other words the ancestors of the Queen lived in Armenia in a gorge where grapes were grown.

20   Redgate, A. E. (2000) p249

21   cited in Armstrong, J. (1982) p212

22   Dudwick, N. (1993) p262

23   Papazian, D. R. (1987) p8

24   Naimark, N. M. (2001) p19

25   Redgate, A. E. (2000) pp263-266

26   McCarthy, J. (2001) p68

27   Redgate, A. E. (2000) p271

28   Armstrong, J. (1982) p211

29   Dudwick, N. (1993) pp262-263.
The Mekhitarists, an Armenian Roman Catholic congregation that established the noted island monastery of San Lazzaro in Venice in 1715. On their island sanctuary the Mekhitarists have long operated a printing press, possessed a fine library, and issued a noted scholarly journal. Another Mekhitarist order has operated from Vienna since 1811. When the Mekhitarists in Venice became bankrupt in the early

eighties, because of bad business ventures, ASALA, one of the Armenian terrorist organisations, threatened to retaliate against the Italian government.

30   Libaridian, G. J. (1983)p263
31   Libaridian, G. J. (1983), pp263-264
32   Libaridian, G. J. (1983) pp263-264
33   Following the Russo-Turkish war 1877-1878, the Armenian Patriarch in Constantinople, Megerdich Khrimian (known affectionately by the term *'Hyrig'* or 'little Father') argued that the Armenians must hence use the 'iron ladle' or armed force if they were ever to achieve their demands. To illustrate his point, Hyrig told a parable. At the Berlin Conference, the European powers had permitted him to meet with them around a large kettle of Armenian festive food, but while the others had iron ladles, Hyrig had only a paper one. Thus, he could not share the meal or achieve Armenian demands. This parable representing the need to employ armed force is well known to most Armenians.

34   Talai, V. A. (1989) p120
35   Gunter, M. M. (1990) p2
36   Talai, V. A. (1989) p120
37   Although it is the oldest Armenian political party, since the failure of its insurrectionary activities in the 1890s, the Marxist Hunchaks have been also the least significant. The Party still exists and celebrated its centenary in 1990. Indeed in Lebanon (where a cohesive and unassimilated Armenian community still exists in Bourj Hammoud, the teeming Armenian quarter of east Beirut, as well as in Anjar, a small city of some 3,000 in the Bekaa Valley) a small Hunchakian militia exists alongside a much larger Dashnak one. The Party also sponsors affiliated groups such as the Nor Serount (New Generation) Cultural Association and the Armenian Sports Association. Hunchak in Armenian means "bell". The name apparently was adopted from the nineteenth century Russian revolutionary leader Alexander Herzen's 'Kolokol' which in Russian means "bell".

38   Throughout its existence, the ARF created in 1890 as a nationalist revolutionary party, has maintained basically the same organisational structure. Early in its existence, the Party joined the Second or Socialist International and remains to this day a member. Socialism, however, has never really been one of its main tenets. At its apex is the Bureau, the Party's supreme executive body. Although the Dashnaks have always maintained an aura of secrecy about their traditions, meetings and leadership, it appears that an Iranian born Armenian, Maroukhian, who lived in Beirut, heads it. In the mid 1980s, given the endemic violence in Lebanon, the Bureau was apparently relocated from Beirut to either Athens or Paris. A Central Committee of the ARF also exists in each country where there is a relatively large Armenian population. A number of other bodies are also associated with the Dashnaks including the Armenian Youth Federation (AYF), and the Armenian General Athletic Union which includes Armenian Boy and Girl Scouts. Each of these subsidiary groups operates transnationally throughout the Diaspora.

39   McCarthy, J. (2001) p70
40   Vratzian, S. (1950) p19
41   McCarthy, J. (2001) p71
42   McCarthy, J. (2001) p66
43   The Muslim majority, however, included both Turks and Kurds in Eastern Anatolia. For a different interpretation of the population see Levon Marashlian (1987) "Population Statistics on Ottoman Armenians in the context of Turkish Historiography" in *Armenian Review* 40, pp1-59
44   Gunter, M. M. (1990) p25

45	Redgate, A. E. (2000) pp270-271
46	Bryce, J. (1896) pp525-26
47	Langer, W. (1951) p157
48	Laqueur, W. (1977) p44
49	McCarthy, J. (2001) p72
50	Papazian, D. R. (1987)p11

51   Member of the Ottoman ruling class could be called Turkish only in that they knew Ottoman Turkish, a literary and court language, quite different from the common Turkish language.

52   The territory inhabited by Turkic peoples stretched from the Balkans to the Great Wall of China and this vast territory was called Turan (the Persian name for the mythological birthplace of Turkic peoples). "Fatherland for the Turks is neither Turkey nor Turkestan", the Young Turks spokesman Ziya Goeckalp wrote, "their famous fatherland is a great and eternal land, Turan" cited in Graber, G. S., 1996, p97. Pan-Turkism in Turkey and Azerbaijan developed simultaneously in the decade preceding the First World War, giving rise to a Turkish cultural renaissance among Azeri Turks.

53	McCarthy, J. (2001) pp73-74
54	McCarthy, J. (2001) p76
55	Hostler, C. W. (1957) p99
56	Graber, G, S. (1996) pp50-53
57	McCarthy, J. (2001) p106
58	Graber, G. S. (1996) p87

59   Quoted and translated from "Proces des Unionistes:Documents microfilms de la bibliotheque du Congres de Washington, in the appendix to *The Trial of Talaat Pasha*, stenographic court records. Also to be found in Tessa Hofmann, *Der Voelkernord an den Armeniern vor Gericht; Der Prozess Talaat Pascha, Berlin 1921* Vienna:Goettingen 1980 cited in Graber, G. S. (1996) pp87-88

60   April 24 is commemorated every year to mourn the victims of the Armenian Genocide. It is known as Martyrs Day.

61	Walker, C. (1980) p207
62	Walker, C. (1980) p207
63	Graber, G. S. (1996) p106
64	Redgate, A. E. (2000) p271
65	Suny, R. G. (1993) p114
66	Naimark, N. M. (2001) p41
67	Walker, C. (1980) p232

68   Bryce 1916, Foreign Office 1917, El-Ghusein 1917, cited in Talai, V. A. (1989) p123

69   Roger. W. Smith. Professor of Government, College of William and Mary cited in Graber, G. S. (1996) pxiii

70   Ambassador Morgenthau's Story, New York: Garden City, 1918, cited in Graber, G. S. (1996) pxii

71   Scholars continue to debate the causes of genocide but an interesting theory suggested by Fein argues that a crucial factor in both the Armenian genocide and the Holocaust, is the rise of new elites within declining states, for whom minorities are outside the universe of moral obligations. Fein proposes an explanation of both the Armenian genocide and the Holocaust as emerging from the potential implications of the political modus operandi adopted by a new elite in a state in decline, legitimating the rationale of the state as the vehicle of change for the dominant group, from which the victim is excluded by definition. In the Armenian case, the facilitat-

ing conditions are: the exclusion of non-Muslims from the Islamic universe of obligation and their inferiority, both legally and socially, in the Ottoman empire; the gradual decline of the Ottoman empire, since the seventeenth century in territory and population, which were further reduced by military defeats in the twentieth century; the ascendancy of the Young Turks and their adaptation of Pan-Turkism as a new basis for legitimising their right to rule; and the alliance of Turkey with Germany in World War I which rendered Turkey immune to protests and sanctions of the western allies, decreasing the visibility of the Armenians giving the Turks the opportunity to repudiate treaties which protected the Armenians. For a full discussion see Helen Fein (1993) *Genocide: A Sociological Perspective*, pp71-5

72   Marienstras, R. (1989) pp119-125
73   Milton, J. E. (1986) pp333-9
74   Dekmejian, R. H. (1997) p436
75   Takooshian, H. (1986-7) p136
76   Takooshian, H. (1986-7), p137
77   Takooshian, H. (1986-87) p138
78   Gunter, M. M. (1990) p35
79   Gavakian, A. (1997) p115
80   Gavakian, A. (1997) p115

Notes to Chapter Four: The Contemporary Armenian Diaspora

1   Gavakian, A. (1997) p76
2   Suny, R. (1998) p198
3   "Two Separate Demonstrations in NYC Planned", *The Armenian Reporter* 10 December 1987, p10 cited in Gunter, M. M. (1990) p29
4   Gunter, M. M. (1990) p27
5   Gunter, M. M. (1990) pp-73-74
6   After almost two thousand years of political presence, no Armenian state existed between 1375 and 1918.
7   Gunter, M. M. (1990) pp148-149
8   Torossian, R. M. (1980) p76
9   Papazian, D. R. (1987) p76
10   Gunter, M. M. (1990) pp148-149
11   Suny, R. (1998) pp281-290
12   Suny, R. (1998) p440
13   See Michael. J. Arlen (1975) *Passage to Ararat*
14   Takooshian, H. (1986) p140
15   Schahgaldian. (1979) pp88-91
16   Schahgaldian. (1979) p91
17   Gavakian, A. (1997) p79
18   The ADL commonly referred to as the Ramgavars have represented the other main political tendency in the Diaspora since its creation in 1921 from the triple merger of the Armenakans, the Verakazmial (Reformed) Hunchaks (who had split from the Hunchaks in 1896), and the Sahmanadir Ramgavars (Constitutional Democratic) Party that had been founded in Cairo in 1908. Over the years the Ramgavars have consisted of affluent merchants possessing a conservative philosophy and broad

minded professionals such as lawyers, doctors and teachers. Despite their conservative instincts, however, the Ramgavars argued that the present geopolitical situation compels them to support Soviet Armenia.

19 Hovannisian, R. G. (1997) pp415-416
20 Sarkissian, K. V. (1969) p482
21 "A Candid Conversation with His Holiness Vazken I" *The Armenian Reporter* 10 December 1987, p10, cited in Gunter, M. M. (1990) p29
22 "A Candid Conversation with His Holiness Vazken I" *The Armenian Reporter* 10 December 1987, p10, cited in Gunter, M. M. (1990) p30
23 Hovannisian, R. G. (1997) p416
24 Cohen, R. (1997) p53
25 Hovannisian, R. G. (1997)p275
26 Dekmejian, R. H. (1997) p419
27 Dekmejian, R. H. (1997) p419
28 Dekmejian, R. H. (1997) p420
29 Cohen, R. (1997) p49
30 Cohen, R. (1997) p49
31 Saroyan, W. (1962) pp87-88
32 The spelling rules of the Armenian language were changed by decree of the Soviet Armenian government in the twenties. The decree met with resistance in the Diaspora where traditional orthography remains in use.
33 Dekmejian, R. H. (1997) p421
34 Gunter, M. M. (1990) p32
35 Milton, E. J. (1986) pp333-9
36 Gunter, M. M. (1990) p103
37 Armenian Weekly 4 April 1987 cited in Gunter, M. M. (1990) p32
38 Armenian Weekly 4 April 1987 cited in Gunter, M. M. (1990) p32
39 Armenian Weekly 4 April 1987 cited in Gunter, M, M. (1990) pp32-33
40 Gunter, M. M. (1990) pp33-34
41 Gunter, M. M. (1990) pp33-34
   The 'Van Operation' was an ASALA strike against the Turkish Consulate in Paris on 24 September 1981, in which one Turkish guard was killed and 56 people held hostage for 16 hours.
42 cited in Gunter, M. M. (1990)
43 Talai, V. A. (1989) p27
44 "Booklet giving history of ASALA's existence gives new insight into the Revolutionary Movement" *The Armenian Reporter* 10 January 1985, pp3-5 cited in Gunter, M. M. (1990)
45 Gunter, M. M. (1990) pp45-46
46 Smith, D. (1983) p2
47 Gunter, M. M. (1990) p37
48 Redgate, A. E. (2000) pp275-276
49 Sassounian, Harout. (1983) cited in the California Courier, p4
50 Gunter, M. M. (1990) p36
51 Torossian, R. M. (1989), p110
52 Gavakian, A. (1997) p100
53 Keshishian, A. (1978)
54 Cohen, R. (1997) p51
55 Gunter, M. M. (1990) p28
56 There is a considerable Armenian presence in Athens of around 15,000 and the Armenian Popular Movement (APM) established its headquarter there in 1980.

57   Gunter, M. M. (1990) pp50-51
58   Diuk & Karatnycky (1993)
59   Financial Times, 16 September 1994
60   Diuk & Karatnycky (1993) pp153-154
61   Diuk & Karatnycky (1993) pp-153-154
62   Diuk & Karatnycky (1993) p163
63   cited in in Gavakian, A. (1997) p171
64   Gavakian, A. (1997) p171
65   Gavakian, A. (1997) p172
66   cited in Gavakian, A. (1997) p172. Manoogian further claimed that "what has happened is that, with the way these schools are usually run, you just begin to attract more and more immigrant students. Local boys never come and parents do not want their children going to schools with nothing but immigrants ... everybody wants you to do a million things but it's a question of whether you do a few things really well or do you do a lot of things? Well probably we are more programme orientated than most"
67   Gavakian, A. (1997) p175
68   Gavakian, A. (1997) p175 ˙
69   Gavakian, A. (1997) p203
70   Gunter, M. M. (1990) p36
71   Gavakian, A. (1997) p174
72   Redgate, A. E. (2000) pp278-279
73   Redgate, A. E. (2000) pp278-279
74   Dalziel, S. (1993) p141
75   Dalziel, S. (1993) p141
76   "Armenia, Turkey take steps towards rapprochement" cited in *EurasiaNet Insight*, 11 June 2002
77   Diuk & Karatnycky (1993) p163
78   Gavakian, A. (1997) p155
79   Gavakian, A. (1997) p155
80   Suny, R. (1998) pp483-484. The collapse of the Soviet Union remains an open topic of investigation by historians and political scientists. See Cook, L. (1994) *The Soviet Social Contract and why it failed*; Dallin & Lapidus (Eds) (1995) *The Soviet System from Crisis to Collapse*; and Walker, R. (1993) *Six Years that Shook the World*
81   Dekmejian, R. H. (1997) p442
82   Suny, R. (1998) pp496-498
83   Suny, R. (1998) pp440-441
84   Information provided by the Ministry of Foreign Affairs of the Republic of Armenia, for the 2000 Armenia Diaspora Conference. The first Armenia-Diaspora conference was convened on 22-23 September 1999 in Yerevan pursuant to a 1998 executive order by President Kocharian.
85   Hye Sharzhoom (2001) p1
86   Hye Sharzhoom (2001) p5
87   Halpin, T (2002) p28
88   Halpin, T. (2002)pp28-29
89   Gunter, M. M. (1990) p51
90   Gunter, M. M. (1990) p52
91   Gavakian, A. (1997) p193

Notes to Chapter Five: Methodology

1   The Armenian Institute is dedicated to making Armenian culture and history a living experience through innovative programmes, educational resources, workshops, academic events, exhibits and performances. Particular attention is paid to contemporary diasporic life and the development of links with Armenia and other communities.

2   Taylor, S. (2002) pp2-3

3   Devine, F. (1996) p152

4   For further discussion on this topic see Weinberg, D. (Ed) (2002) *Qualitative Research Methods*

5   Stoker, G. (1995) p14

6   Ramazanoglu & Holland (2002) p46

7   Devine, F. (1996) p140

8   Keat & Urry (1975) p217

9   Devine, F. (1996) p140

10   McCracken, G. (1998) p16

11   McCracken, G. (1998) p16

12   McCracken, G. (1998) p17

13   McCracken, G. (1998) p18

14   One interviewee asked me if my surname had ever been a barrier to employment, as she had trained as a teacher and had been advised to change her name if she wished to procure a teaching post.

15   Kikumura, A. (1986) pp140-141

16   Damaris, R. (2001) p2

17   Taylor, S. (2002) p3

18   Ramazanoglu & Holland (2002) pp118-119

19   Stansfield, J. H. (1993) pp42-43

20   Razavi, (1992) p161

21   Kikumura, A. (1986) pp140-141. Interestingly, Robert Merton is believed to be the founder of focus group interviewing.

22   Vaughn, et al, (1996) pp15-16

23   Vaughn, et al, (1996) p5

24   Vaughn, et al, (1996) p6

25   Slim, et al, (1993) p119. It is also advisable to produce a moderator's guide to assist the course of the focus group from the beginning to end and keep within time constraints. This can be excessively detailed or a general plan providing the major questions and probes. See Appendix A.

26   Slim, et al, (1993) p119

27   Vaughn, et al, (1996) pp7-14

28   Vaughn, et al, (1996) p148

29   Armenia Diaspora Conference May 27-28 2002 Yerevan. The conference was divided into four thematic sessions: Political Relations/Armenia-Diaspora Organisational and Structural Issues; Information and Media; Economic and Social Development; Education, Culture and Science.

30   Vaughn, et al, (1996) p151

31   Vaughn, et al, (1996) p154

32   Chamberlayne, et al, (2000) p141

33   Devine, F. (1995) p138

34   May, T. (2001) p1224

35   Spradley, J. (1979) p131

36   Spradley, J. (1979) p82
37   Spradley, J. (1979) p83
38   Slim, et al, (1993) p116
39   Devine, F. (1995) p137
40   Many of these associations such as the Armenian Institute and Armenian Studies Group operate from London, however, many members of the Manchester community are involved in these organisations.
41   McCracken, G. (1999) p27
42   McCracken, G. (1999) p28
43   Rubin, Lilian. B. (1979)
44   Stansfield, J, H. (1993) pp51-52
45   Coffey. (1999) p1

Notes to Chapter Six: The Manchester Armenians

1   The Manchester Recorder, p6
2   George, J. (2002) p5
3   George, J. (2002) p49
4   Cohen, R. (1997) p187
5   See Bourdieu, P. & Wacquant, L. (1992) *An Invitation to Reflexive Sociology* and Castells, M (2000) *The Network Society*
6   Dekmejian, R. H. (1997) p437
7   Cohen, R. (1997) p171
8   Gold, S. J. (2002) pp33-35
9   Massey, et al, (1993) pp431-66
10   Cohen, R. (1997) pp163-165
11   Mirak, R.(1997) p399
12   See Henry, S. (1978) *Cultural Persistence and Socio-economic mobility: A comparative study of assimilation among Armenians and Japanese in Los Angeles*; Tashjian, J. H. (1947) *The Armenians of the United States and Canada*
13   Williams, B. F. (1996) p429
14   Anthia, F. & Yuval-Davis, N. (1996) p5
15   Gold, S. J. (2002) pp57-58
16   Talai, V. (1989) p3
17   Walker, C. J. (1980) p12
18   Talai, V. (1989) p78
19   One of my respondents said to me that as soon as she saw my first name on the letter, she knew I was not Armenian.
20   Root, M. P. (1992) pp-181-189
21   Root, M. P. (1992) pp181-189
22   Talai, V. (1989) pp98-99
23   Talai, V. (1989) p100
24   Dekmejian, R. H. (1997) p439
25   Cohen, R. (1997) p129
26   Chambers, I.. (1993) p133
27   Mirak, R. (1997) p408
28   George,J. (2002) pp139-140. One such lecture I attended was given by Professor Armen Aivazian, Professor of Political Science at the American University of Yerevan. Its title 'Ottoman decision making and exercise on extermination during the Armenian rebellion of the 1720's'

29   Dekmejian, R. H.(1997) p438
30   Smith, A. D. (1992) p441
31   Cohen, R. (1997) p189
32   Milton, E. J. (1986) p337
33   George, J. (2002) pp227-228
34   Dudwick, N. (1993) p262
35   cited in Talai, V. (1989) p88
36   Gavakian, A. (1997) pp153-154
37   Said, E. W. (1994) p143
38   The most recent organisation to be set up is DA Connection UK, a cultural and
      humanitarian organisation set up last year by a group of young Anglo-Armenians.
      The aim is to improve the everyday lives of Armenian children through education.
      They organise summer projects in rural areas of Armenia and Karabagh for
      children who would otherwise be wandering the streets during the summer period.
      DA Connection also renovates their village schools and provides a basic medical
      check up for each child. Through continuous contact with the villagers, cultural ties
      are promoted between the Republic of Armenia, the European Union and The
      Armenian Diaspora.
39   Hall, S. (1991) pp35-36
40   Gavakian, A. (1997) p141
41   A good listing of the American organisations can be found in Hamo Vassillian's
      American-Armenian   Almanac.   It   is   also   available   on   line   at
      www.armenian.com/org
42   Acronymn made from the Armenian letters HMEM which stands for Armenian
      General Athletic Union. This is a sports organisation with Dashnak leadership with
      branches in Lebanon and the United States.
43   Bakalian, A. (1994) p158
44   cited in Gavakian, A. (1997)
45   The plight of the Ottoman Armenian population and its struggle for civil rights and
      administrative reforms became known to western commentators as the Armenian
      Question.
46   Adalian, R. P. (1989) pp81-114
47   Hansen, M. L. (1962)
48   Gans, H. J. (1979) p11
49   Arlen, M. J. (1975)
50   Toloyan, K. (2002) p8
51   Dekmejian, H. R. (1997) p436
52   cited in Gavakian, A. (1997) p232
53   cited in Gavakian, A. (1997) p233
54   Ayanian, A. (1987) pp13-29
55   Toloyan, K. & Beledian, K. (1998) pp5-6
56   For a full discussion see Panossian, R. (1998)
57   Braziel, J. E. & Mannur, A. (2003) p9
58   Mirak, R. (1997) p409
59   Suny, R. G. (1993) p4
60   Dekmejian, R. H. (1988) p421
61   Suny, R. G. (1993) p5
62   Hovannisian, R. G. (1997) p69
63   As far as I am aware there are no immigrants from the Republic of Armenia living
      in Manchester. There is reference to Tamara Gmbikian and her teenage daughter
      from Yerevan who were welcomed into the community in 1992 in Joan George's

book 'Merchants in Exile' (p228). Tamara a Russian language teacher and interpreter took a part time business course and her daughter was sent to a 'good' local
school. She went on to study Law at Canterbury and has now graduated with a first
class degree. Tamara joined Baroness Cox on one of her many mercy mission to
the Nagorno Karabagh, acting as an honorary interpreter.

64   Talai, V. (1989) p44
65   Gold, S. J. (2002) p115
66   Bakalian, A. (1997) p123
67   Edwards, J. (1985) p110

Notes to Chapter Seven: Summary

1   Appadurai, A. (1996)
2   Cohen, R. (1997) p163
3   Rapport, N. & Dawson, A. (Ed) (1998) p23
4   Hall, J. (1994)
5   Even in the largest Diaspora communities, Armenians seldom account for more
     than one per cent of the population.
6   Dekmejian, H. R. (1997)
7   Bakalian, A. (1993)
8   Gans, H. J. (1979) p9
9   Clifford, J. (1997) pp267-8

BIBLIOGRAPHY

Adalian, R. P. (1989) "The Historical Evolution of The Armenian Diaspora", *The Journal of Modern Hellenism* No 6

Adelman, H. (1996) *The International Response to Conflict & Genocide*, London: Overseas Development Institute

Allen, J. & Hamnett, C. (1995) *In a Shrinking World: Global Unevenness and Inequality*, Oxford & New York: Oxford University Press

Anderson, B. (Revised Edition) (1991) *Imagined Communities*, London: Verso

Anderson, B. (1983) *Imagined Communities*, London & New York: Verso

Anthias, F. & Yuval Davis, N. (1996) *Racialized Boundaries*, London: Routledge

Appadurai, A. (1996) *Modernity at Large: Cultural Dimensions of Globalisation*, Cambridge: Cambridge University Press

Appadurai, A. Disjuncture & Difference in the Global Cultural Economy in Inda & Rosaldo (2002) *The Anthropology of Globalisation*, London: Blackwell

Appadurai, A. Global Ethnoscapes: Notes and Queries for a Transnational Anthropology in Taylor, S. (Ed) (2002) *Ethnographic Research*, London: Sage

Arlen, M. J. (1975) *Passage to Ararat*, New York: Farrar, Straus, Giraux,

Armenian International Magazine (AIM), Aug-Sept 1999 & April 2002

Armstrong, J. (1982) *Nations before Nationalism*, Chapel Hill: University of North Carolina Press

Avakian, A. S. "Armenians in America: How many and where?" *In Ararat Quarterly* Vol 18 No 1 Winter 1977

Ayanian, M. A. & J. Z. (1987) "Armenian Political Violence on American Networks: An analysis of content" in *Armenian Review* 4 (1-57)

Bakalian. A. (1993) *American Armenians: From Being to Feeling*, New York: New Brunswick Publications

Ballard, R. (Ed) (1994) *Desh Pardesh — The South Asian Presence in Britain*, London: Hurst

Banks, M. (1996) *Ethnicity: Anthropological Constructions*, London: Routledge

Barr, A. & Toye J. (2000) "Its not what you know—its who you know! Economic Analyses of Social Capital" in *Development Research Insights*, 34:1-2

Barth, F. (1969) *Ethnic Groups and Boundaries*, Boston: Little Brown & Co

Beck, U. (2002) What is Globalisation? in Held, D. & McGrew, A. (Eds) *The Global Transformations Reader*, London: Blackwell

Beloff, Max. (Ed) (1990) *Beyond the Soviet Union: the fragmentation of power*, Aldershot: Ashgate Publications

Berridge, G. R. & Heater, D. (1992) *International Politics*, London: Harvester Wheatsheaf

Bhabha, H. Frontlines/Borderposts in Bammer, A. (Ed) (1994) *Displacements: Cultural Identities in Question*, Bloomington: Indiana University Press

Bhabha, H. (1990) *Nation & Narration*, London: Routledge

Bhabha, H. (1994) *The Location of Culture*, London: Routledge

Bourdieu, P. & Wacquant, L. (1992) *An Invitation to Reflexive Sociology*, Chicago: University of Chicago Press

Bottomore, T. (Ed) (1964) *Karl Marx Early Writings*, New York: New York University Press

Brah, Avtar. (1996) *Cartographies of Diaspora*, London: Routledge

Braziel, J. E. & Mannur, A. (Eds) (2003) *Theorizing Diaspora*, London: Blackwell

Bremmer, I. & Taras, R. (Eds) (1993) *Nations & Politics in the Soviet Successor States*, Cambridge: Cambridge University Press

Bromley, Y. V. *Soviet Ethnography: Main Trends*, Moscow: USSR Academy of Sciences

Bryce, J. (Fourth Ed) (1896) *Transcaucasia and Ararat*, London: Macmillan & Co

Burney, C. "Avant Les Armeniens: Les Ouranteens guerriers et battiseurs" in Dedeyan, G. (Ed) (1982) *Histoire des Armeniens,* Tolouse: Editions Privat

Castells, M. The Network Society in Held, D. & McGrew, A. (Eds) (2000) *The Global Transformations Reader*, London: Blackwell

Castles, S. & Miller, M. (1998) *The Age of Migration: International Population Movements in The Modern World*, Guildford: Guildford Press

Chahin, M. (Second Ed) (2001) *The Kingdom of Armenia*, Kent: Curzon Press

Chambers, I. (1993) *Migrancy Culture & Identity*, London: Routledge

Chamberlayne, P. Bornat, J. & Wengraf, T. (2000) *The Turn to Biographical Methods in Social Science*, London: Routledge

Clifford, J. (1997) *Routes: Travel and Translation in the late Twentieth Century*, Cambridge: Cambridge University Press

Clifford, J. (1994) "Diasporas" in *Cultural Anthropology* 9 (3)

Coffey, A. (1999) *The Ethnographic Self: Fieldwork and the Representation of Identity*, London: Sage Publications

Cohen, A. (1969) *Custom & Politics in Urban Africa*, Berkeley: University of California Press

Cohen, A. P. (1985) *The Symbolic Construction of Community*, London: Routledge

Cohen, R. (Ed) (1995) *The Cambridge Survey of World Migration*, Cambridge: Cambridge University Press

Cohen, R. (1996) "Diasporas and the Nation State: From Victims to Challengers", *International Affairs* Vol 72 (3)

Cohen, R. (1997) *Global Diasporas*, London: University College

Collins, P. H. (1986) "Learning from the outsider within: the sociological significance of Black Feminist thought" in *Social Problems* 33

Comaroff, John & Jean. (1992) *Ethnography and the Historical Imagination*, New York: Westview Press

Constantinides, P. The Greek Cypriots: Factors in the maintenance of ethnic identity in Watson, J. L. (Ed) (1977) *Between Two Cultures*, London: Blackwell

Cook, L. J. (1994) "The Soviet Social Contract and Why It Failed", *Russian Research Centre Studies*, Cambridge, Mass: Harvard University Press

Dallin, A. & Lapidus, G. (Eds) (1995) *The Soviet System from Crisis to Collapse*, New York: Westview Press

Dalziel, S. (1993) *The Rise and Fall of the Soviet Empire*, Madison: Magna

Damaris, R. (2001) "The Insider/Outsider conundrum in feminist interviewing: update on the debate" in *Revisiting Feminist Research Methodologies*, Status of Women Canada Research Division

Dekmejian, R. H. The Armenian Diaspora in Hovanissian, R. G. (Ed) (1997) *The Armenian People from Ancient to Modern Times,* Vol II, New York: MacMillan

Deutsch, K. W. (Second Ed) (1966) *Nationalism & Social Communication*, Cambridge, Mass: MIT Press

Devine, F. Qualitative Methods, in Marsh, D. & Stoker, G. (Eds) (1996) *Theory & Methods in Political Science*, London: MacMillan

Diuk, N. & Karatnycky, A. (1993) *New Nations Rising: The Fall of the Soviets and the Challenge of Independence*, Hoboken: John Wiley

Dudwick, N. Armenia: The Nation Awakes in Bremmer, I. & Taras, R. (Eds) (1993) *Nations & Politics in the Soviet Successor States*, Cambridge: Cambridge University Press

Edwards, J. (1985) *Language Society & Identity*, Oxford: Basil Blackwell

Eller, J. D. (1999) *From Culture to Ethnicity to Conflict: An Anthropological Perspective on International Ethnic Conflict*, Ann Arbor: University of Michigan Press

Enloe, C. Religion & Ethnicity in Sugar, P. (Ed) (1980) *Ethnic Diversity & Conflict in Eastern Europe*, Santa Barbara: ABC-Clio

Epstein, A. L. (1978) *Ethos & Identity*, London: Tavistock

Eriksen, Thomas Hylland. (1993) *Ethnicity & Nationalism: Anthropological Perspectives*, London: Pluto Press

Eriksen, Thomas Hylland. (Second Ed) (2001) *Small Places, Large Issues: An Introduction to Social and Cultural Anthropology*, London: Pluto Press

Featherstone, M. (Ed) (1990) *Global Culture: Nationalism, Globalisation and Modernity*, London: Sage

Fein, H. (1993) *Genocide: A Sociological Perspective*, London: Sage

Friedman, J. (1987) "Prolegomena to the adventures of Phallus in Blunderland: An anti-anti discourse" in *Culture and History* No 1

Friedman, J. Being in the World: Globalisation and Localisation in Featherstone, M. (Ed) (1990) *Global Culture: Nationalism, Globalisation and Modernity*, London: Sage

Friedman, J. Global Crises, The Struggle for Cultural Identity & Intellectual Pork Barrelling, Cosmopolitans versus Locals, Ethnics and Nationals in an era of De-Hegemonization in Werbner, P. & Modood, T. (2000) *Debating Cultural Hybridity*, London: Zed Books

Gans, H. J. "Symbolic Ethnicity, the future of ethnic groups and cultures in America" in *Ethnic and Racial Studies*, Vol 2, No 1 January 1979

Gans, H. J. Ethnicity & Social Change in Glazer, N. & Moynihan, D. P. (Eds) (1975) *Ethnicity: Theory & Experience*, Cambridge, Mass: Harvard University Press

Gavakian, A. (1997) *Homeland, Diaspora & Nationalism: The Re-imagination of American-Armenian Identity*, Sydney: University of Sydney, Dept of Government & Public Administration

Geertz, C. The Integrative Revolution in Geertz, C. (Ed) (1963) *Old Societies & New States*, New York: New York Free Press

Geertz, C. (1985) *A Contemporary Critique of Historical Materialism—The Nation State and Violence*, Cambridge: Polity Press

George, J. (2002) *Merchants in Exile*, London: Gomides Institute

Gilbert, P. (2000) *Peoples, Culture & Nations in Political Philosophy*, Edinburgh: Edinburgh University Press

Giddens, A. The Globalizing of Modernity in Held, D. & McGrew, A. (2002) *The Global Transformations Reader*, London: Blackwell

Gillespie, M. (1994) *Television, Ethnicity & Cultural Change*, London: Routledge

Gold, S. J. (2002) *The Israeli Diaspora*, London: Routledge

Gorvett, J. 11 June 2002, "Armenia, Turkey take steps towards rapprochement" *www.Eurasianet*

Graber, G. S. (1996) *Caravans to Oblivion*, Hoboken: John Wiley

Gunter, M. M. Transnational Armenian Activism in Beloff, M. (Ed) (1990) *Beyond the Soviet Union, the fragmentation of power*, Aldershot: Ashgate

Hall, J. R. & Neitz, M. J. (1993) Culture: *A Sociological Perspective*, Upper Saddle River: Prentice Hall

Hall, S. Cultural Identity & Diaspora in Rutherford, J. (Ed) (1990) *Identity, Community, Culture & Difference*, London: Lawrence & Wishart

Hall, S. (1992) "Our Mongrel Selves" in *New Statesmen & Society*, Supplement 19 June, 1992

Hall, S. Cultural Identity & Diaspora in Braziel, J. E. & Mannur, A. (Eds) (2003) *Theorizing Diaspora*, London: Blackwell

Hall, S. (1996) *Critical Dialogues in Cultural Studies*, London: Routledge

Hall, S. (1997) *Representation: Cultural Representations and Signifying Practices*, London: Sage

Hall, S. Morley, D. & Chen, K. (Eds) (1996) *Critical Dialogues in Cultural Studies*, London: Sage

Halpin, T. "History's Reckoning: Turning the Tide Against Denial" in *Armenian International Magazine (AIM)*, April 2002

Hansen, M. L. (1962) "The Third Generation in America" in *Commentary* 14, 496

Held, D. & McGrew, A. (Eds) (2000) *The Global Transformations Reader*, London: Blackwell

Henry, S. (1978) *Cultural Persistence and Socioeconomic mobility: A comparative study of assimilation among Armenians and Japanese in Los Angeles*, Los Angeles: R & E Associates

Hirst, P. & Thompson, G. (Second Ed) (1999) *Globalisation in Question: The International Economy and the Possibilities of Governance*, London: Polity Press

Hobsbawm, E. & Ranger, T. (1983) *The Invention of Tradition*, Cambridge: Cambridge University Press

Hobsbawm, E. (1990) *Nations & Nationalism since 1780*, Cambridge: Cambridge University Press

Hostler, C. W. (1957) *Turkism and the Soviets*, London & New York: Allen & Unwin

Hovannisian, R. G. (1992) *The Armenian Genocide*, London: Macmillan

Hovannisian, R. G. (Ed) (1997) *The Armenian People from Ancient to Modern Times*, Vol II, London & New York: Macmillan

Huntingdon, S. P. (2002) *The Clash of Civilizations: And the Remaking of World Order*, New York: New York Free Press

Huntindon, S. P. (1993) "The Clash of Civilizations" in *Foreign Affairs* Vol 72, n3, p22(28)

Hutchinson, J. & Smith, A. D. (Eds) (1994) *Nationalism*, Oxford: Oxford University Press

Hutchinson, J. & Smith, A. D. (Eds) (1996) *Ethnicity*, Oxford: Oxford University Press

Hutnyk, J. Adorno at Womad: South Asia Crossovers and the Limits of Hybridity in Werbner, P. & Modood, T. (2000) *Debating Cultural Hybridity*, London: Zed Books

Hye Sharzoom (2001) Vol 22 No 4 (74) Newspaper of The CSU Fresno Armenian Students & Armenian Studies Programme

Inda, J. X. & Rosaldo, R. (Eds) (2002) *The Anthropology of Globalisation*, London: Blackwell

Jabagchourian, J. (2001) Eighty Sixth Anniversary of Armenian Genocide Commemorated, New York: Hye Sharzhoom

Jenkins, K. (1999) *Rethinking History*, London: Routledge

Jenkins, R. (1997) *Rethinking Ethnicity*, Arguments & Explorations, London: Sage

Krejci, J. & Velimsky, V. (1981) *Ethnic & Political Nations*, London: Croom Helm

Keat, R. & Urry, J. (1975) *Social Theory and Science*, London: Routledge

Keshishian, A. (1969) *The Witness of the Armenian Church in a Diaspora Situation*, New York: Armenian Apostolic Church

Kellehear, A. (1993) *The Unobtrusive Researcher: A Guide to Methods*, New York: Allen & Unwin

Khacharian, H. (12.12.02) "Armenia: Repatriation may not solve problem of exodus" www.eurasianet

Kikumura, A. (1986) Family Life Histories in Perks, R. & Thomson, A. (2000) *The Oral History Reader*, London: Routledge

Kivisto, P. "Social spaces, transnational immigrant communities, and the politics of incorporation" in *Ethnicities*, Vol 3 No 1 March 2003

Kotkin, J. (1993) *How Race, Religion & Identity determine success in the New Global Economy*, Toronto: Random House Inc

Koutcharian, G. (1989) "Der Siedlungsraum unter dem Einfluss der Historisch-Politischer Ereign isse seil dem Berliner Kongress 1878". Berlin: Eine Polilisch-Geographische Analyse und Dokumentation

Lacqueur, W. (1977) *Terrorism*, Boston & Toronto: Little, Brown & Co

Lang, D. M. (Third Ed) (1980) *Armenia: Cradle of Civilization*, London: Allen & Unwin

Langer, W. (Second Ed) (1951) *The Diplomacy of Imperialism* 1890-1902, London: Macmillan

Lash, S. & Friedman, J. (Eds) (1991) *Modernity and Identity*, Oxford: Blackwell

Lee, R. M. (2000) *Unobtrusive Methods in Social Research*, Milton Keynes: Open University Press

Libaridian, G. J. (Ed) (1983) "Modernization & Armenian Society" in *Armenian Review* Vol 36 No 1 & 3

Lowe, L. Heterogeneity, Hybridity & Multiplicity in Braziel, J. E. & Mannur, A. (Eds) (2003) *Theorizing Diaspora*, London: Blackwell

Marashlian, L. (1987) "Population Statistics on Ottoman Armenians in the context of Turkish Historiography" in *Armenian Review* 40

Marienstras, R. (1989) On the notion of Diaspora in Chaliand, G. (Ed) *Minority Peoples in the Age of Nation States*, London: Pluto

Marsh, D. & Stoker, G. (Eds) (1995) *Theory & Methods in Political Science*, London: Macmillan

Massey, et al. (1993) "International Migration: A Review and Appraisal", in *Population and Development Review* 19 (3) pp431-66

May, T. (Third Ed) (2001) *Social Research: Issues, methods and process*, Milton Keynes: Open University Press

McCarthy, J. (2001) *The Ottoman Peoples and the End of Empire*, Oxford: Oxford University Press

McCarthy, J. (1983) *Muslims & Minorities: The Population of Ottoman Anatolia and the End of the Empire*, New York & London: New York University Press

McCracken, G. (1988) *The Long Interview: Qualitative Research Methods*, London: Sage

McNeill, W. H. (1986) *Polyethnicity & National Unity in World History*, Toronto: Toronto University Press

Milton, J. E. Diasporas & International Relations in Sheffer, G. (Ed) (1986) *Modern Diasporas in International Politics*, London: Croom Held

Minassian, A. Ter. (1984) *Nationalism & Socialism in the Armenian Revolutionary Movement (1887-1912)*, Cambridge, Mass: The Zoryan Institute

Mirak, R. The American Armenians in Hovannisian, R. G. (Ed) (1997) *The Armenian People from Ancient to Modern Vol II*, London & New York: MacMillan

Moerman, M. (1965) "Who are the Lue? Ethnic Identification in a Complex Civilization" in *American Anthropologist* Vol 67

Naimark, N. M. (2001) *Fires of Hatred, Ethnic Cleansing in Twentieth Century Europe*, Cambridge, Mass: Harvard University Press

Nash, M. (1989) *The Cauldron of Ethnicity in the Modern World*, Chicago: Chicago University Press

Nersessian, S. Der. (1945) *Armenia and the Byzantine Empire*, Cambridge, Mass: Harvard University Press

Nonini, D. & Ong, A. Introduction: Chinese Transnationalism as an alternative modernity in Ong, Aihwa, & Nonini. (Eds) (1997) *Ungrounded Empires: The Cultural Politics of Modern Chinese Transnationalism*, New York: Routledge

Panossian, R. (1998) "Between Ambivalence and Intrusion: Politics of Identity in Armenia Diaspora Relations "in *Diaspora: A Journal of Transnational Studies* 7:2

Papazian, D. R. (1987) *The Armenians*, Ann Arbor: University of Michigan

Perks, R. & Thompson, A. (Second Ed) (2000) *The Oral History Reader*, London: Routledge

Ranger, T. Samad, Yunas. Stuart, O. (Eds) (1996) *Culture, Identity and Politics: Ethnic Minorities in Britain*, Aldershot: Avebury Publications

Rapport, N. & Dawson, A. (Eds) (1998) *Migrants of Identity: Perceptions of Home in a World of Movement*, Oxford & New York: Berg Publications

Rapport, N. & Overing, J. (2000) *Social and Cultural Anthropology*, London: Routledge

Ramazanoglu, C. & Holland, J. (2002) *Feminist Methodology: Challenges and Choices*, London: Sage

Razavi, Fieldwork in familiar settings; the role of politics at the national, community and household levels in Devereux, S. & Hoddinott, J. (Eds) (1992) *Fieldwork in Developing Countries*, Boulder: Lynne Rienner

Redgate, A. E. (2000) *The Armenians*, London: Blackwell

Rex, J. (1986) *Race & Ethnicity*, Milton Keynes: Open University Press

Riggs, F. W. (1999) *Diaspora: Some Conceptual considerations*, Washington: International Studies Association (ISA)

Root, M. P. (Ed) (1992) *Racially mixed people in America*, London: Sage

Rosenau, J. (1990) *Turbulence in World Politics*, Princeton: Princeton University Press

Rosenberg, J. (2001) *The Follies of Globalisation Theory: Polemical Essays*, London: Verso

Rouse, R. Mexican Migration and the Social Space of Postmodernism in Inda & Rosaldo (Eds) (2002) *The Anthropology of Globalisation*, London: Blackwell

Rubin, L. B. (1979) *Women of a Certain Age: The Mid-Life Search for Self*, New York: Harper & Row

Said, E. W. (2000) *Reflections on Exile*, London: Granta Publications

Said, E. W. Orientalism Re-considered in Said, E. W. (2000) *Reflections on Exile*, London: Granta Publications

Said, E. W. The Clash of Definitions in Said, E. W. (2000) *Reflections on Exile*, London: Granta Publications

Said, E. W. (2000) *The Edward Said Reader*, London: Granta Publications

Said, E. W. (1993) Representations of the Intellectual—*The 1993 Reith Lectures*, London: Vintage

Saffran, W. (1991) "Diasporas in Modern Societies, Myths of Homeland and Return" in *Diaspora* Vol 1, No 1

Sanguin, A. L. (1994) "Les reseaux des Diasporas", Cahiers de Geographie du Quebec Vol 38 (105)

Sarkissian, K. V. The Armenian Church in Arberry, A. J. (1969) *Religion in the Middle East: Three Religions in Concord and Conflict*, Cambridge: Cambridge University Press

Saroyan, W. (1962) *"Here comes, there goes, you know who": An autobiography*, London: Peter Davis

Sassounian, H. (1983) Third Generation Hyes Haven't Lost the Feel in *California Courier*

Schahgaldian, N. B. (1979) *The Political Integration of an Immigrant Community into a Composite Society*, New York: Columbia University

Schiller, Glick, Basch, Szanton & Blanc. (Eds) (1992) *Towards a Transnational Perspective on Migration: Race, Class, Ethnicity & Nationalism Reconsidered*, New York: New York Academy of Sciences

Scholte, J. A. (2002) *What is Globalisation—The Definitional Issue—Again*, Warwick: CSGR (Centre for Study of Globalisation & Regionalization) Working Paper 109/02

Schopflin, G. (2000) *Nations Identity Power*, New York: New York University Press

Shain, Y. (2000) "American Jews & The Construction of Israel's Jewish Identity" in *Diaspora: A Journal of Transnational Studies* 9:2

Sheffer, G. A new field of study: Modern Diasporas in International Politics, in Sheffer, G. (Ed) (1986) *Modern Diasporas in International Politics*, London: Croom Helm

Skeldon, Ronald. (1997) *Migration and Development: A Global Perspective*, London: Longman

Slim, Thompson, Bennett & Cross. (1993) Ways of Listening in Perks, R. & Thomson, A. (Eds) (2000) *The Oral History Reader*, London: Routledge

Smith, A. D. (1992) "Chosen Peoples: Why Ethnic Groups survive" in *Ethnic & Racial Studies* 15:3

Smith, A. D. (2003) *Chosen People—Sacred Sources of National Identity*, Oxford: Oxford University Press

Smith, D. (1983) Terrorism mars Armenian Image, *California Courier*

Smith, G. (Ed) (1992) *The Nationalities Question in the Soviet Union*, London: Longman

Spradley, J. (1979) *The Ethnographic Interview*, New York: Holt Rinehart & Winston

Stansfield, J. H. & Rutledge, M. D. (Eds) (1993) *Race & Ethnicity in Research Methods*, London: Sage

Suny, R. G. (1993) *Looking Toward Ararat: Armenia in Modern History*, Bloomington: Indiana University Press

Suny, R. G. (1998) *The Soviet Experiment: Russia, the USSR and the Successor States*, Oxford: Oxford University Press

Tabibian, J. (1983) "Modernization, Political Culture and Political Economy in the Diaspora", *Armenian Review* Vol 3

Tabibian, J. "The Risk of Democratization" in *Armenian International Magazine (AIM)* August—September 1999

Takooshian, H. 1986-87, "Armenian Immigration to the United States from the Middle East" in *Journal of Armenian Studies*, Vol 3

Talai, V. A. (1989) *Armenians in London*, Manchester: Manchester University Press

Tashjian, J. H. (1947) *The Armenians of the United States and Canada*, Boston: Hairenik Press

Taylor, S. (Ed) (2002) *Ethnographic Research*, London: Sage

The Manchester Historical Recorder, Reprinted by Neil Richardson, Ringley Road, Manchester

Toloyan, K. & Beledian, K. (1998) "Fresh Perspectives on Armenia-Diaspora Relations", *Armenian Forum*

Toloyan, K. (2002) *Redefining Diasporas: Old Approaches, New Identities*, London: Armenian Institute

Tonkin, E. McDonald, M. & Chapman, M. (1989) *History & Ethnicity*, London: Routledge

Torossian, R. M. (1980) *The Contemporary Armenian Nationalist Movement*, Ann Arbor: Ann Arbor Publications

Vaughn, S. Shay Schumm, J. & Sinagub, J. (1996) *Focus Group Interviews*, London: Sage

Vertovec, S. & Cohen, R. (Eds) (1999) *Migration, Diasporas & Transnationalism*, Cheltenham: Edward Elgar

Vratzian, S. (1950) "The Armenian Revolution and the Armenian Revolutionary Federation", *The Armenian Review* Vol 3

Walker, C. J. (1980) *Armenia, The Survival of a Nation*, London: Croom Held

Walker, R. (1993) *Six Years that Shook the World*, Manchester: Manchester University Press

Wallerstein, I. Culture as the Ideological Battleground of the Modern World System, in Featherstone, M. (Ed) (1990) *Global Culture*, London, Sage

Webb, E. J. Campbell, D. T. Schwartz, K. D. and Sechrest, L. (1996) *Unobtrusive Measures: Non-reactive Research in the Social Sciences,* Chicago: Rand McNally

Weber, M. The Nation in Gerth, H. H. & Wright-Mills, C. (Eds & Translators) (1948) *Max Weber—Essays in Sociology,* London: Routledge & Kegan Paul

Weber, M. Ethnic Groups in Roth, G. & Wittich, C. (Eds) (1978) *Economy & Society Vol I,* Berkeley: University of California Press

Weinberg, D. (Ed) (2002) *Qualitative Research Methods,* London: Blackwell

Werbner, P. (2002) *Imagined Diaspora among Manchester Pakistanis,* Oxford: Oxford University Press

Werbner, P. (1980) "From Rags to Riches: Manchester Pakistanis in the Textile Trade" in *New Community* 9 (1&2)

Werbner, P. The Dialectics of Cultural Hybridity in Werbner, P. & Modood, T. (2000) *Debating Cultural Hybridity,* London: Zed Publications

Werbner, P. & Modood, T. (2000) *Debating Cultural Hybridity,* London: Zed Publications

Williams, B. F. Skinfold not Kinfolk: Comparative Reflection on the identity of Participant Observation in two Field Situations in Wolf, D. L. (Ed) (1996) *Feminist Dilemmas in Fieldwork,* Boulder: Westview Press

Williams, P. & Chrisman, L. (Eds) (1996) *Colonial Discourse and Post-Colonial Theory: A Reader,* New York: Columbia University Press

Wolf, D. L. (Ed) (1996) *Feminist Dilemmas in Fieldwork,* Boulder: Westview Press

Yuval Davis, N. (1997) Ethnicity Gender & Multiculturalism in *Debating Cultural Hybridity,* London: Zed Publications

INDEX